IMAGES
of America

BARTLETT

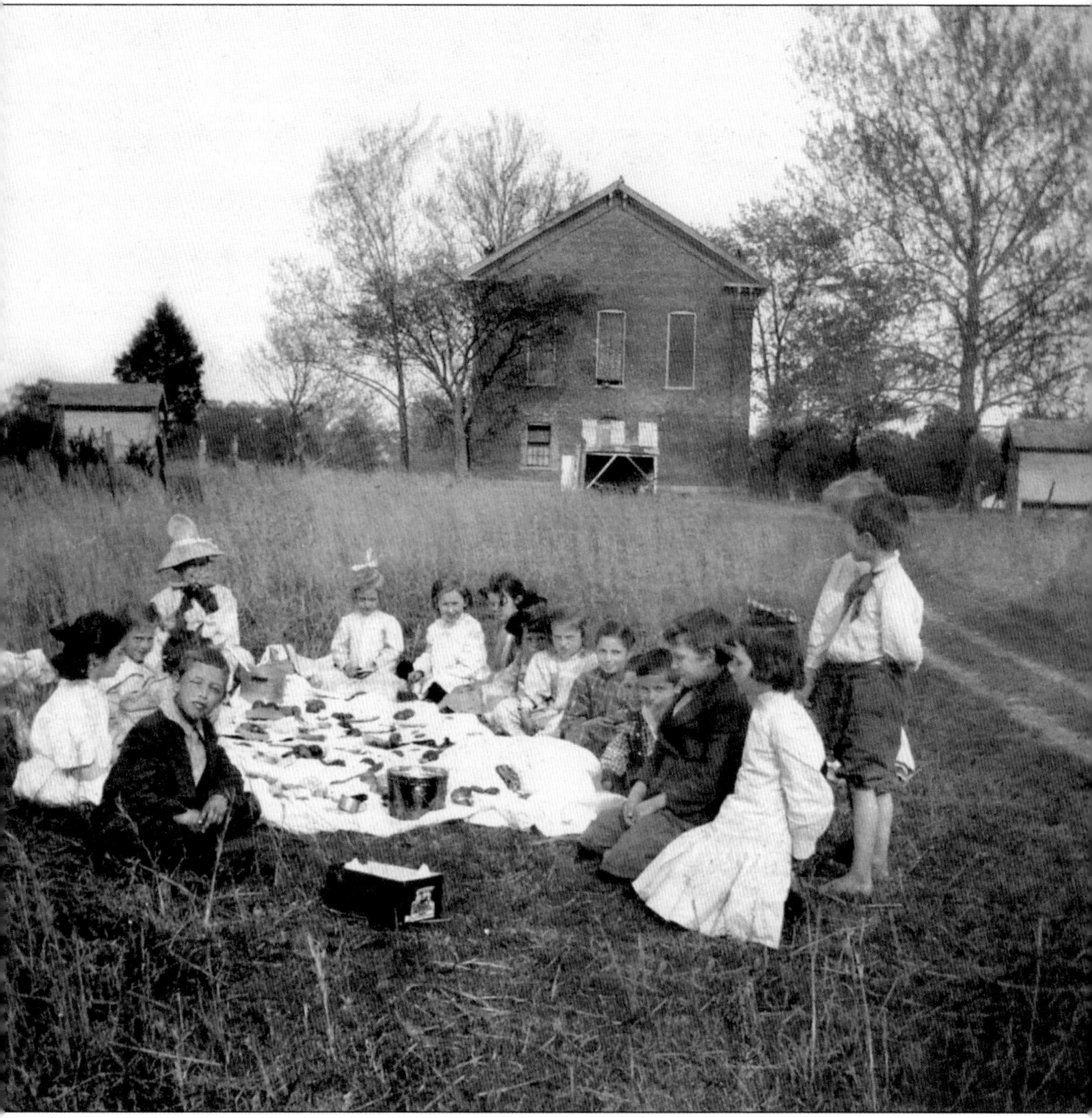

Students spread out a blanket for a picnic behind the Bartlett Courthouse School in 1915. After the circuit courts left Bartlett, Nicholas Blackwell allowed the building to be used as a school. The Bartlett Training Institute, as it was officially known, operated until 1917, when Nicholas Blackwell High School was built just west of its location on Woodlawn Street. (Courtesy of the Bartlett Historical Society.)

On the Cover: Kate Bond was the granddaughter of Dr. Samuel Bond, who settled in Ellendale in the 1830s. She inherited her parents' homestead on Stage Road and became one of Shelby County's leading horticulturists. She provided the flowers for the opening of the Claridge and Peabody Hotels in the 1920s and filled the local hospitals with her beautiful arrangements. Kate Bond Elementary School was named in her honor and is today one of the leading schools in Shelby County. (Courtesy of the Bartlett Historical Society.)

IMAGES
of America

BARTLETT

Robert W. Dye

ARCADIA
PUBLISHING

ISBN 978-0-7385-6673-3

Published by Arcadia Publishing
Charleston, South Carolina

Printed in the United States of America

Library of Congress Control Number: 2009933393

For all general information contact Arcadia Publishing at:
Telephone 843-853-2070
Fax 843-853-0044
E-mail sales@arcadiapublishing.com
For customer service and orders:
Toll-Free 1-888-313-2665

Visit us on the Internet at www.arcadiapublishing.com

This book is dedicated to Elva Bledsoe and the members of the Bartlett Historical Society who have preserved the memories and images of Bartlett, Tennessee, for future generations. All royalties from the sale of this book go directly to the Bartlett Historical Society.

Contents

ACKNOWLEDGMENTS

The images used in this book tell the story of a community made up of individuals who made a difference over the years in Bartlett. The Bartlett Historical Society should be highlighted for its commitment to preserving the history of the town. It is through its efforts that future generations will learn of our past and remember those citizens who laid the foundation for Bartlett.

Thanks to the Memphis Room of the Memphis Public Library, the Mississippi Valley Collection of the University of Memphis, and the Shelby County Archives for their help and assistance. Thanks also to David McGuire, Jo Ann Jones, and Betty Ruffin for sharing their family photographs. A special thanks goes to Jonathan K. T. Smith, who has provided a foundation for all those who will write of Bartlett in the future. His meticulous research and love of the city is very much appreciated. For those wishing additional reading on the history of Bartlett, please read his book, *Bartlett: A Beautiful City*, available through the Bartlett Historical Society, located in the historic Nicholas Gotten House at 2969 Court Street.

Unless otherwise noted, all images are from the collection of the Bartlett Historical Society.

Introduction

In the middle of the 19th century, 64 percent of the U.S. population was farmers, with the average farm containing over 200 acres. Those who settled in the Bartlett area did so for its rich soil and long growing season. In 1843, John Blackwell purchased 3,000 acres of prime farmland on the Memphis to Somerville Road, now known as Stage Road, from the heirs of Joseph Cotton for $16,000. This was equal to over $500,000 today. The farm was noted as being one of the most productive in Shelby County. Shelby County was the leading cotton-growing county in Tennessee, producing over 3,500 bales of cotton annually. From the early 1800s until the late 1960s, Bartlett was an agricultural town producing cotton, soybeans, and flowers, and beginning in the early 1900s, dairy farms began to dominate the landscape. The larger dairies, such as the Norwood Dairy and Cedar Grove Dairy on Raleigh LaGrange Road, were full processing plants. Klinke, Clifton, Tate, Haefker, Albright, and others operated smaller dairies in Bartlett. The Blackwells, Williamsons, and Warners grew strawberries, watermelons, and other fruits and vegetables, often employing the youth of the area to pick their crops in the summer. Several farms grew flowers in the Bartlett area, but the largest by far was operated by Kate Bond. Born in 1886, she lived her entire life near Bartlett at the corner of Kate Bond Road and Stage Road. She provided flowers for the opening of the Claridge and Peabody Hotels in the 1920s and regularly donated flowers to local hospitals. For many years, she sold her flowers at the Crosstown Curb Market in Memphis. In the spring, when her daffodils were in full bloom, people would drive to Bartlett just to see her flowers. When a new school was built near her home in the 1990s, it was named Kate Bond Elementary in her honor.

As the *Memphis Daily Argus* reported on August 22, 1866, "In the fall of 1865 the citizens of Union Depot endeavored to secure a name for the place by which the depot and the post office should be known and have wisely settled upon the name of Bartlett in honor of one of the oldest citizens of the county and most liberal of the village inhabitants [Gabriel Maston Bartlett]. Bartlett will soon be incorporated as soon as the legislature meets."

The first election was held on May 2, 1867, with the results as follows: Gabriel Bartlett was elected mayor; W. T. Pryor, Dr. W. B. Wright, J. B. Mercer, H. L. Priddy, and Nicholas Blackwell were chosen as aldermen; and Nicholas Gotten became constable.

Legislation was passed in 1869 whereby a circuit court could be established for three terms a year in Bartlett. Dr. Nicholas Blackwell and his business partner, Dr. William T. Pryor, owned most of the land in the town and decided to donate a lot for a town square. In 1870, bids were taken for the construction of the courthouse, and the winning bid was James Oglesby for $12,449. A brick kiln was set up and bricks made onsite for the two-story courthouse. With the increased business from the courts, the town of Bartlett grew, adding a hotel, several saloons, and various general stores. The courts were closed in 1885, and the courthouse was used for the next 32 years as a school. Bartlett citizens discovered that an unincorporated city could not serve liquor. In an attempt to curb the use of alcohol, they voted to dissolve the city charter in 1885, thus ridding the town of its saloons. The town reapplied to gain its charter, but due to the depopulation from the loss of the circuit courts, it was denied. The town was finally rechartered in 1905 with the same form of government as before.

Despite the many photographs in this book, there is one image that is missed more than any other. That is the photograph of the founder of the city that so many call home today. Gabriel Maston Bartlett was born in Robertson County, Tennessee, on November 27, 1821. The family had moved to Tennessee from South Carolina along with the Blackwells. At the time, Tennessee was a wilderness, Memphis had a population of only a few thousand, and Native Americans were still a frequent sight in West Tennessee. In his early 20s, Gabriel Bartlett visited his cousin John Blackwell, who lived in Fayette County, Tennessee, and while there, he met Elizabeth Glasgow, whom he married on December 3, 1846. The next year, he and his bride purchased a large tract of land in Green Bottom next to the Goodwood plantation, recently purchased by his cousin John Blackwell. In 1848, Gabriel Bartlett was elected justice of the peace for Civil District 7, a position he held until his death. Sadly, Elizabeth died in childbirth in 1851, leaving Gabriel with a young son, Tommy. Gabriel Bartlett was a Democrat, active in the Methodist Episcopal church, and an advocate of the temperance movement. Major Bartlett, as he became known, was elected a state representative from Shelby County in 1855, serving on the elections and banking committees. In 1854, Bartlett married Rebecca Cross and purchased the Pruden home, about 3 miles west of his former residence. His estate, covering almost 400 acres, had fruit trees, vegetable gardens, wheat fields, a cotton gin, and a corn mill. This property today is the Bartlett Historic District. In 1859, Bartlett hired a surveyor to lay out his property for the purpose of creating a town. Lots were sold, and slowly a community emerged. The Civil War put a halt to most business in the area, and his vision of a town was put on hold. Union Depot, as the town was called, consisted of a train station, a large plantation home, and several smaller homes. In his memoirs, Union general Lew Wallace mentioned what a beautiful and peaceful place the town was. In 1864, Bartlett became business partners with J. W. Gould and R. L. Yancey, operating as cotton factors on Front Street in Memphis. The store supplied groceries, hardware, and cotton supplies to the local farmers. The business folded in 1868 and left Bartlett in great debt. He sold his land holdings to Nicholas Blackwell and William Pryor for $24,000, and they carried on with his vision of a town. In 1866, the small community was incorporated and named in honor of the man who first decided to develop the land, Gabriel Bartlett. Bartlett became the city's first mayor and helped to lay the foundation for the great city it is today. Bartlett would not live to see his city grow as he had hoped, passing away in 1876 while visiting his sister in Robertson County. He did not leave much in the way of possessions. There are no photographs and no diaries or ledgers to tell us about this man. What he left was a seed of a community planted in the fertile ground of a place he called home, a place we today call Bartlett, Tennessee.

One

Early History

After the Revolutionary War, veterans could receive a specific number of acres of land in the west. The west at that time was the land east of the Mississippi River and west of the Cumberland Mountains. Land speculators would buy up these claims and proceed to hire surveyors to find the best land and have it surveyed and certified. By 1838, over 8 million acres of land had been claimed by North Carolinians. Three of the major land grants in the Bartlett area were to William Polk, Richard Smith, and George Doherty. The Polk land grant of 5,000 acres was surveyed by John Ralston and processed in 1820. This land was north of Stage Road to the Loosahatchie River. John Ralston also surveyed 2,560 acres in what would become Ellendale for Richard Smith in 1822. George Doherty's 3,000 acres were surveyed by William Lawrence and processed in 1822. This tract ran from Bartlett Road east along both sides of Stage Road to Germantown Road. The owners made their money by selling the subdivided parcels to investors or to farmers looking for better land to grow their crops. In 1829, the Memphis to Somerville Road was cut through Shelby County. This would eventually become known as Stage Road. During the relocation of the Native Americans, known as the Trail of Tears, one of the routes passed along the Memphis to Somerville Road in 1832. Raleigh LaGrange Road was laid out in 1829. In 1854, Bartlett Road was laid out from Stage Road toward Raleigh LaGrange Road. In 1856, the New Brownsville Road was laid out toward Memphis-Arlington Road from Stage Road. This road is today known as Sycamore View Road.

In 1851, a contract was issued to build a plank road out from Memphis toward the Fayette County line. Wood planks were laid to give easier access for wagons traveling along the road. Tollgates were built at intervals to collect payments for use of the road. There was a tollgate at Stage Road and the railroad tracks and another just past Germantown Road. Today the only thing left from this time is a small cemetery called Tollgate Cemetery just east of Germantown Road. Tolls for passage along the road were 35¢ for buggies and wagons and 10¢ for those on horseback. The venture did not succeed, and the tollgate in Union Depot was closed in 1856. By the start of the Civil War, the upkeep on the plank road was abandoned and Stage Road reverted back to a dirt road. In 1929, State Highway 1/U.S. Highway 70 was laid out from Memphis towards Nashville. Where it crossed Stage Road has long been known as Four Way.

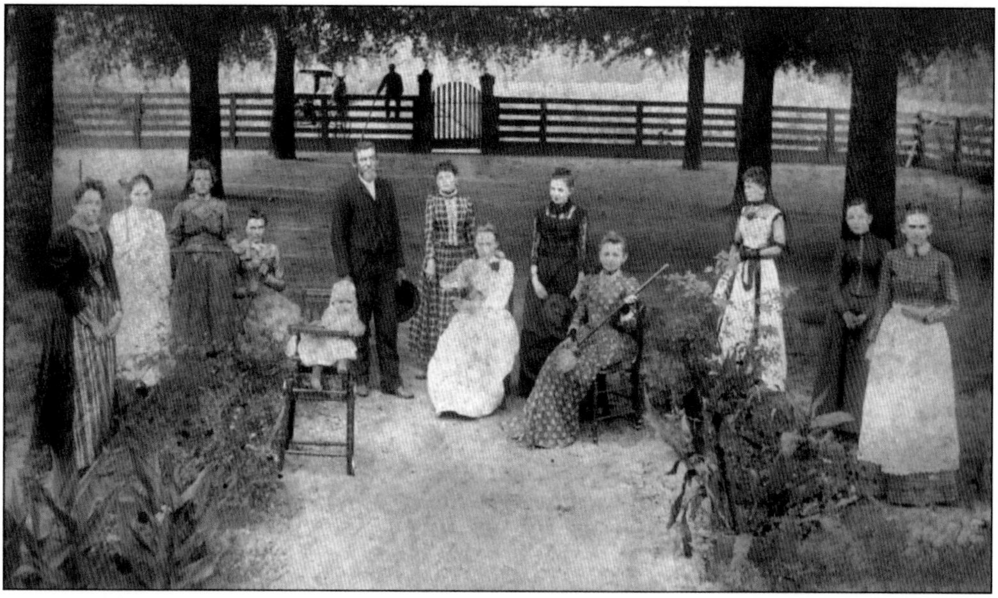

The Bond family, shown here in 1900, arrived in the Bartlett area around 1830, settling in the Ellendale community northeast of Bartlett. Among the first Bonds were Dr. Washington Bond, Dr. Samuel Bond, John Bond, and Newton Bond, all brothers who moved from Alabama. The home of Dr. Samuel Bond, Cedar Hall, was built in 1845; it still stands in Ellendale today and is listed on the National Register of Historic Places.

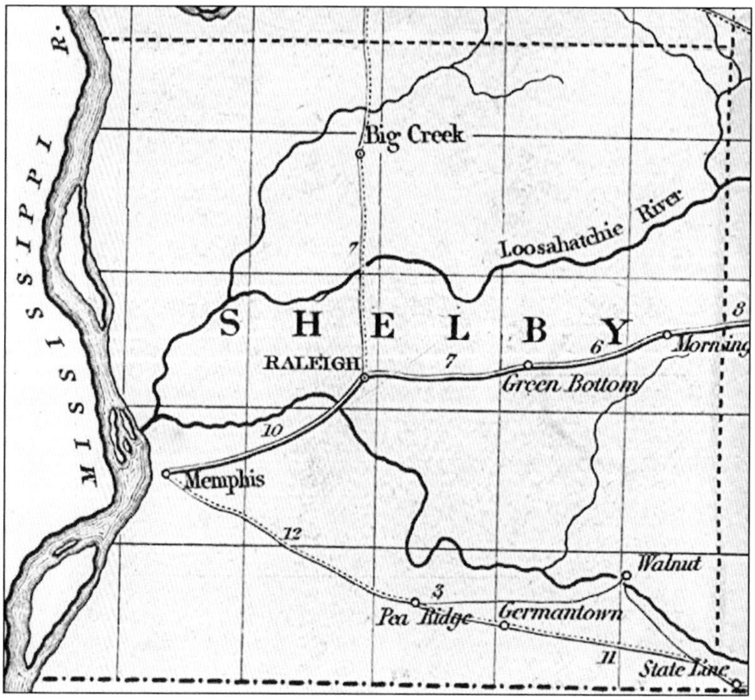

In 1839, when this map was created, there was no Bartlett and no Union Depot, only a small community on the Memphis to Somerville Road near Kate Bond Road called Green Bottom.

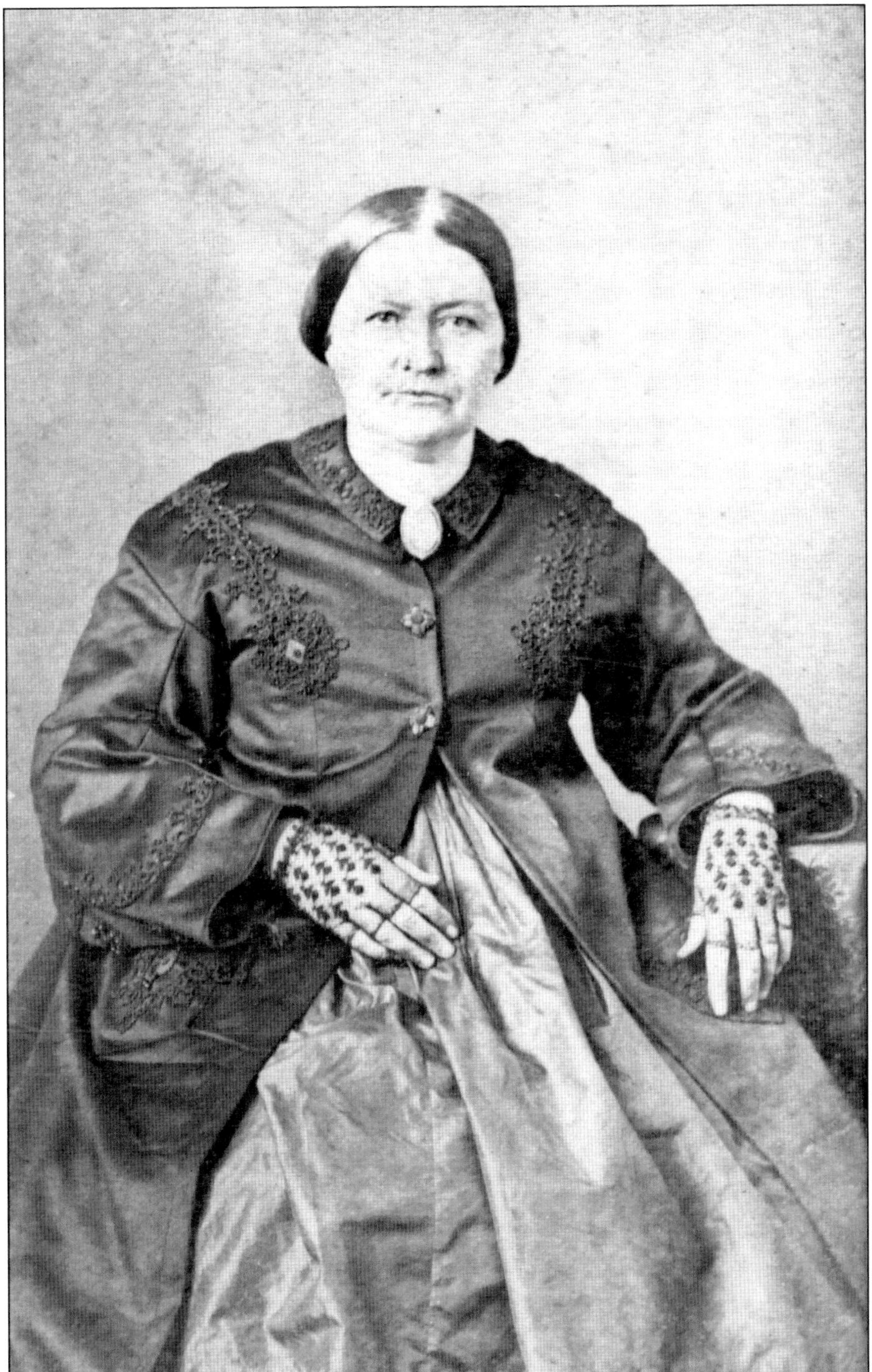

Martha Alexander Ward was born in 1823 and moved to Bartlett in 1832 with her family. She was the daughter of Adam R. Alexander, a planter and political rival of Davy Crockett. In 1845, she married Joseph Ward and lived on a large farm surrounded by 600 acres on Stage Road between Sycamore View Road and Alturia Road.

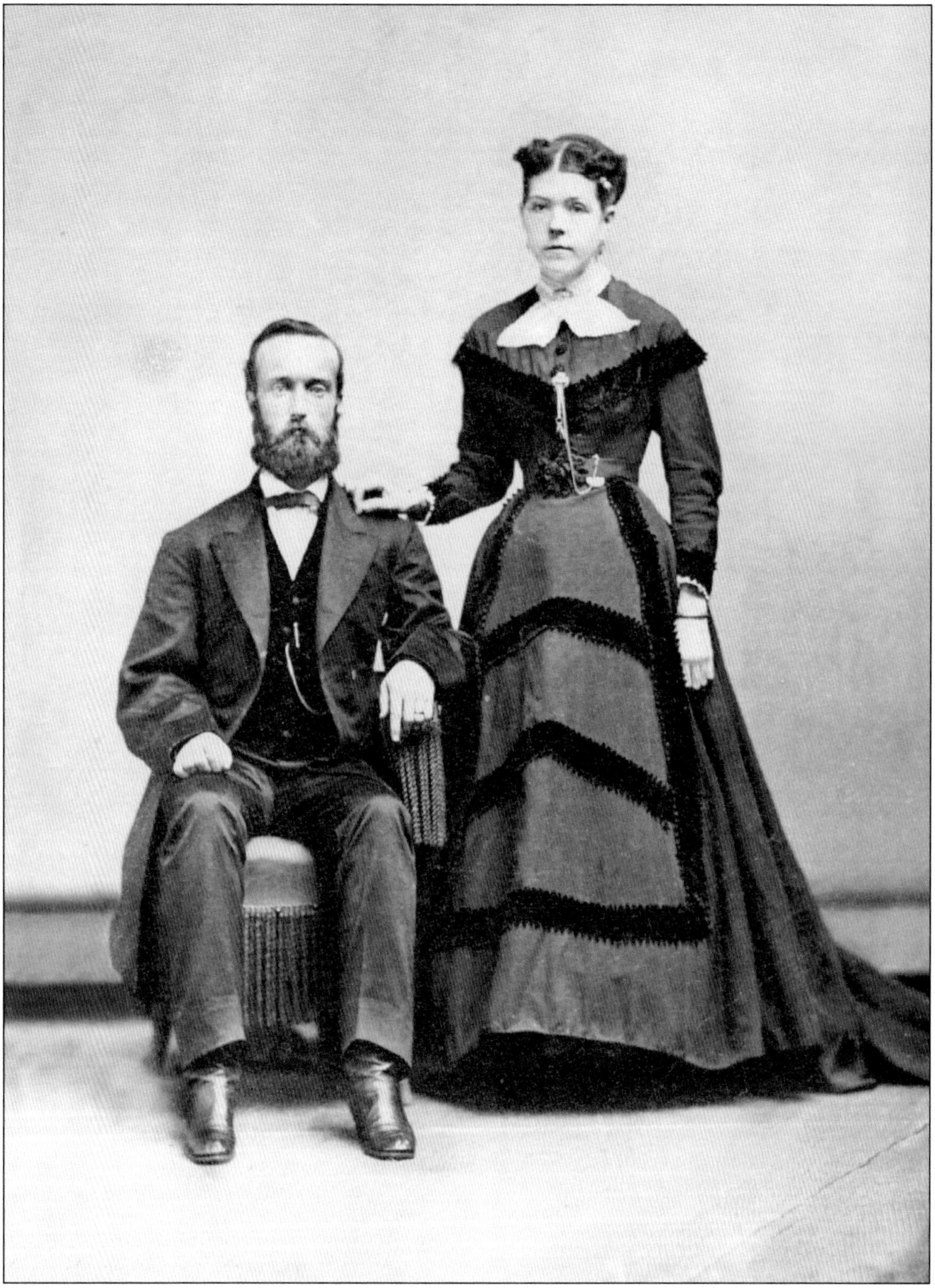

Nicholas Blackwell moved to Bartlett just after the Civil War and became a leading physician and land developer in the area. In 1866, he married Lucy Virginia Ward, whose family owned a large farm on Stage Road. Virginia was the granddaughter of Col. Adam R. Alexander, a political rival of Davy Crockett. Sadly, Virginia died in 1872, leaving Nicholas with their only child, Willie Bugg Blackwell.

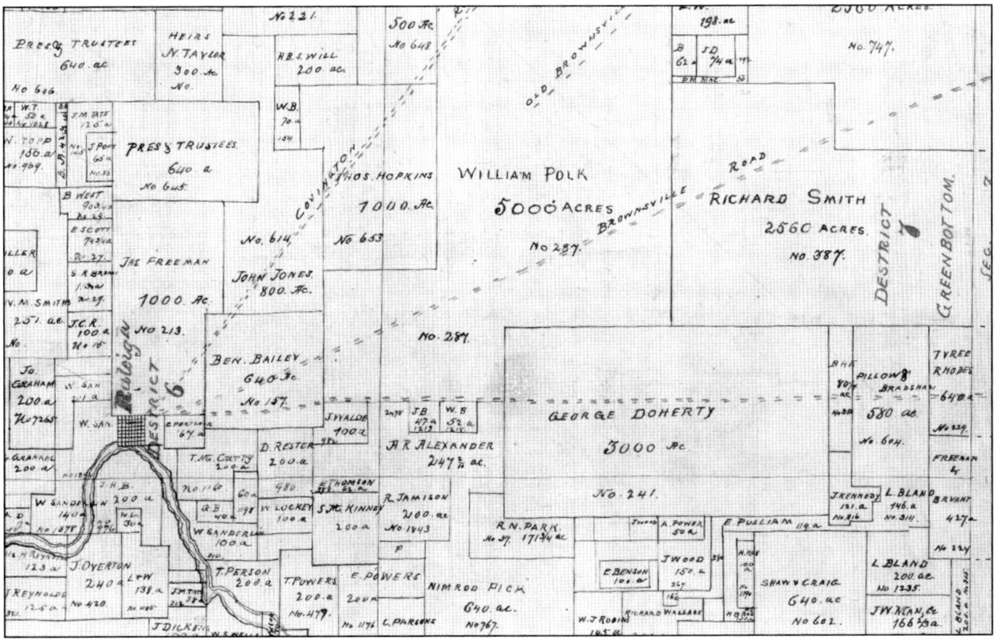

This 1850 Wherry Map shows the land grants in the Bartlett area as they appeared in 1830. The three largest were the Polk, Smith, and Doherty grants made in the early 1820s.

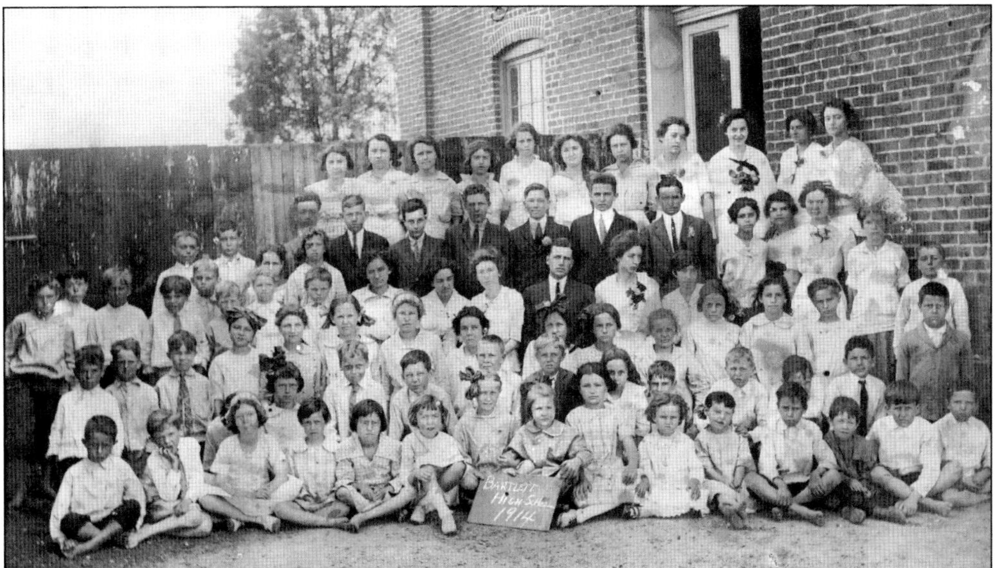
An early photograph, taken in 1914, shows the Bartlett Courthouse School. All grades, 1 through 12, attended in the same building. In 1917, a new modern school, Nicholas Blackwell High School, was built just west of the courthouse.

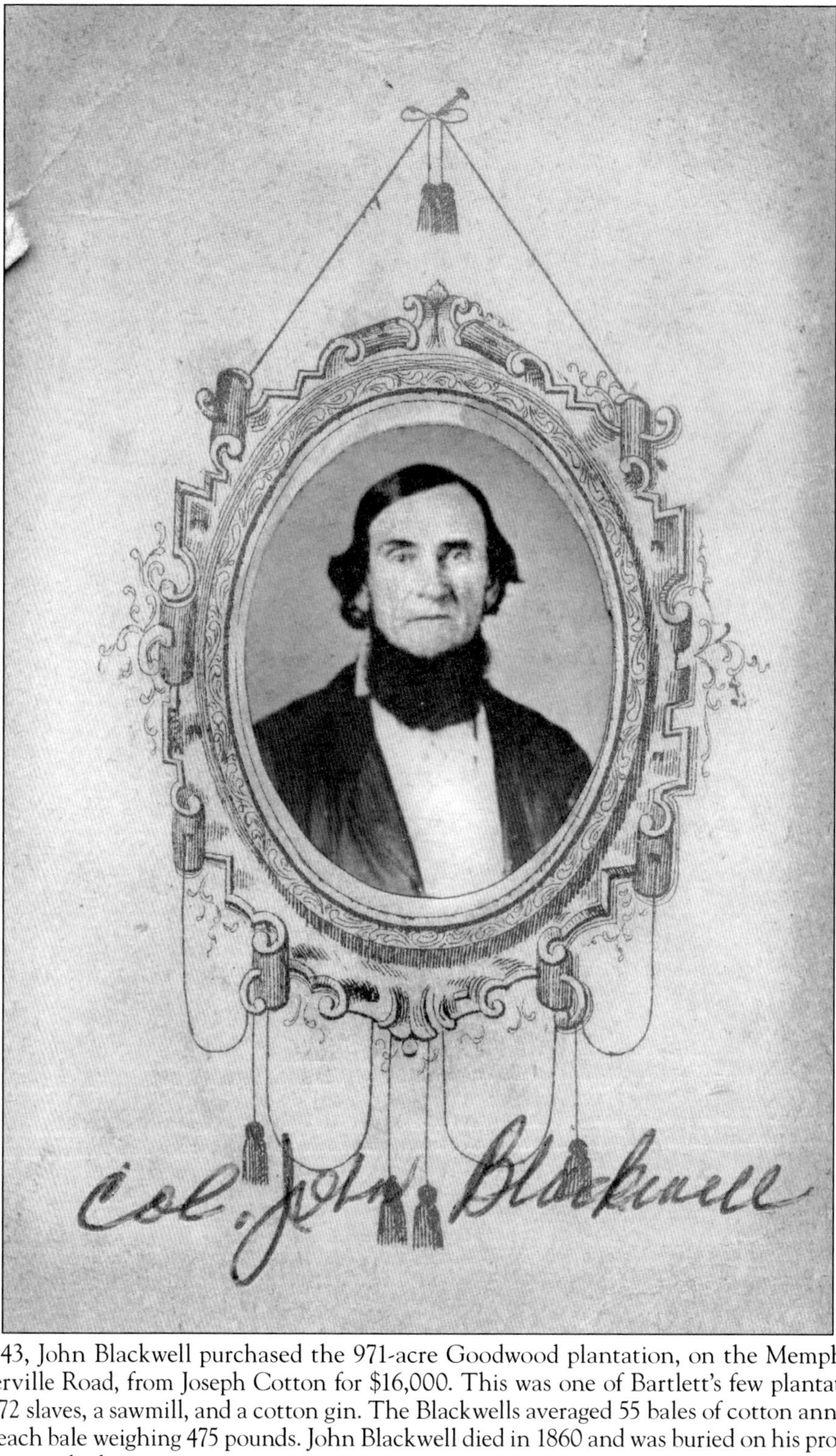

In 1843, John Blackwell purchased the 971-acre Goodwood plantation, on the Memphis to Somerville Road, from Joseph Cotton for $16,000. This was one of Bartlett's few plantations, with 72 slaves, a sawmill, and a cotton gin. The Blackwells averaged 55 bales of cotton annually, with each bale weighing 475 pounds. John Blackwell died in 1860 and was buried on his property in an unmarked grave.

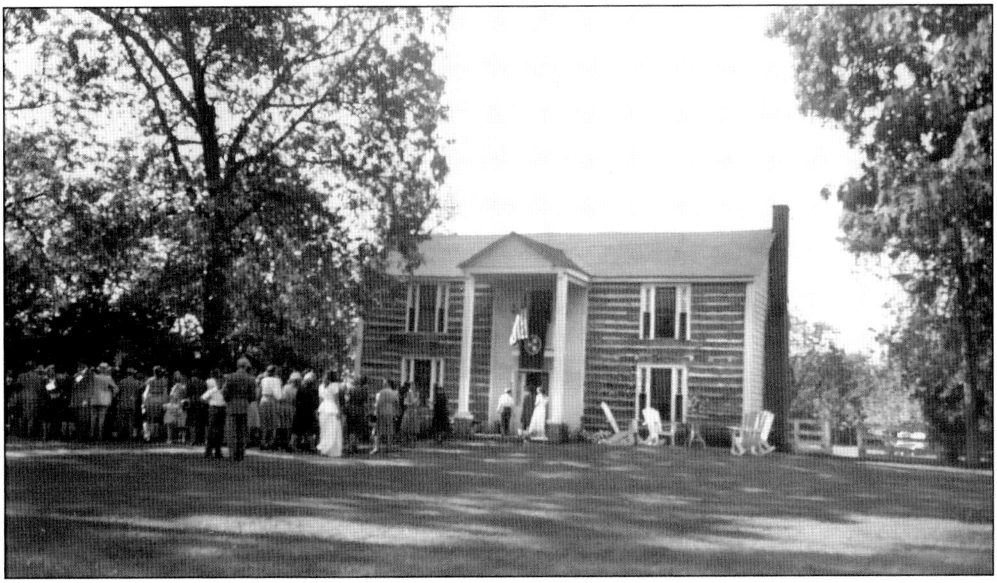

Davies Manor was originally a single-room log cabin that was added onto over the years. The builder is unknown, but it is believed to have been constructed in the 1830s and is today the oldest home in Bartlett.

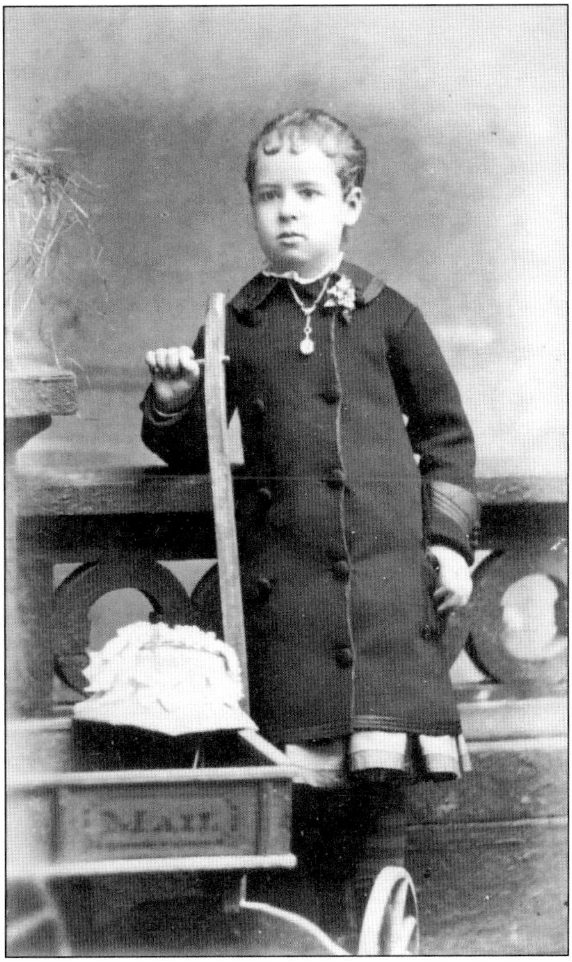

The Arbuckle family arrived in Bartlett in 1891 and lived at the corner of Main Street and Sycamore View Road in the old Dr. Benjamin Eddins home. Mary Arbuckle grew up in Bartlett and attended the Bartlett Courthouse School.

TENNESSEE STATE GAZETTEER

BARTLETT.

A thriving village of 450 people, settled in 1863, incorporated in 1867, and located in Shelby county, 11 miles from Memphis, the seat of justice, and 220 from Nashville. It is a station on the L. & N. and G. S. R. R., and has one steam saw and grist mill, 4 churches, Methodist, Baptist, Cumberland Presbyterian and Colored Baptist, 1 white and 1 colored school. Cotton is the principal product and shipment. Express, southern. Mail daily. W. B. Wright, postmaster.

Business Directory.

Barteau, C. R., lawyer.
Bartlett, G. M., magistrate.
Blackwell, N., Physician.
Brooks, John M., lawyer.
Brown, M. L., county surveyor.
Cochran, John F., physician.
Cross, W. R., General Store.
Eddins, H. B., eclectic physician.
Fairs, E., express agent.
Forgay, Abraham, carpenter.
Gotten, N., miller.
Johnston, Rev. B. W., (Methodist).
Kimbro, B. J., lawyer.
King, T. J., grocer.
Means, R. P., physician.
Mercer, T. D., hotel.
Mercer, W. T., butcher.
Moon, Jacob, blacksmith.
Priddy, H. L., general store.
Ray, J. E. R., judge.
Reeves, B. T., lawyer.
Reeves, W. G., lawyer.
Shelby, D. G., lawyer.
Smith, Sullivan, undertaker.
Wesson, J. N., saloon.
Wolfe, Wm. wagonmaker.
Wright & Moody, General Store.

The *Tennessee Gazetteer* of 1877 listed Bartlett as a "thriving village of 450 people." By now, the circuit courts of Shelby County had established a courthouse in Bartlett, and the city was growing, with six lawyers, a hotel, and a saloon.

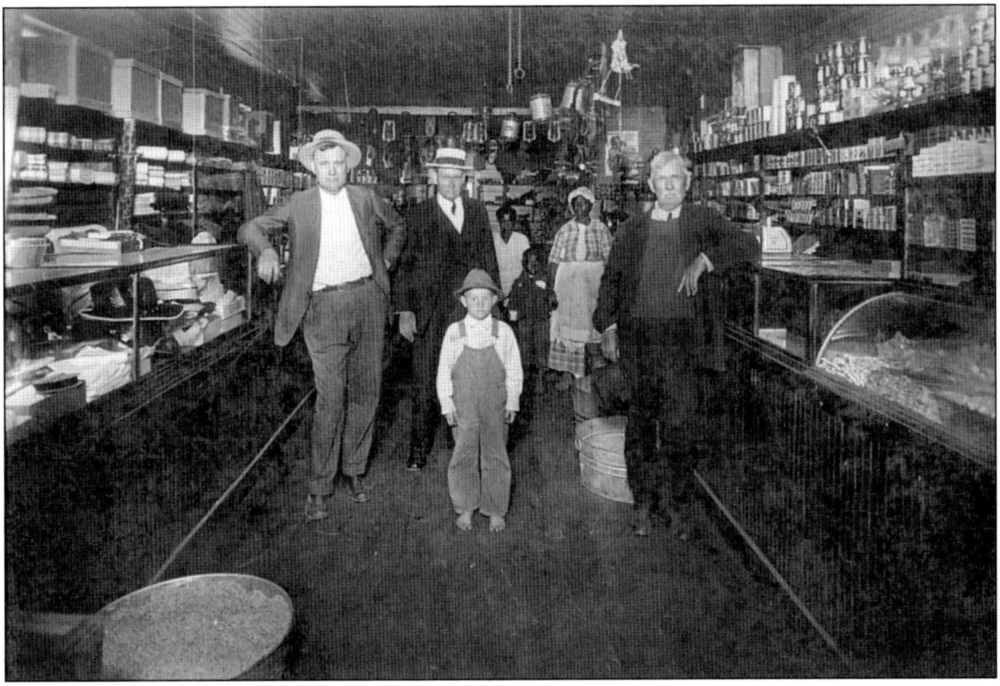

The B. P. Herring Store, located in Ellendale, was built in the early 1900s. The small boy in the front is Brack Herring, a longtime Ellendale resident.

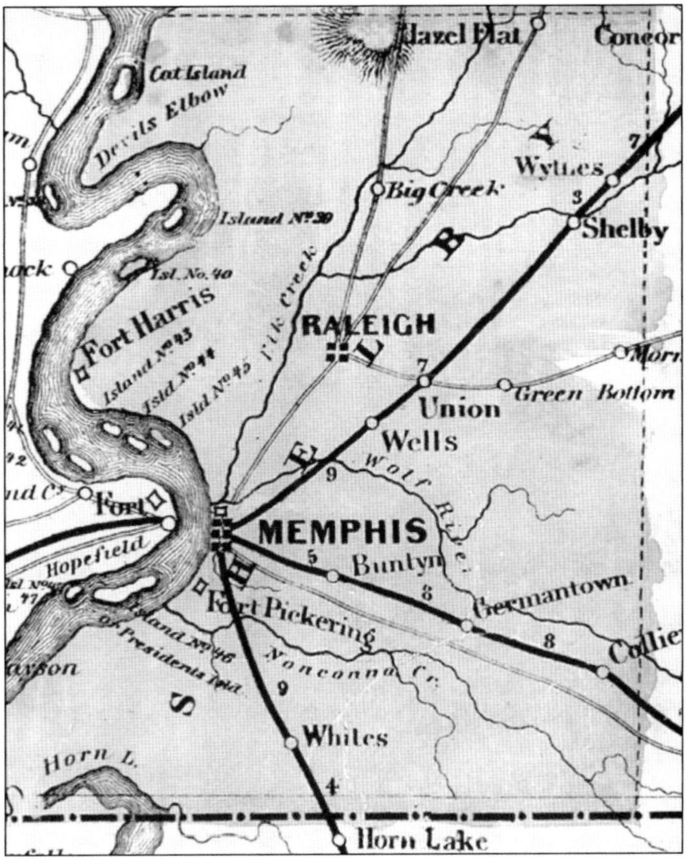

An 1857 map of Shelby County shows Union Depot and Green Bottom, which encompass much of Bartlett today. Big Creek in northern Shelby County was one of the county's first communities, established in 1808.

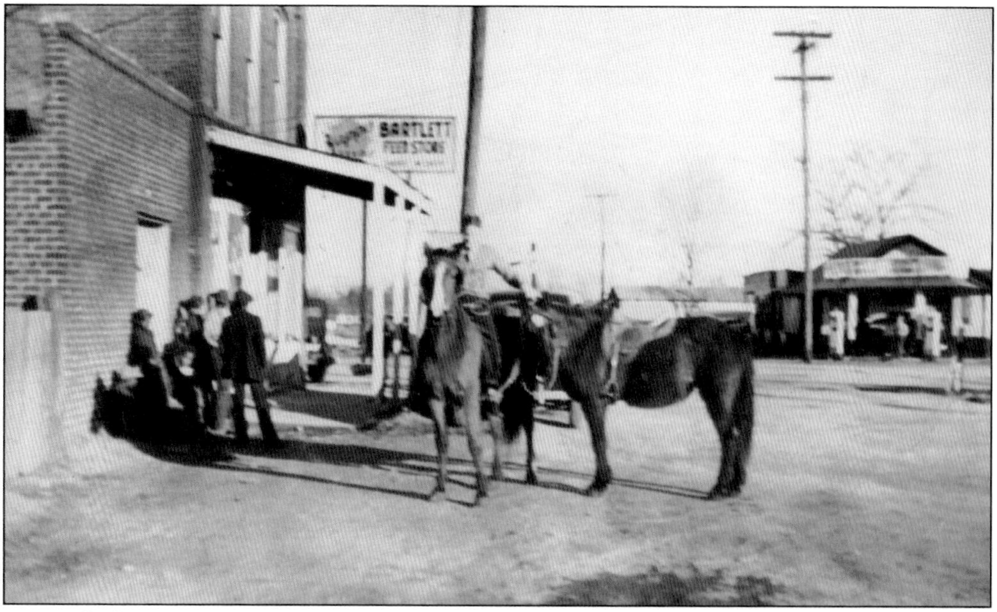

A view looks east down Stage Road from present-day Court Street around 1930. The gas station on the far right is where Warr and Geurin garage is located today.

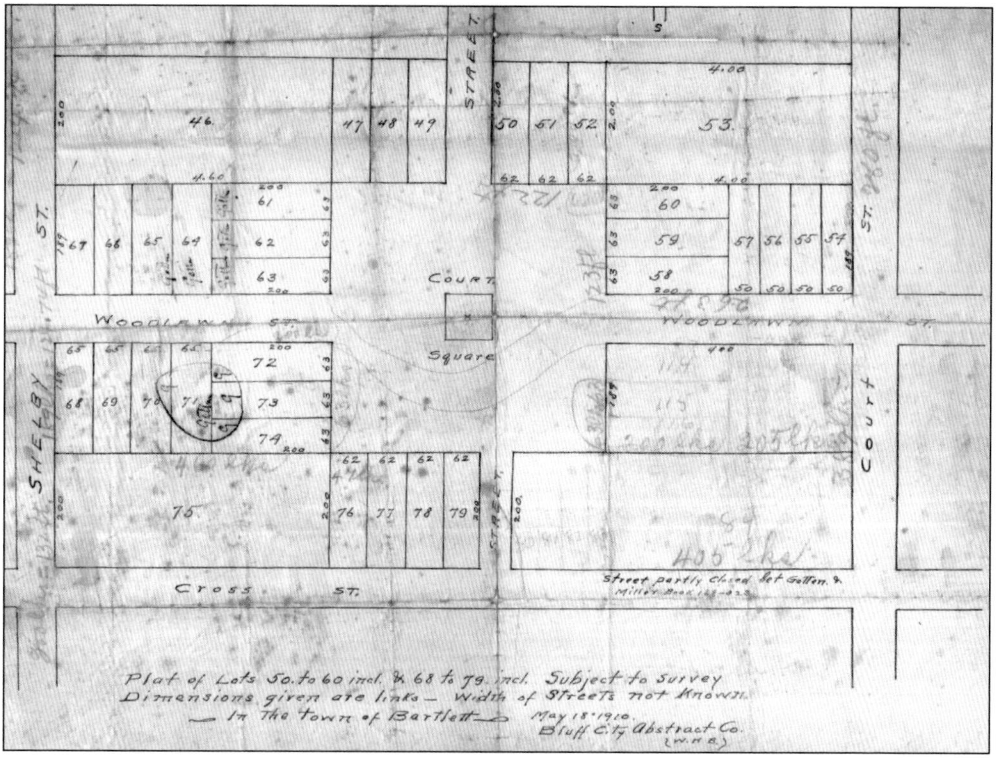

The town of Bartlett had intended to have a town square surrounding its courthouse. One of the first lots sold was to Nicholas Gotten. The circuit courts came to Bartlett in 1870, but by 1885, they were returned to Memphis. The plan for a court square to be located where Bartlett High School is today was never realized, with only the plat map above showing its location.

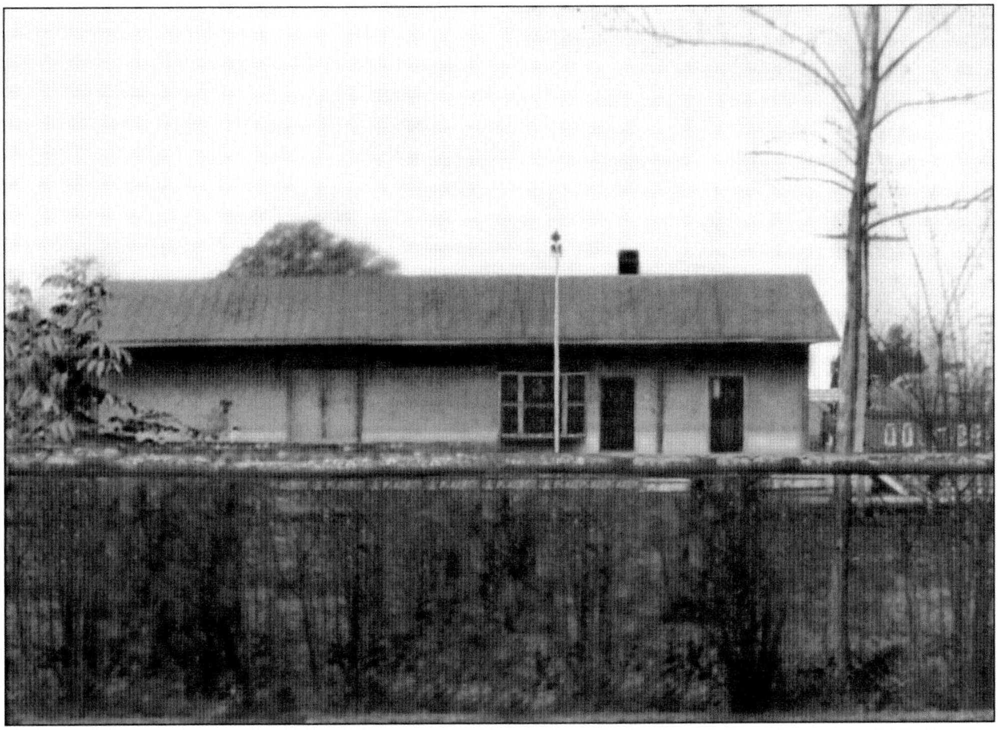

The Memphis and Ohio Railroad began laying tracks in 1852 from Memphis toward Nashville. A depot was built about 12 miles out from Memphis and was named Union Depot. It crossed the Memphis to Somerville Road, now known as Stage Road. The depot survived the Civil War and was a focal point of Bartlett until 1940, when it was torn down.

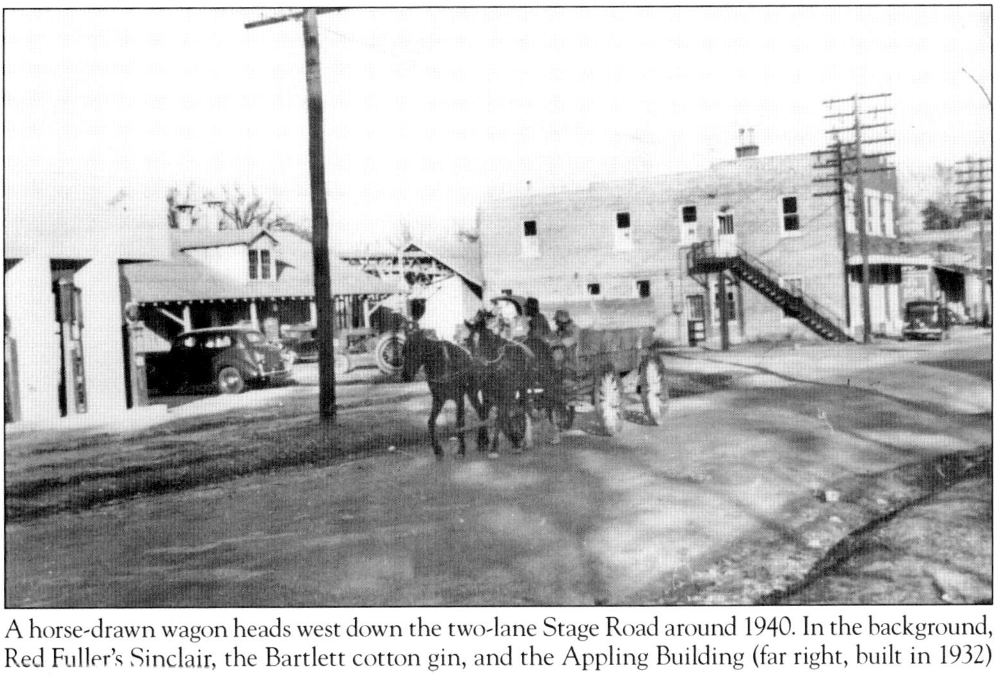

A horse-drawn wagon heads west down the two-lane Stage Road around 1940. In the background, Red Fuller's Sinclair, the Bartlett cotton gin, and the Appling Building (far right, built in 1932) can be seen.

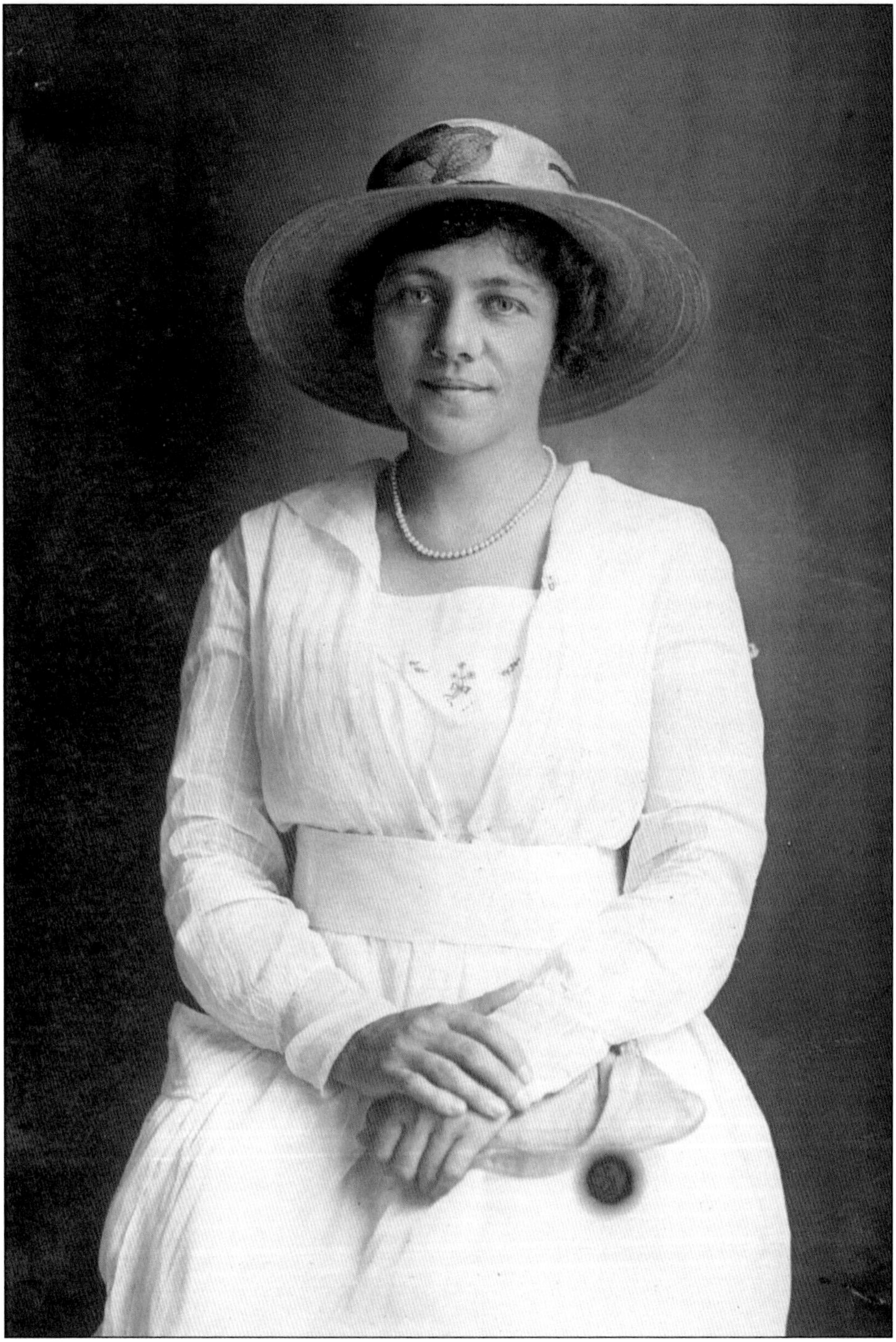

Nannie Bartlett, shown above around 1905, was the granddaughter of Gabriel Maston Bartlett, the founder of Bartlett. She had one daughter who had no children. Nannie Bartlett passed away in 1951, leaving no possessions related to her family. For many years, a large painting of Gabriel Bartlett hung in her home. After her death in 1951, the painting disappeared and today there is not a single known image of Gabriel Bartlett.

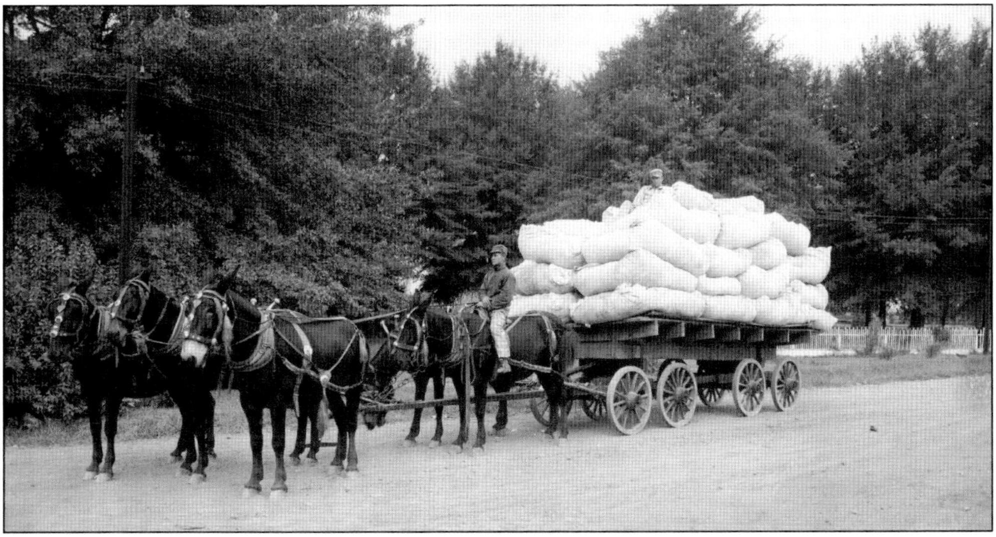

Before the railroad was completed in 1855, cotton had to be hauled to the gin or to Memphis by horse-drawn wagon. Travel was difficult on the muddy road of early Shelby County. For a time, cotton could be hauled down the Wolf River from Raleigh.

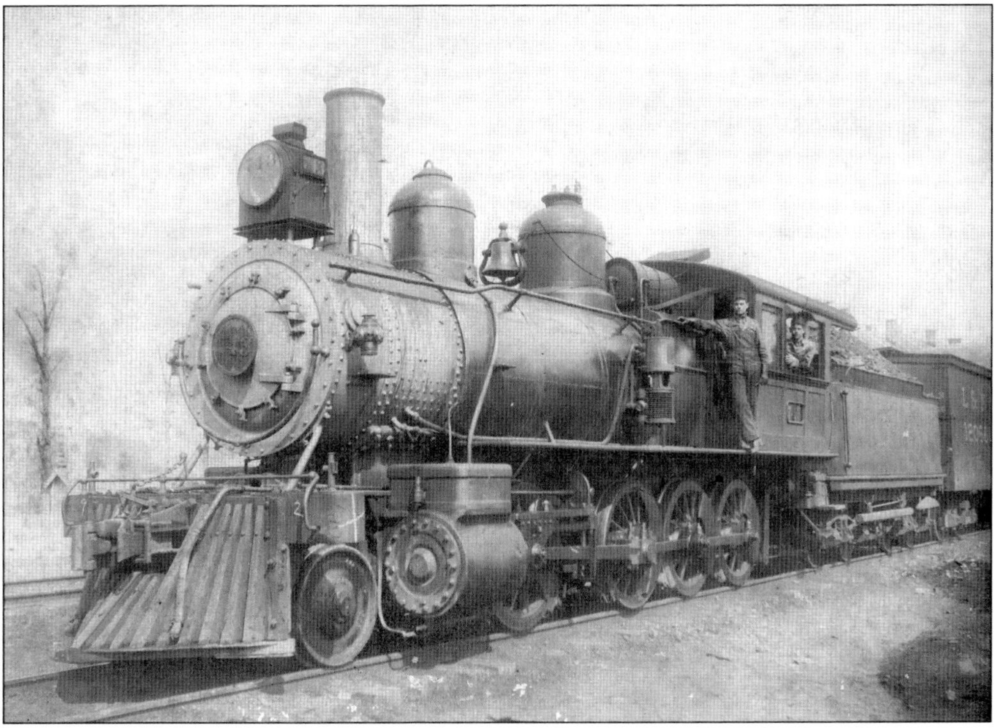

The railroad in Bartlett brought food, furnishings, and building materials to the growing community. The mail was picked up daily from a large mailbag hung on a pole located next to the depot. As the train passed, a hook would grab the outgoing mail. For many years, businessmen who worked in downtown Memphis traveled from Bartlett to Memphis daily on the train.

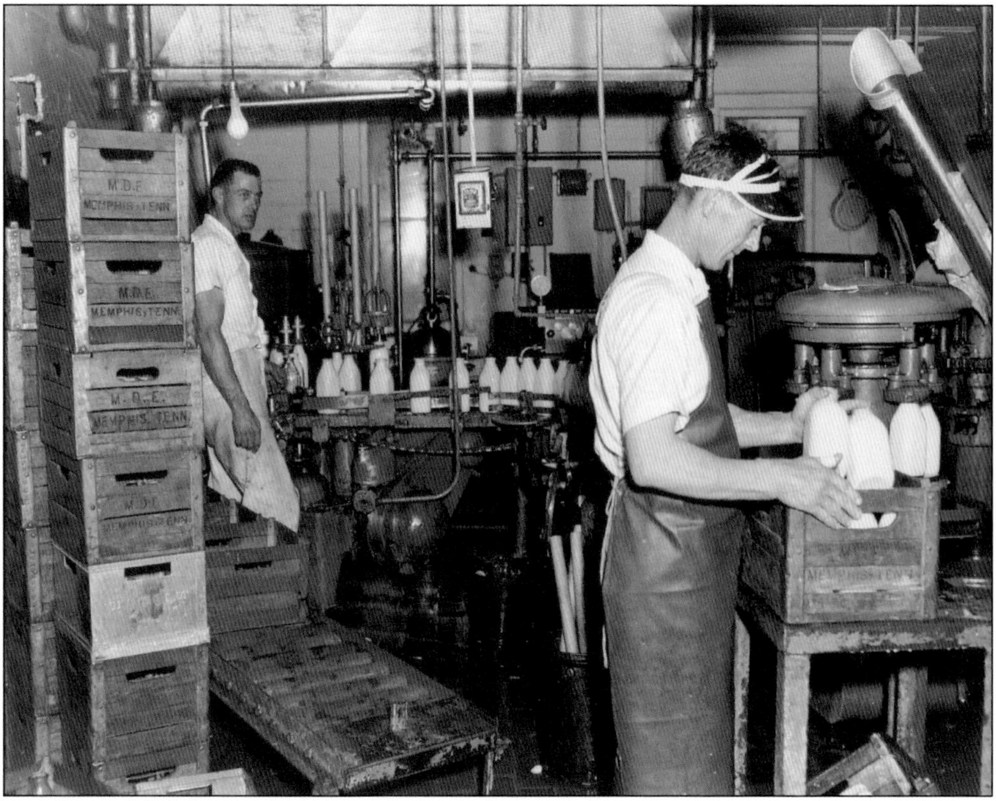

Due to the infestation of the boll weevil on cotton and land, which had been depleted from years of farming, cattle dairies saw a dramatic upswing beginning in the 1920s. By the 1950s, there were as many as 20 dairies in the Bartlett area. The largest were Cedar Grove (shown above), Norwood Brothers, and the Klinke Dairy.

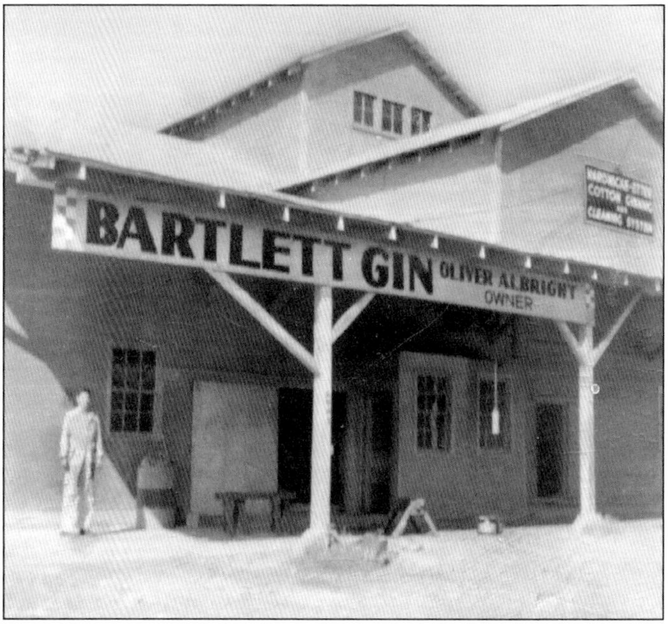

The Bartlett cotton gin, shown here in 1952, was owned by the Albright family and operated as a cotton processing plant, creating large 450-pound bales of cotton. Once pressed into bales, the cotton would be loaded onto trains and sent to warehouses in Memphis.

Most families in Bartlett had some type of garden. The larger farms would sometimes hire the local school kids to help pick crops in the summer.

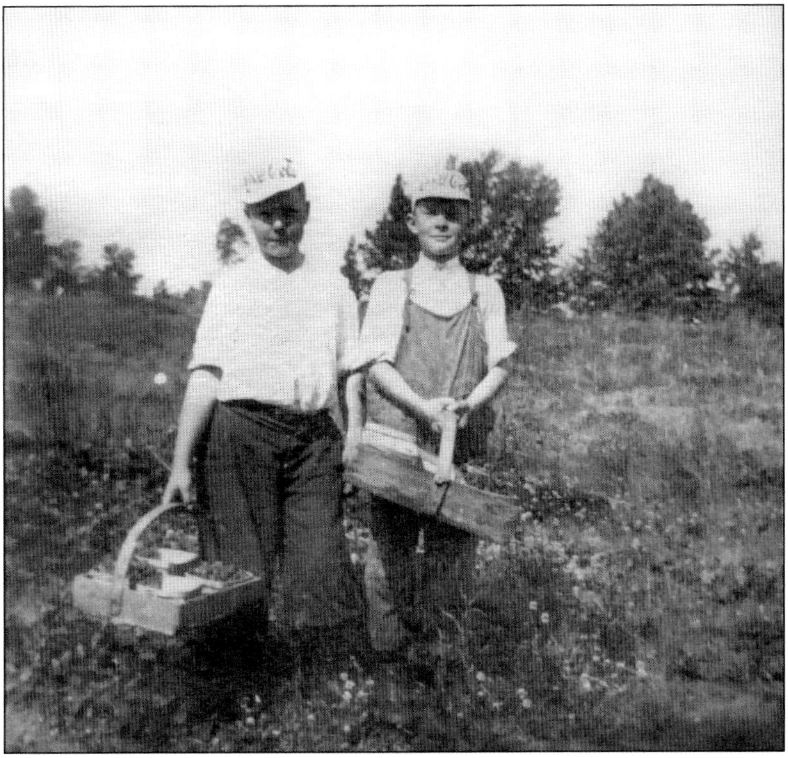

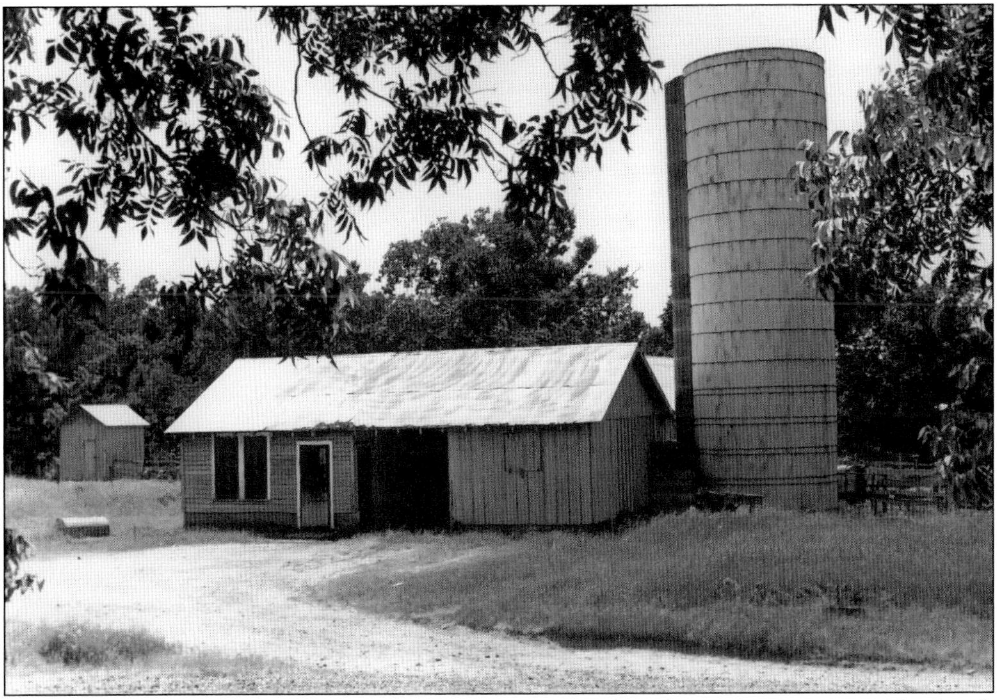

The Warner farm was located on Raleigh LaGrange Road in the Cedar Grove neighborhood. The farm was known for its large strawberry and watermelon fields. The Warners moved to the Bartlett area from Germany in the 1850s.

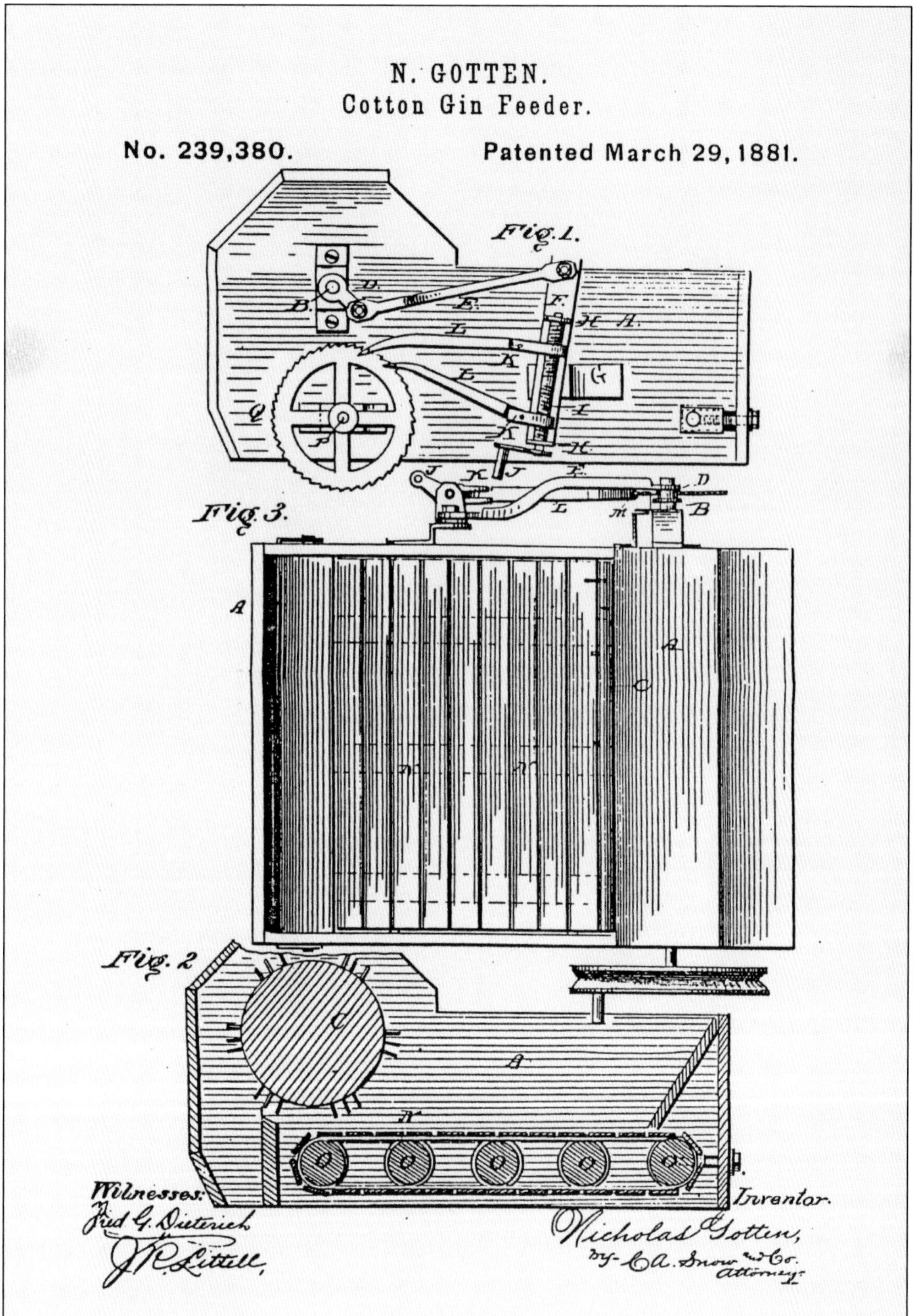

Nicholas Gotten applied for and was issued a U.S. patent for an improvement to a cotton gin feeder on March 29, 1881. Gotten served under Nathan Bedford Forrest during the Civil War as a Confederate cavalryman. He also volunteered his services as a blacksmith.

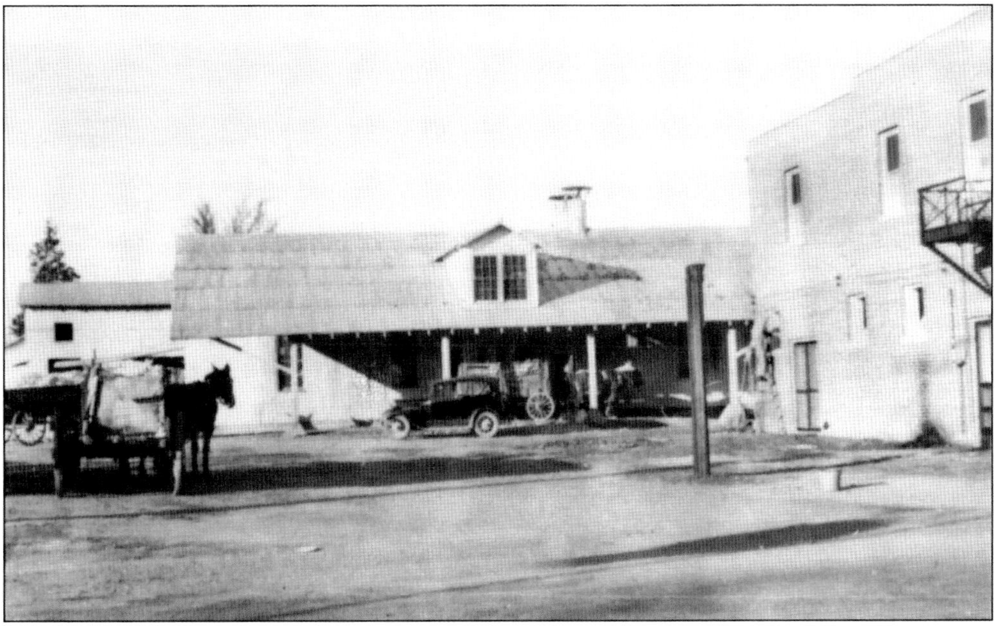

The first cotton gin in Bartlett was established just after the Civil War. The gin shown here in the 1930s was operated by Nicholas Gotten and served an area of over 10 miles around Bartlett.

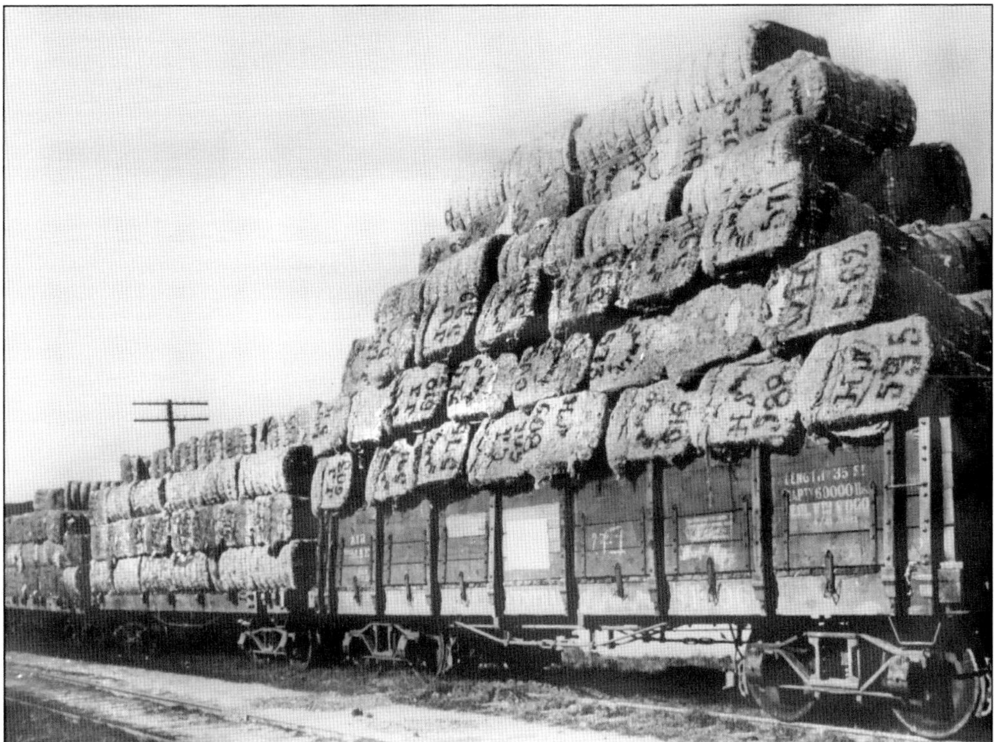

Before the railroad was laid out to Bartlett in 1855, cotton had to be hauled by wagon over unpredictable dirt roads. With the advent of the rail lines, cotton could be hauled quickly and safely to warehouses in south Memphis before being delivered to cotton mills in the northeast.

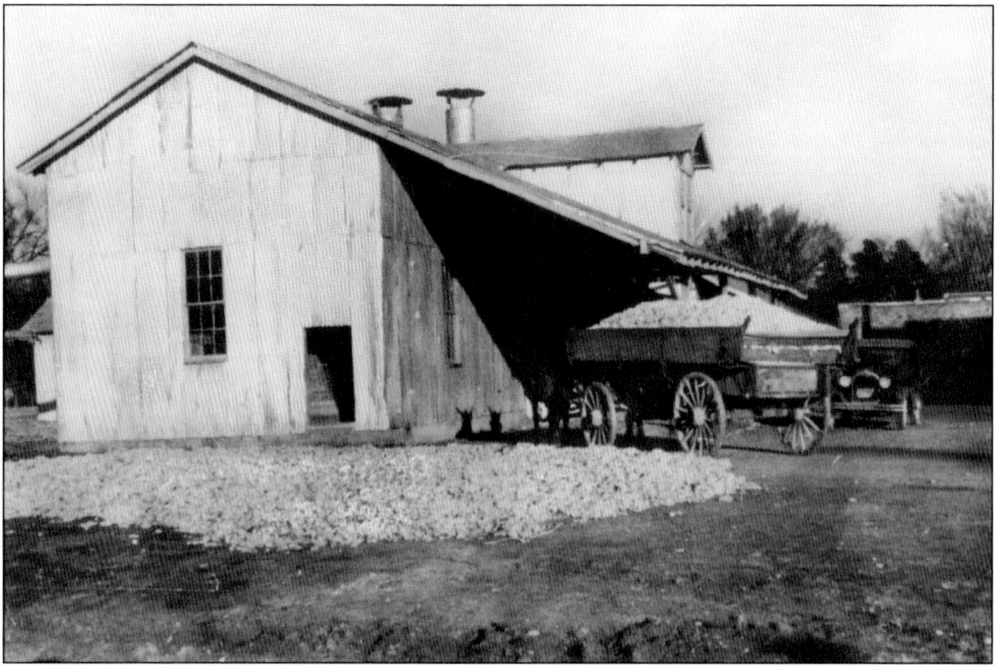

The Bartlett cotton gin would take the raw cotton brought in by horse-drawn wagons and process it into bales weighing up to 450 pounds each.

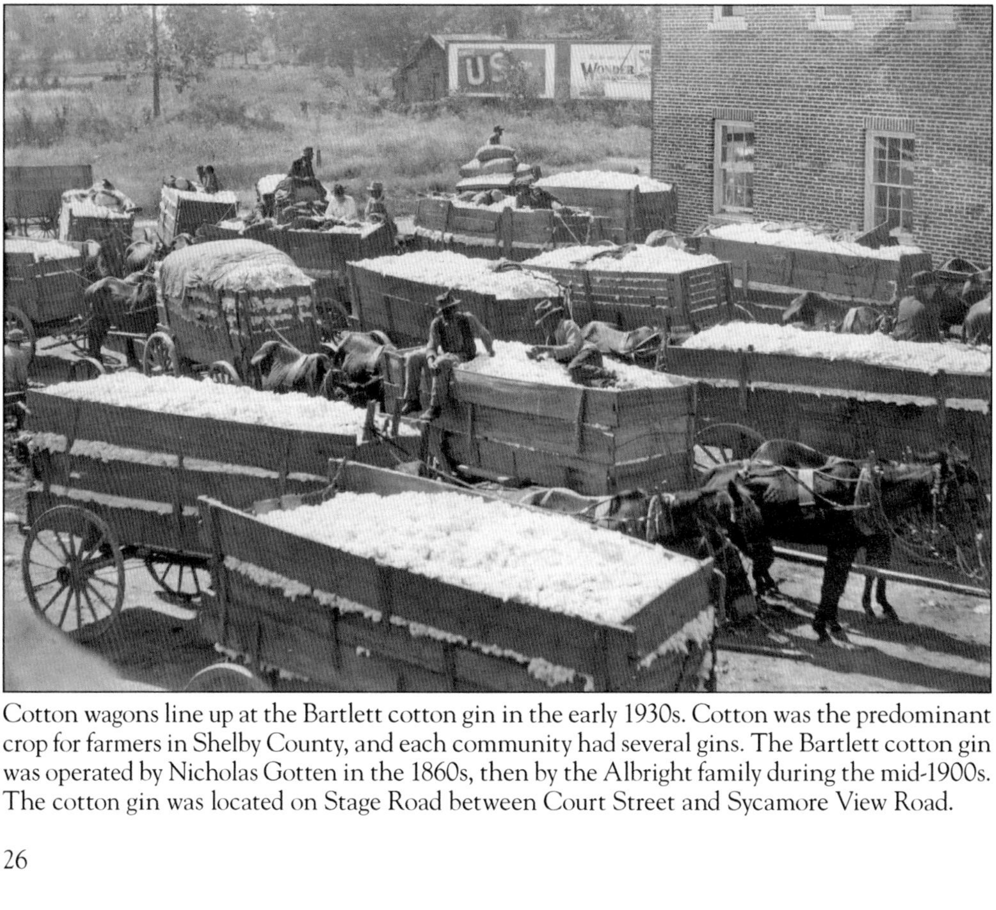

Cotton wagons line up at the Bartlett cotton gin in the early 1930s. Cotton was the predominant crop for farmers in Shelby County, and each community had several gins. The Bartlett cotton gin was operated by Nicholas Gotten in the 1860s, then by the Albright family during the mid-1900s. The cotton gin was located on Stage Road between Court Street and Sycamore View Road.

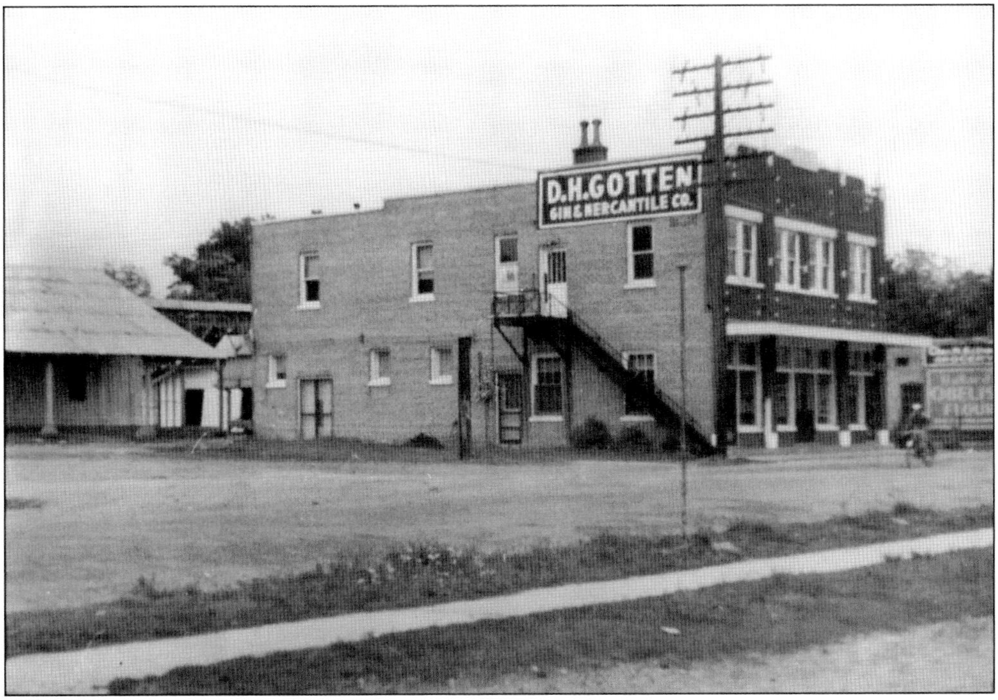

The Appling building, constructed in 1932, was the first multi-story commercial building in Bartlett. The upper floor was used for social functions, including the meetings of the Eastern Star.

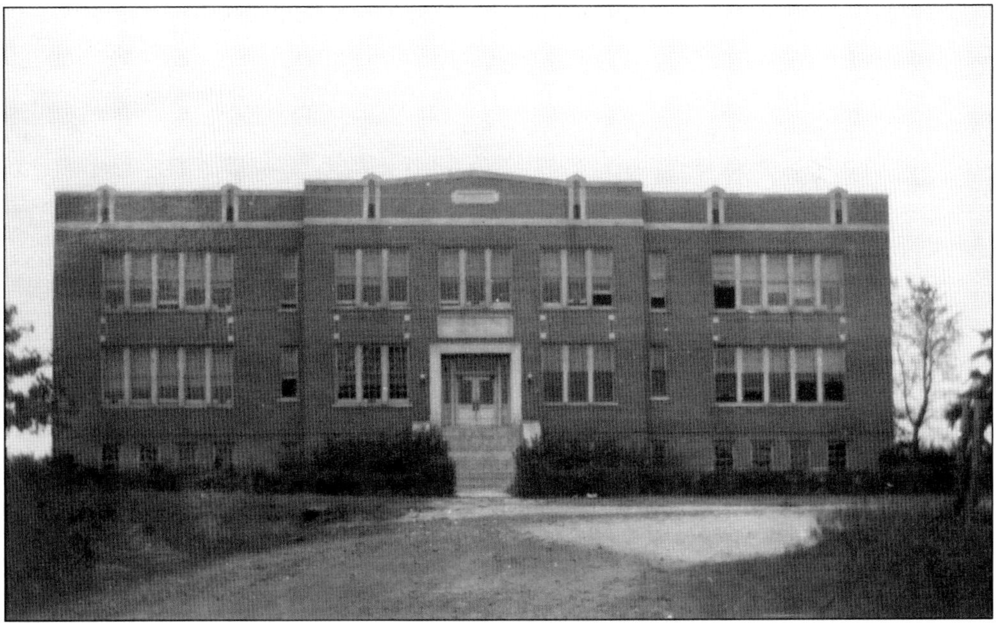

Bartlett High School was built in 1917 on land donated by the Blackwell family and was named in honor of Nicholas Blackwell, Bartlett's longtime physician and second mayor.

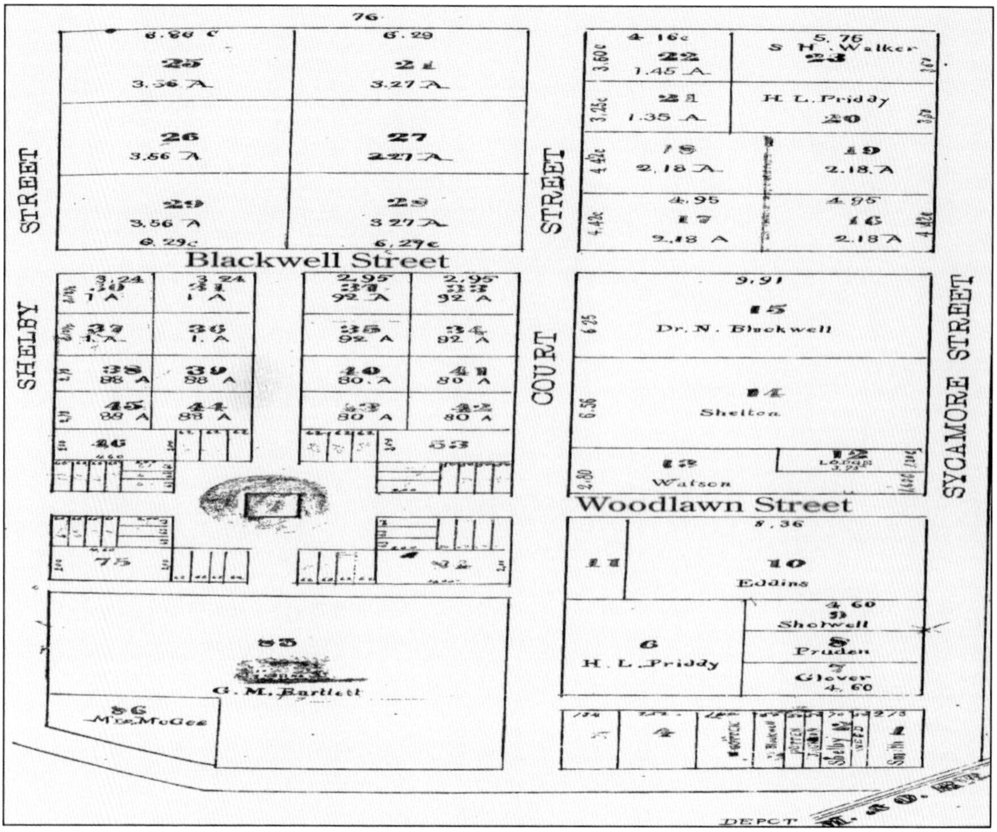

This 1872 plat map shows the properties of the Bartlett Historic District. When Gabriel Bartlett sold his land to Nicholas Blackwell and William Pryor, he had already sold many of the lots or deeded them for public use.

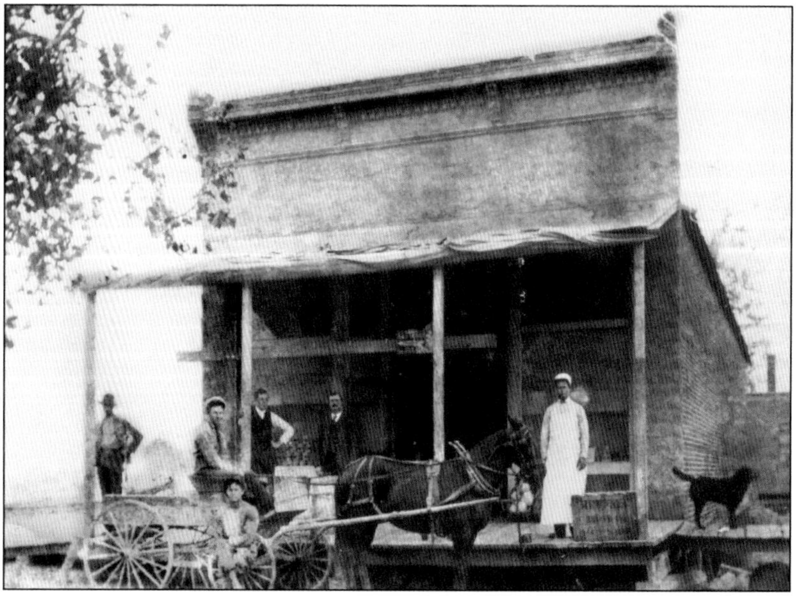

The Tatum Store was located on the north side of Stage Road just east of the railroad tracks next door to the Bartlett Baptist Church. For many years, the store was the place to buy groceries and to learn the latest news of the community.

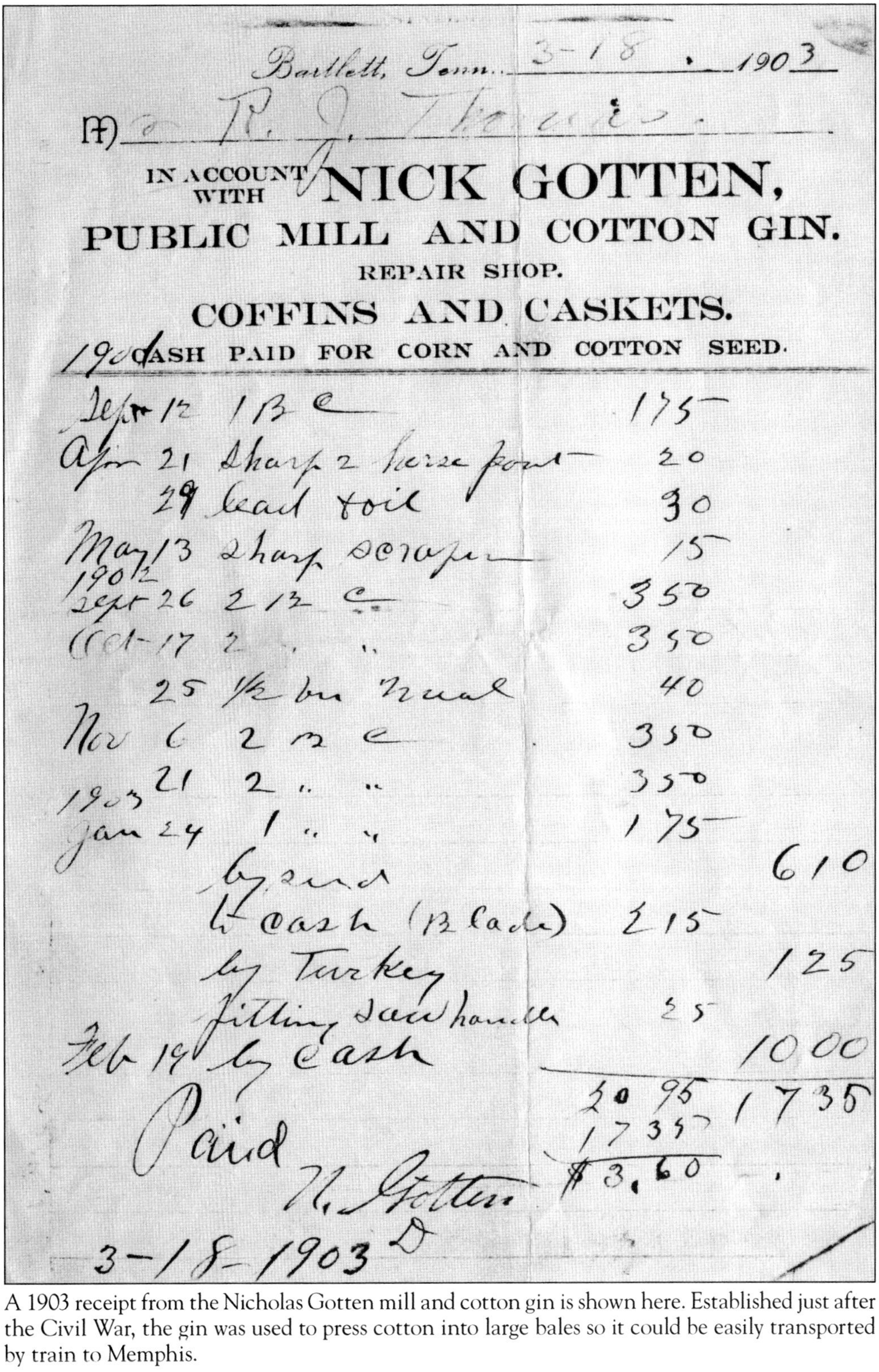
Bartlett, Tenn. 3-18 . 1903

M R. J. Thomas

IN ACCOUNT WITH NICK GOTTEN,

PUBLIC MILL AND COTTON GIN.

REPAIR SHOP.

COFFINS AND CASKETS.

1901 CASH PAID FOR CORN AND COTTON SEED.

Sept 12 1 B C 175
Apr 21 Sharp 2 horse point 20
29 lead & oil 30
May 13 Sharp scraper 15
1902 Sept 26 2 B C 350
Oct 17 2 " " 350
25 1/2 bu meal 40
Nov 6 2 B C 350
21 2 " " 350
1903 Jan 24 1 " " 175
by seed 610
by cash (B Cade) 215
by Turkey 125
fitting saw handle 25
Feb 19 by cash 1000
2095 1735
1735
$3.60
Paid
N. Gotten
3-18-1903 D

A 1903 receipt from the Nicholas Gotten mill and cotton gin is shown here. Established just after the Civil War, the gin was used to press cotton into large bales so it could be easily transported by train to Memphis.

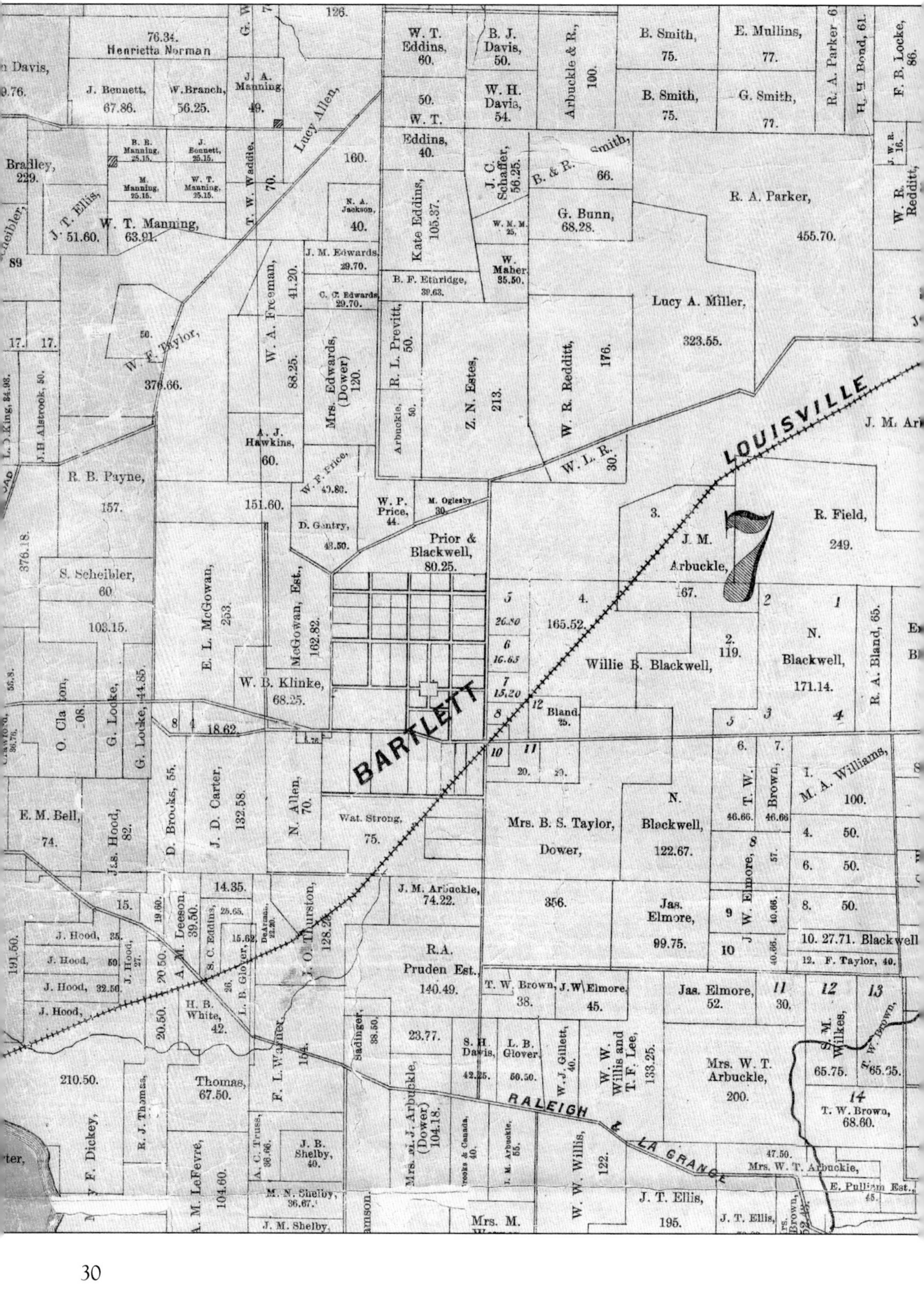

LOUISVILLE
BARTLETT
RALEIGH & LA GRANGE
7
Henrietta Norman 76.34.
J. Bennett, 67.86.
W. Branch, 56.25.
J. A. Manning, 49.
Lucy Allen,
W. T. Eddins, 60.
B. J. Davis, 50.
Arbuckle & R., 100.
B. Smith, 75.
E. Mullins, 77.
B. Smith, 75.
G. Smith, 77.
R. A. Parker 61
F. B. Locke, 86.
W. H. Davis, 54.
W. T. Eddins, 40.
Bradley, 229.
J. T. Ellis, 51.60.
W. T. Manning, 63.91.
T. W. Waddie, 70.
160.
N. A. Jackson, 40.
Kate Eddins, 105.37.
J. C. Schaffer, 56.25.
B. & R. Smith, 66.
G. Bunn, 68.28.
R. A. Parker, 455.70.
W. R. Redditt,
J. M. Edwards, 29.70.
B. F. Ethridge, 39.63.
W. Maher, 35.50.
W. A. Freeman, 41.20.
W. F. Taylor, 376.66.
W. A. Freeman, 88.25.
Mrs. Edwards, (Dower) 120.
R. L. Previtt, 50.
Z. N. Estes, 213.
W. R. Redditt, 176.
Lucy A. Miller, 323.55.
A. J. Hawkins, 60.
W. L. R. 30.
J. M. Ar
R. B. Payne, 157.
151.60.
W. F. Price, 40.80.
W. P. Price, 44.
M. Oglesby, 30.
D. Gentry, 43.50.
Prior & Blackwell, 80.25.
J. M. Arbuckle, 167.
R. Field, 249.
S. Scheibler, 60
103.15.
E. L. McGowan, 253.
McGowan, Est. 162.82.
165.52.
Willie B. Blackwell,
N. Blackwell, 171.14.
R. A. Bland, 65.
W. B. Klinke, 68.25.
O. Clayton,
G. Locke,
G. Locke, 44.85.
18.62.
Bland. 25.
E. M. Bell, 74.
Jas. Hood, 82.
D. Brooks, 55.
J. D. Carter, 132.58.
N. Allen, 70.
Wat. Strong, 75.
Mrs. B. S. Taylor, Dower, 356.
N. Blackwell, 122.67.
T. W. Brown, 46.66 46.66
M. A. Williams, 100.
J. W. Elmore,
14.35.
J. O. Thurston, 128.28
J. M. Arbuckle, 74.22.
Jas. Elmore, 99.75.
10. 27.71. Blackwell
12. F. Taylor, 40.
J. Hood,
A. M. Deeson, 39.50.
S. C. Eddins,
L. B. Glover,
R.A. Pruden Est. 140.49.
T. W. Brown, 38.
J. W. Elmore, 45.
Jas. Elmore, 52.
S. M. Wilkes, 65.75.
H. B. White, 42.
F. L. Warner, 154.
Sadinger, 38.50.
23.77.
S. H. Davis, 42.25.
L. B. Glover, 50.50.
W. J. Gillett, 40.
W. W. Willis and T. F. Lee, 133.25.
Mrs. W. T. Arbuckle, 200.
T. W. Brown, 68.60.
210.50.
R. J. Thomas,
Thomas, 67.50.
F. Dickey,
A. M. LeFevre, 104.60.
A. C. Truss, 36.66.
J. B. Shelby, 40.
M. N. Shelby, 36.67.
J. M. Shelby,
Mrs. J. J. Arbuckle, (Dower) 104.18.
W. W. Willis, 122.
J. T. Ellis, 195.
J. T. Ellis,
Mrs. W. T. Arbuckle,
E. Pulliam Est., 45.
Mrs. M.

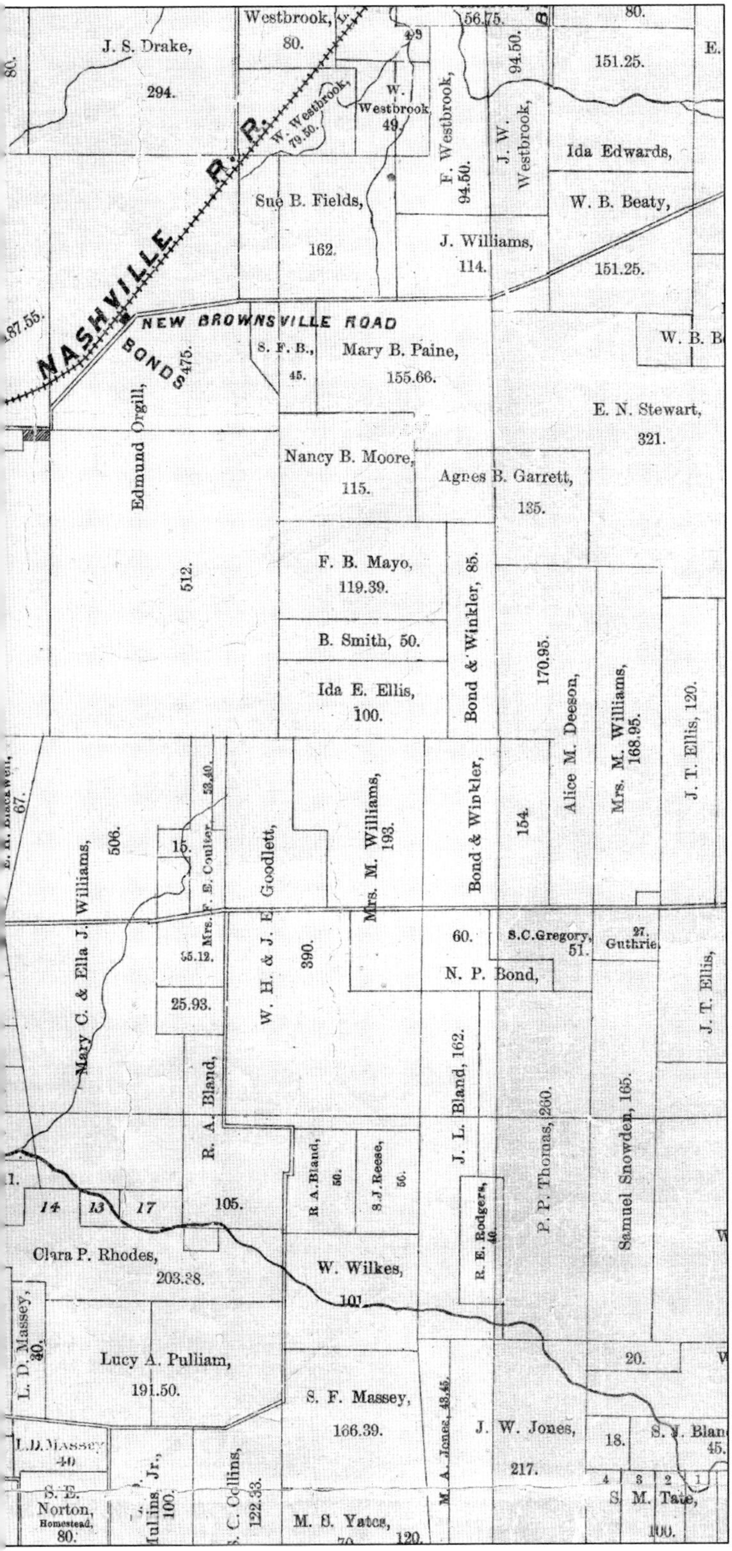

The Bartlett area was made up of large and small farms, shown on this 1896 Williamson plat map. The road bisecting the center of the map is the Memphis to Somerville Road, laid out in 1828 and known today as Stage Road.

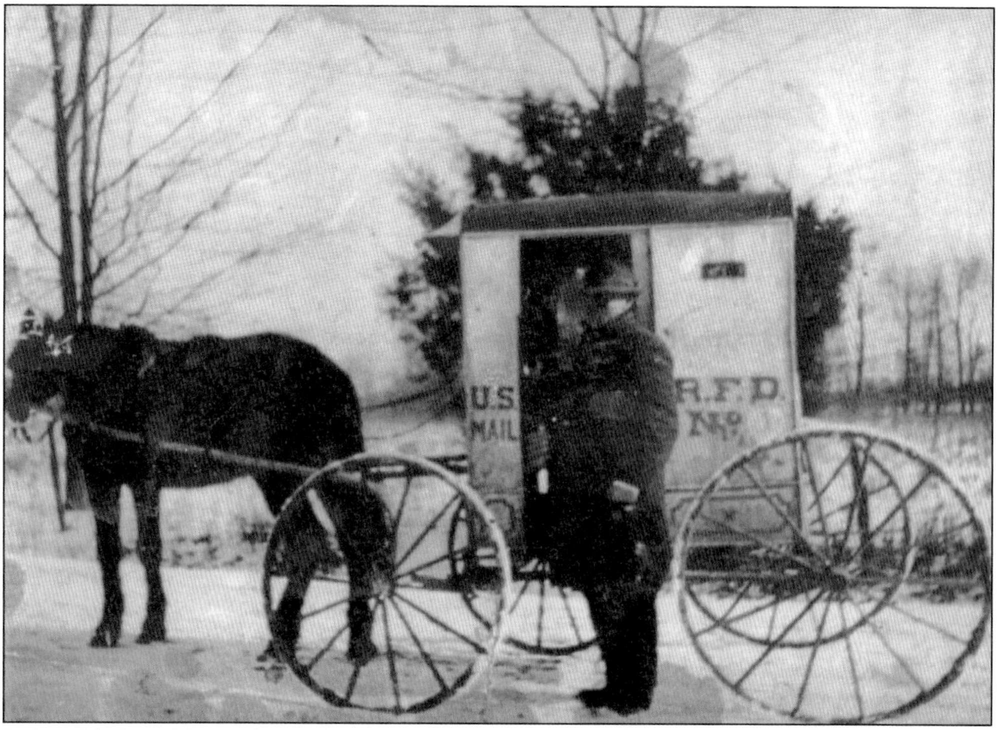

Robert Bledsoe delivers the mail in a horse-drawn wagon in this photograph from 1915. He would often keep heated bricks on the floorboard to keep warm during the winter. He also would deliver medicine and food to those who were unable to get out of the house.

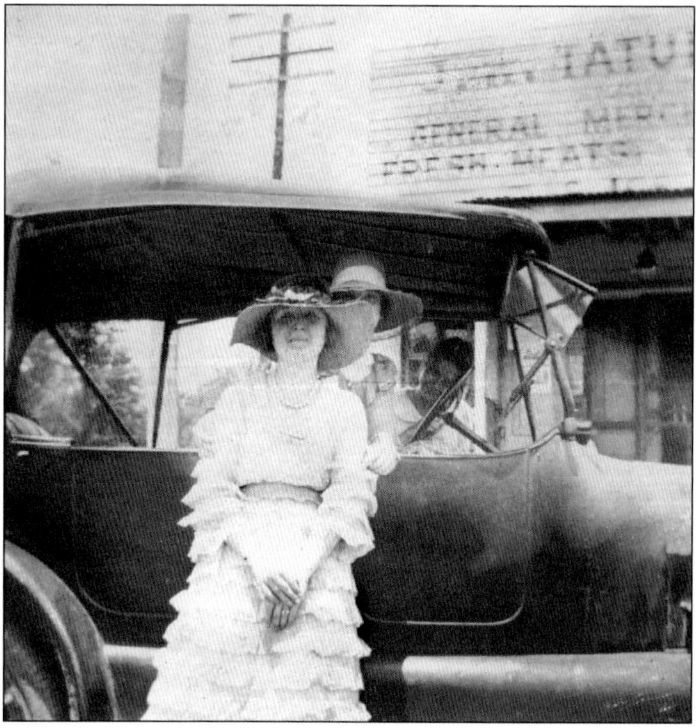

The Tatum Store was a popular hangout in the 1920s for Bartlett youth. For many years, John Hood Tatum operated the grocery store, located just west of the Bartlett Baptist Church on Stage Road.

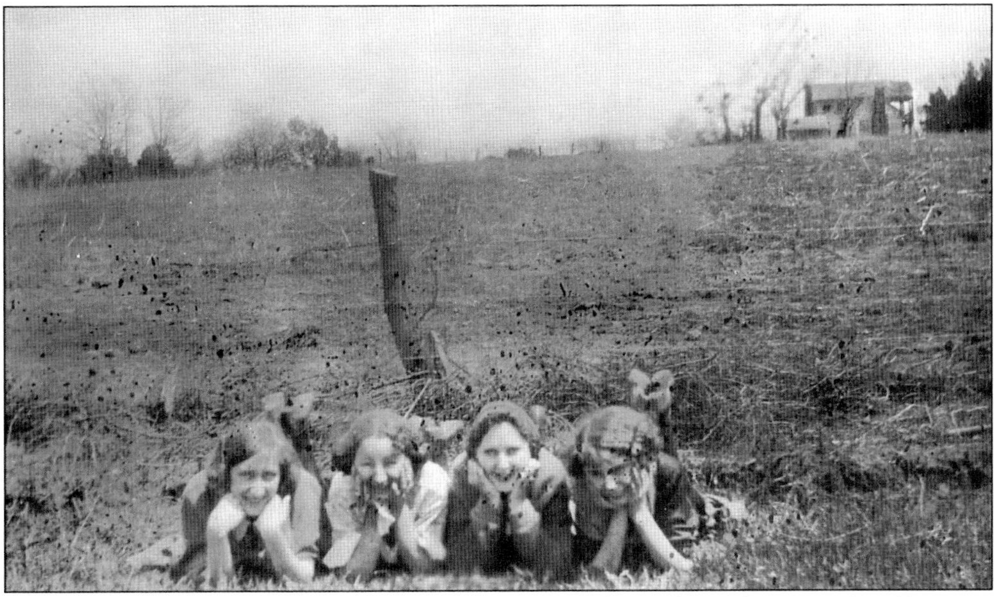

This is the only known photograph of the Gabriel Bartlett home, located on Stage Road between Shelby and Court Streets. It was originally built for the Pruden family in the 1840s, and Bartlett purchased it in 1855. The home was torn down in the early 1920s.

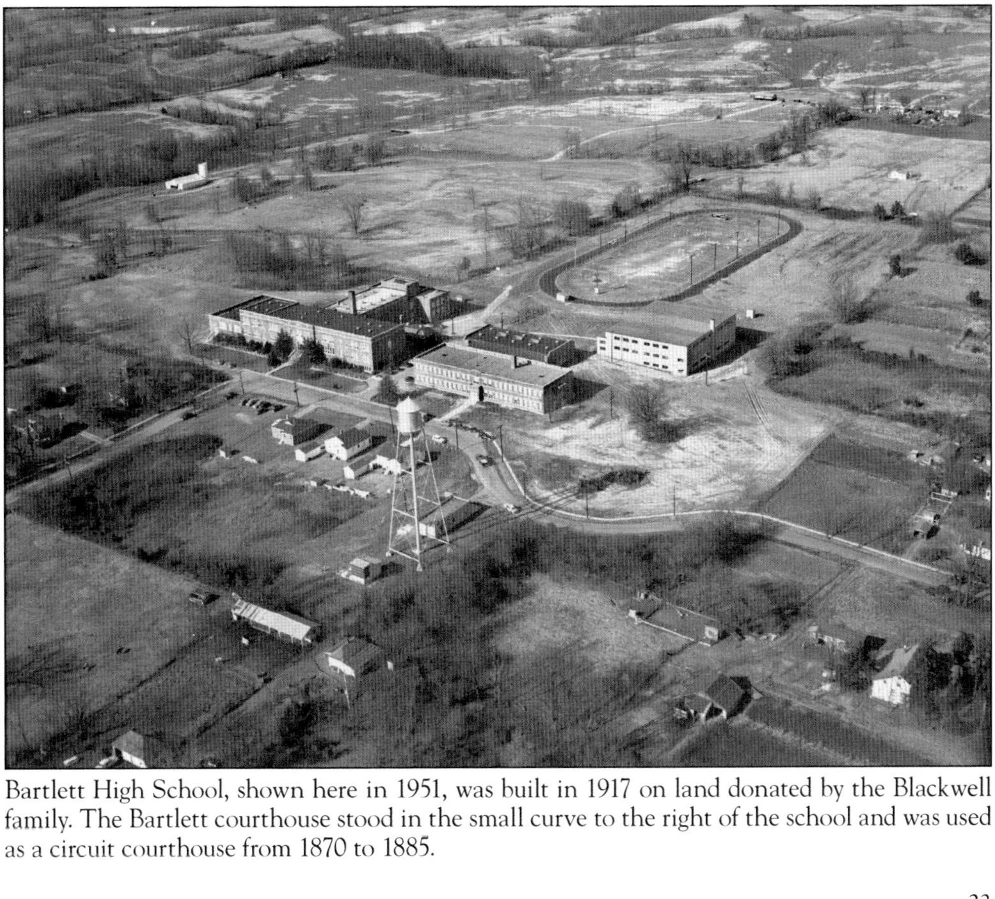

Bartlett High School, shown here in 1951, was built in 1917 on land donated by the Blackwell family. The Bartlett courthouse stood in the small curve to the right of the school and was used as a circuit courthouse from 1870 to 1885.

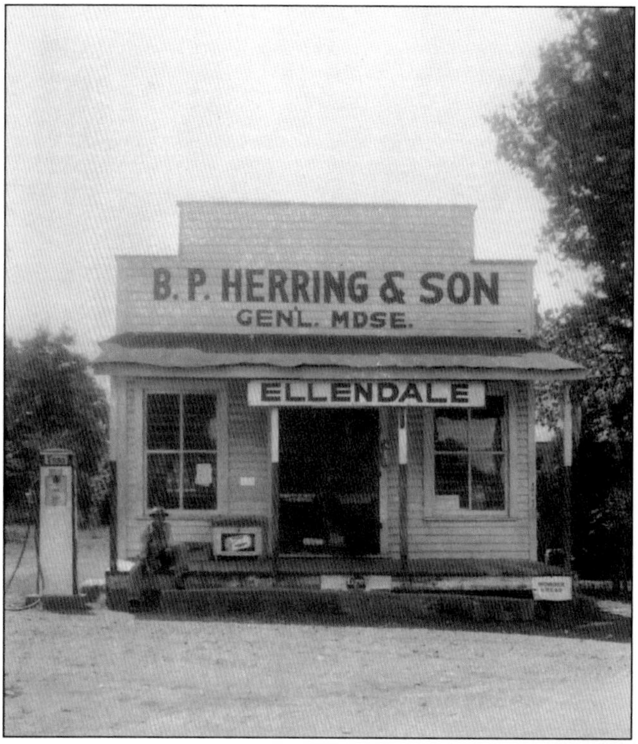

The exterior of the B. P. Herring Store, located at Memphis-Arlington Road and Broadway Road in Ellendale, is shown here around 1940.

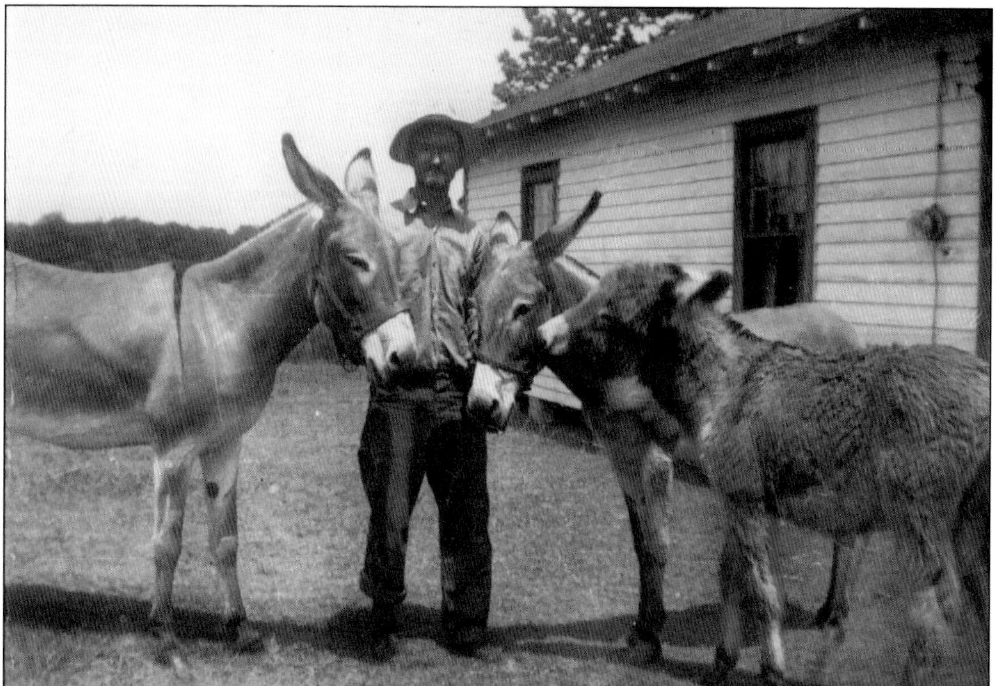

Neville Plesant shows off three of his mules at his farm in Ellendale. In the late 1800s, Memphis was known as the world's largest mule market. Up to 800 mules could be sold in a single day at the Memphis auction houses.

Two

People

The citizens of a community are its lifeblood. They sit on the PTA, volunteer when there is a fire or disaster, run for political office, and help when a neighbor is in need. Bartlett has been blessed from its earliest days to have citizens who looked beyond themselves to the greater need of the community. They wanted to make Bartlett a great place to live, not only for themselves but also for their children and grandchildren. Over the years, there have been countless acts of generosity and giving by the Bartlett community. Just after the Civil War, a benefit was held for Bob Hall, who was blinded during the war. The community gathered food and supplies for his family. Music was played, led by Gabriel Bartlett on violin. When Gabriel Bartlett first laid out the town, some of the best parcels of land were donated for churches, schools, and civic meetinghouses. In 1866, Gabriel Bartlett donated the land and paid for the first freedman school in Bartlett, located on Memphis-Arlington Road.

There is probably no greater service that one can give to their community than to enlist in the military. During the Civil War, those who enlisted included Nicholas Gotten, Nicholas and James Blackwell, and Col. Clark Russell Barteau. During World War II, Jane Hawkins served in the army nurse corps and assisted on Normandy Beach just days after the initial D-Day invasion. Her husband, Mac Hawkins, also served in the European theater. Many others also served, including John George, who fought in the Battle of the Bulge, receiving the Purple Heart for his injuries. Walter K. Singleton was the most decorated soldier to call Bartlett home. He received the Medal of Honor for his heroic actions in the Vietnam War, giving his life to save the lives of his fellow soldiers. Today Singleton Parkway is named in his honor.

On December 25, 1956, a fire broke out in the home of Mr. and Mrs. B. L. Jones, located south of Bartlett on Raleigh LaGrange Road. The home was totally destroyed, but the family, including their daughter and five grandchildren, escaped without harm. Their neighbors took them in, collected food and furniture, and even bought presents for the children, so even though all was lost, they could have Christmas presents. When the article ran in the *Commercial Appeal* telling of the good deed, even more money and gifts were donated to help. When asked why they helped their neighbors, they simply said it was the right thing to do.

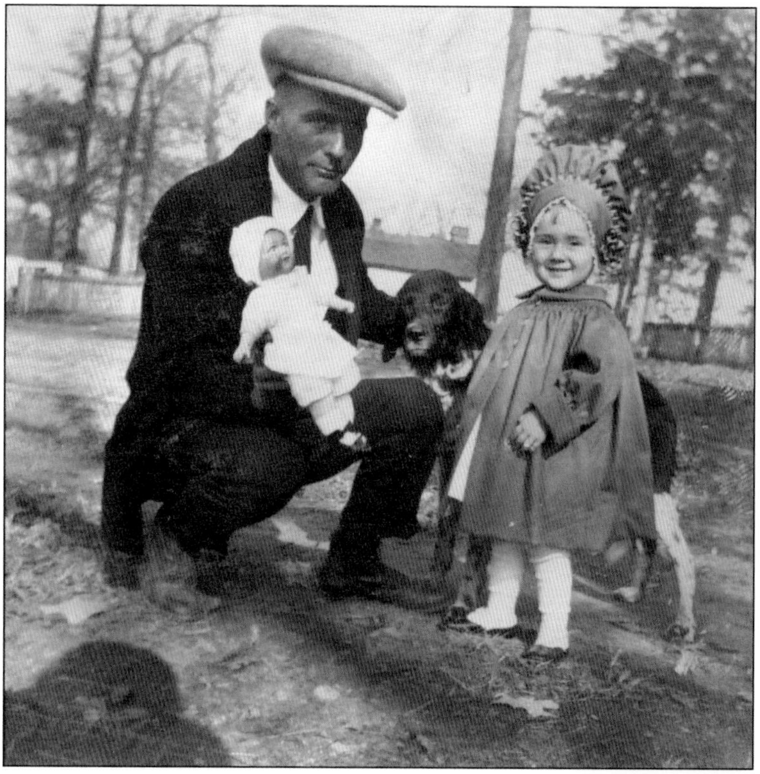

Betty Miller, shown here with her father in 1925 at the Blackwell home on Sycamore View Road, grew up in Bartlett but moved to Memphis, where she became a noted stage actress.

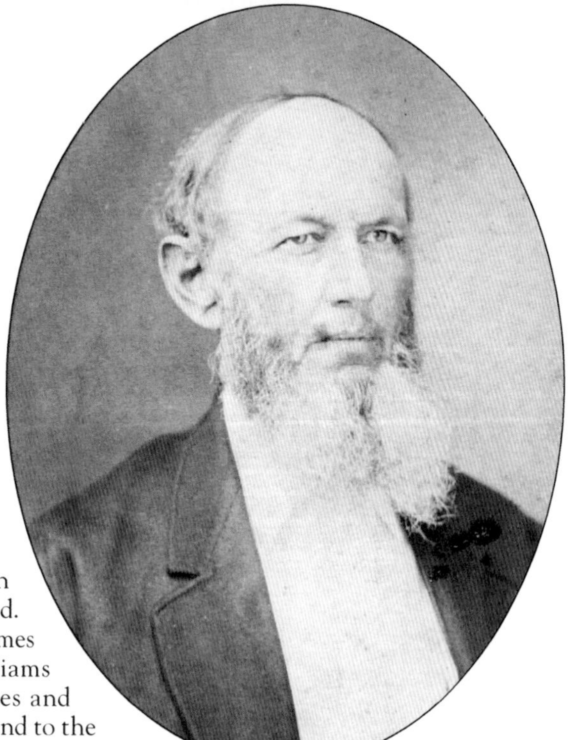

Harvey Williams operated a large farm, called Elder Grove, at what is today the north side of Stage Road at Highway 70. According to the 1850 census, he had $15,000 in real estate, $12,000 in "personnel value," and 600 acres of land. His daughter Emma Williams married James Blackwell, and they lived on the Williams property. Mamie Blackwell Rock, James and Emma's daughter, donated part of this land to the Baptist Children's Home.

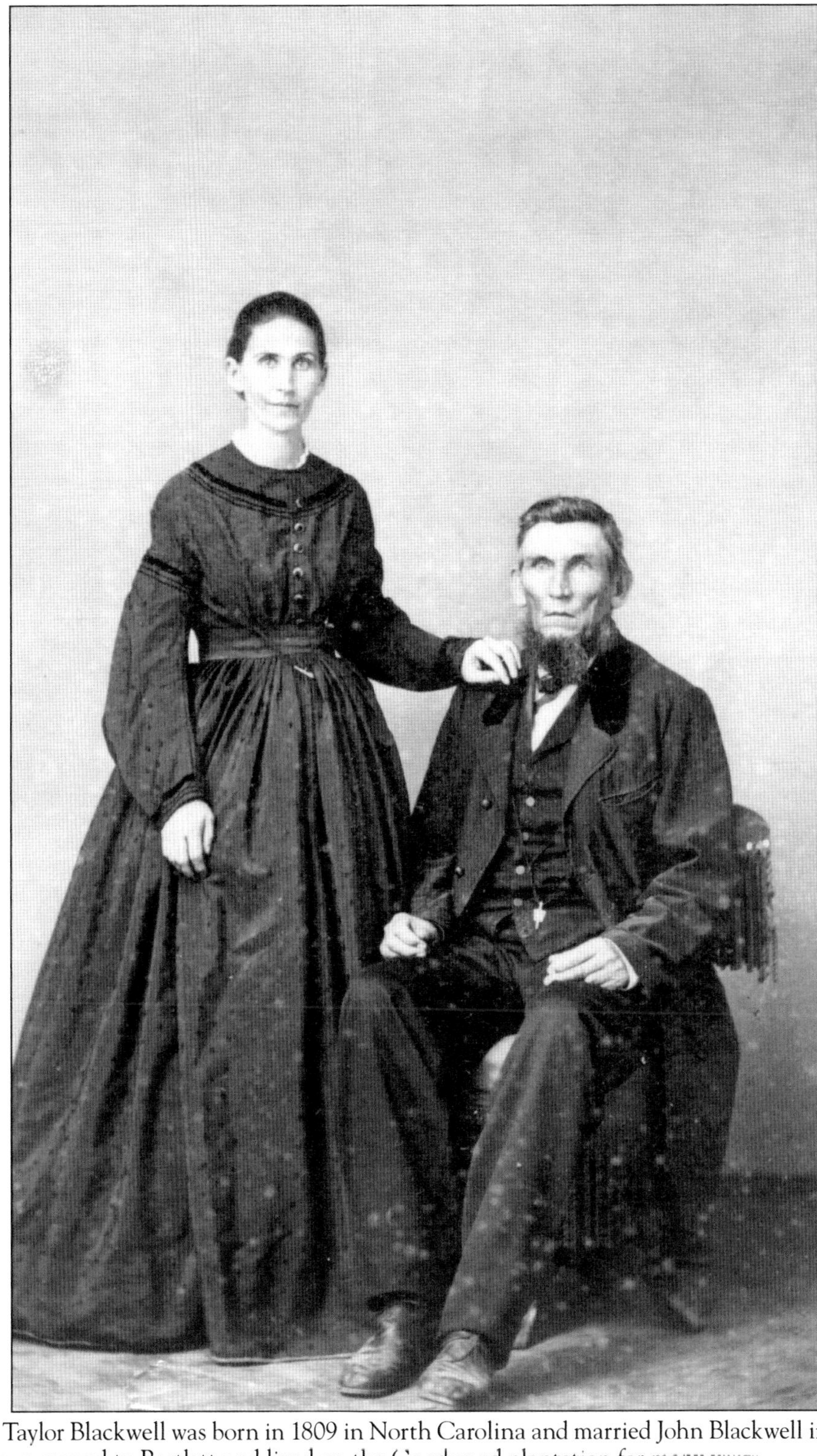

Mary Taylor Blackwell was born in 1809 in North Carolina and married John Blackwell in 1843. She soon moved to Bartlett and lived on the Goodwood plantation for many years.

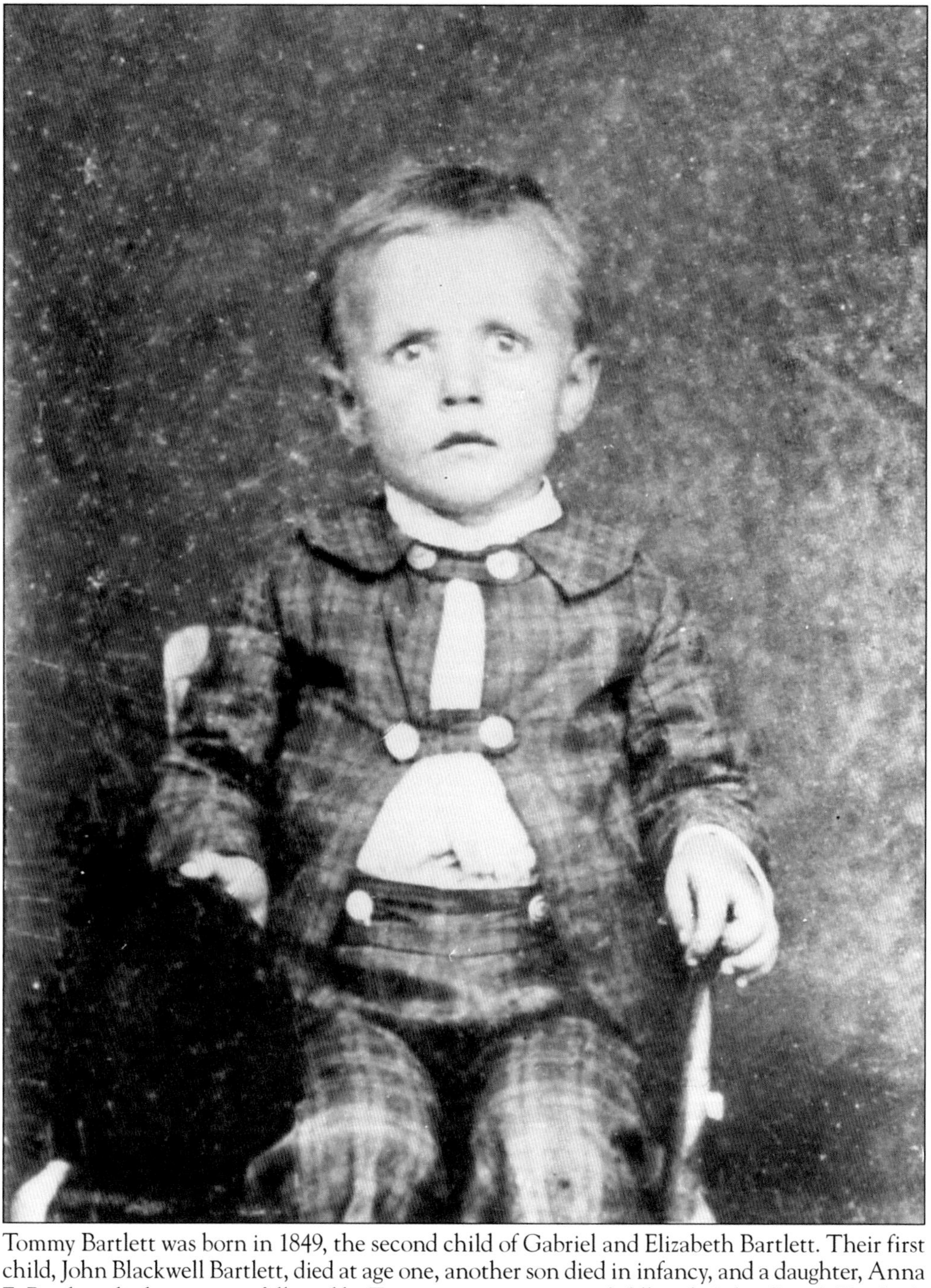

Tommy Bartlett was born in 1849, the second child of Gabriel and Elizabeth Bartlett. Their first child, John Blackwell Bartlett, died at age one, another son died in infancy, and a daughter, Anna E. Bartlett, died at age two, followed by Tommy passing away in childhood. Gabriel's wife Elizabeth passed away during the birth of their fourth child, Anna. Of Gabriel Bartlett's nine children with two wives, only one survived into adulthood, Robert Capitol Bartlett (1855–1923).

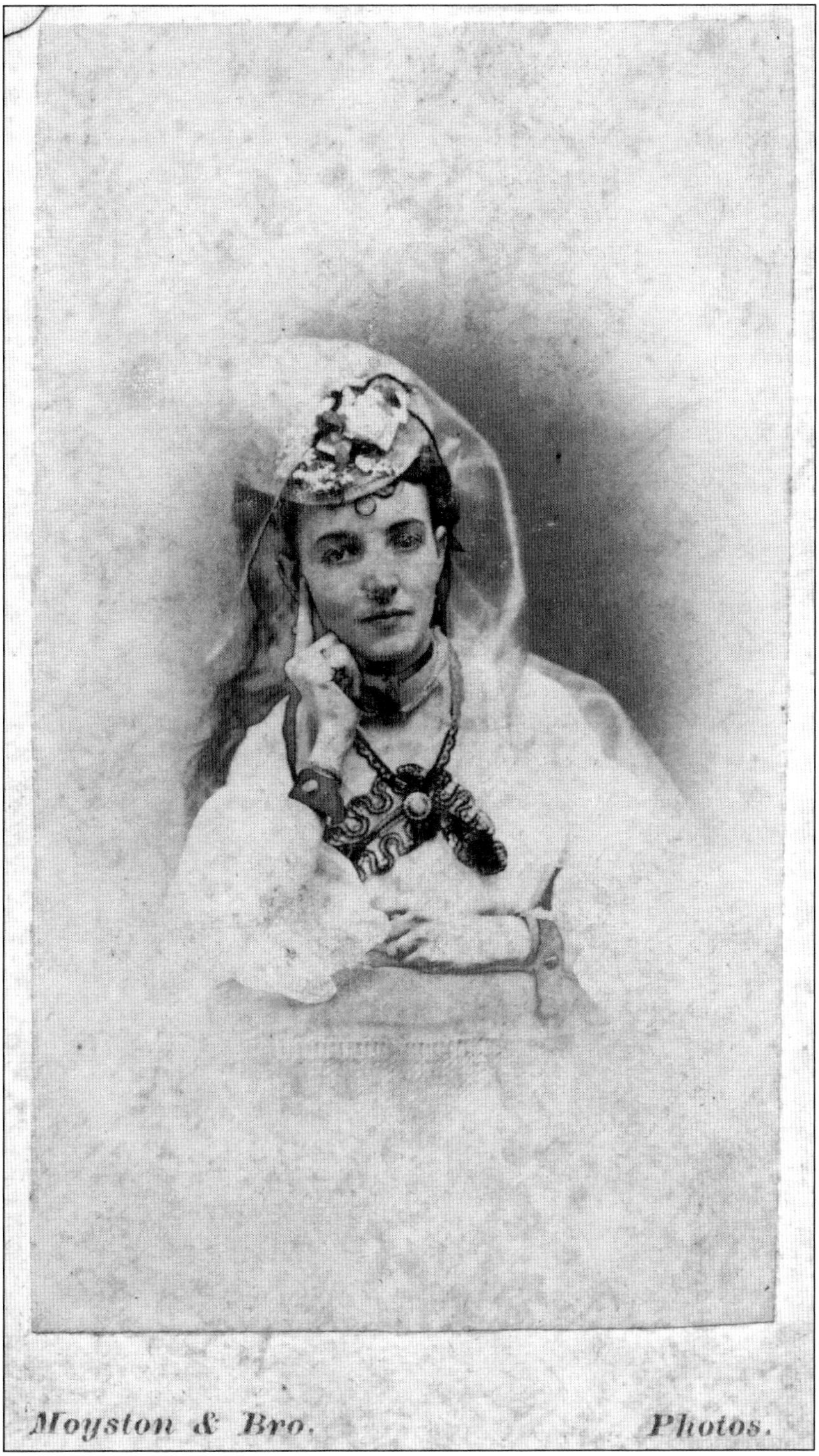

Marie E. Pruden was born in Bartlett in 1848 and lived in the large home on Stage Road that would, in 1854, be purchased by Gabriel Bartlett. Her father, James Pruden, was one of the original settlers in the area and was a founding elder of the Prosperity Baptist Church.

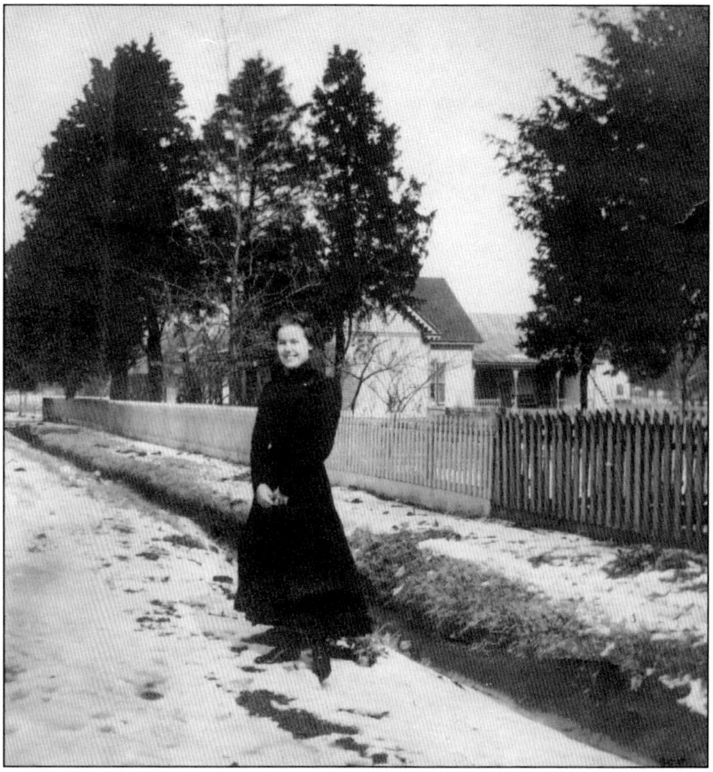

Louise Miller, granddaughter of Nicholas Blackwell, stands on Court Street around 1915. The Mabel Richmond house can be seen in the background.

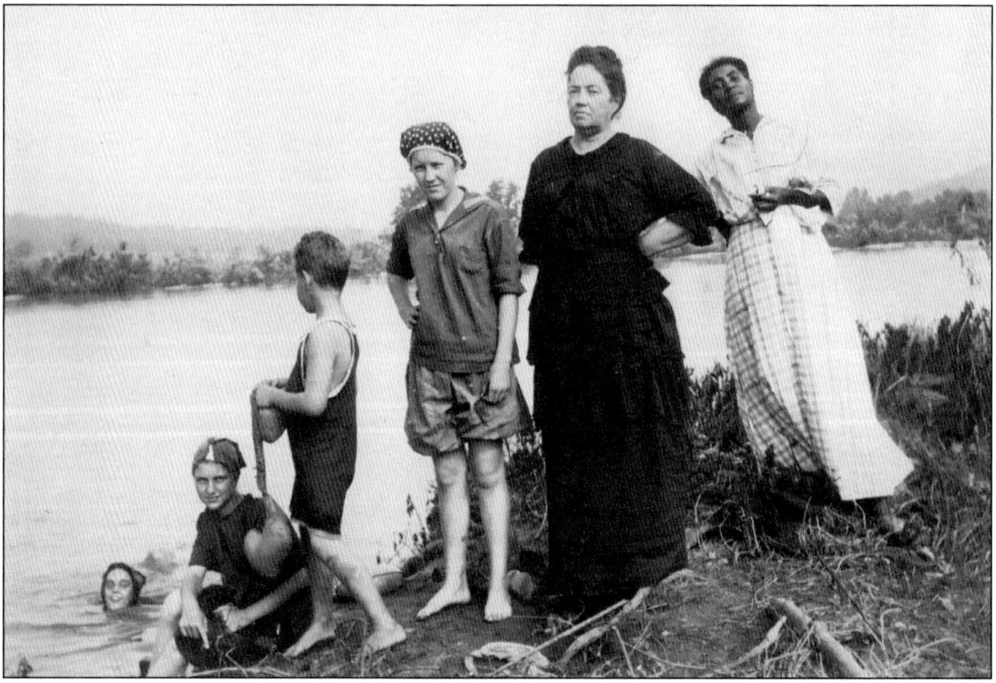

Clara Gowen and family are seen here at the Wolf River around 1920. The Wolf River was the main waterway in Shelby County and had natural sand beaches and rope swings hanging out over the river.

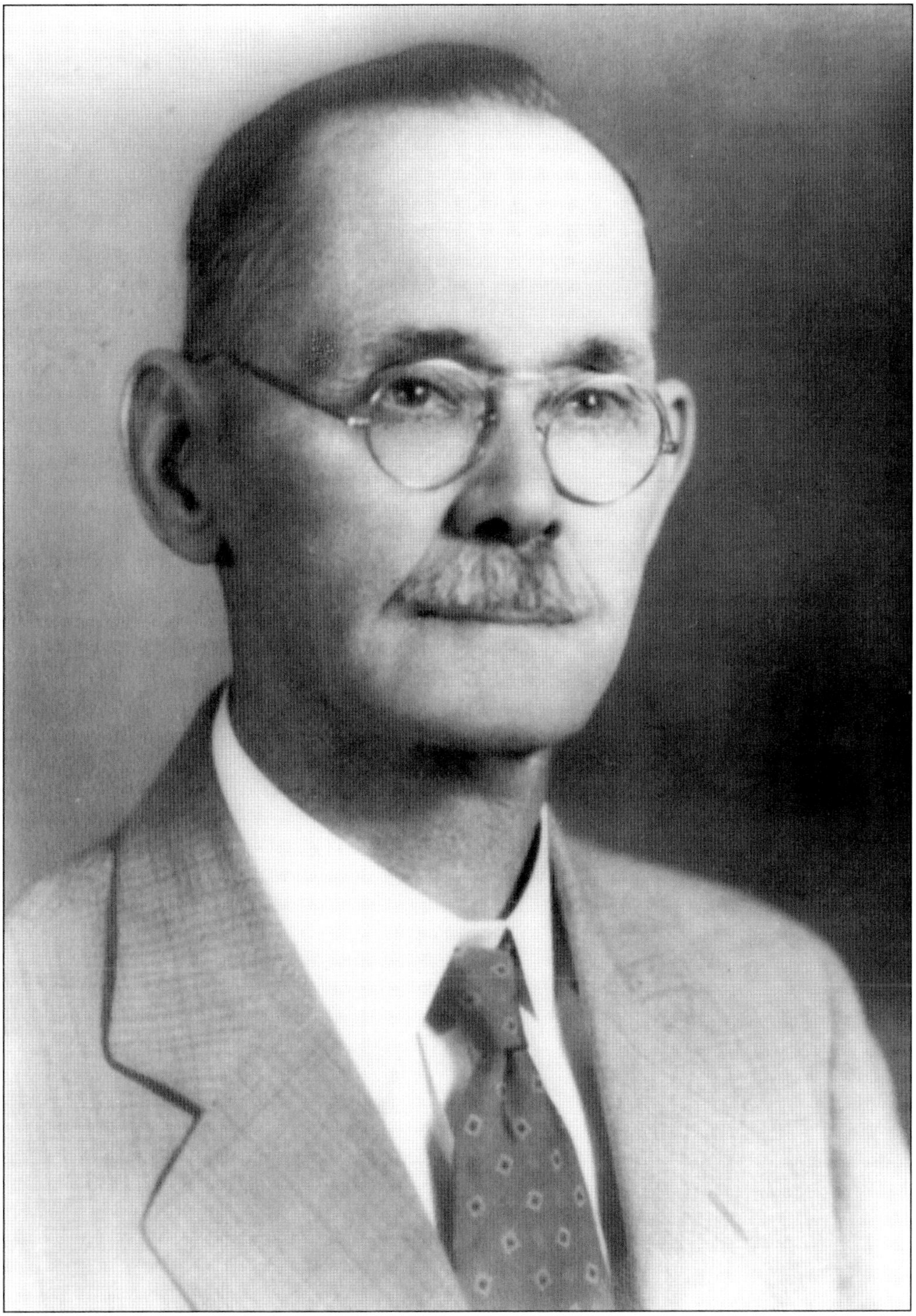

Clarence Gowen was a lifelong Bartlett resident, mayor, and historian. In 1949, he wrote the first history of the Bartlett Baptist Church. As a member of the Shelby County Court, he was on the building commission overseeing the construction of the Memphis Auditorium, later known as Ellis Auditorium.

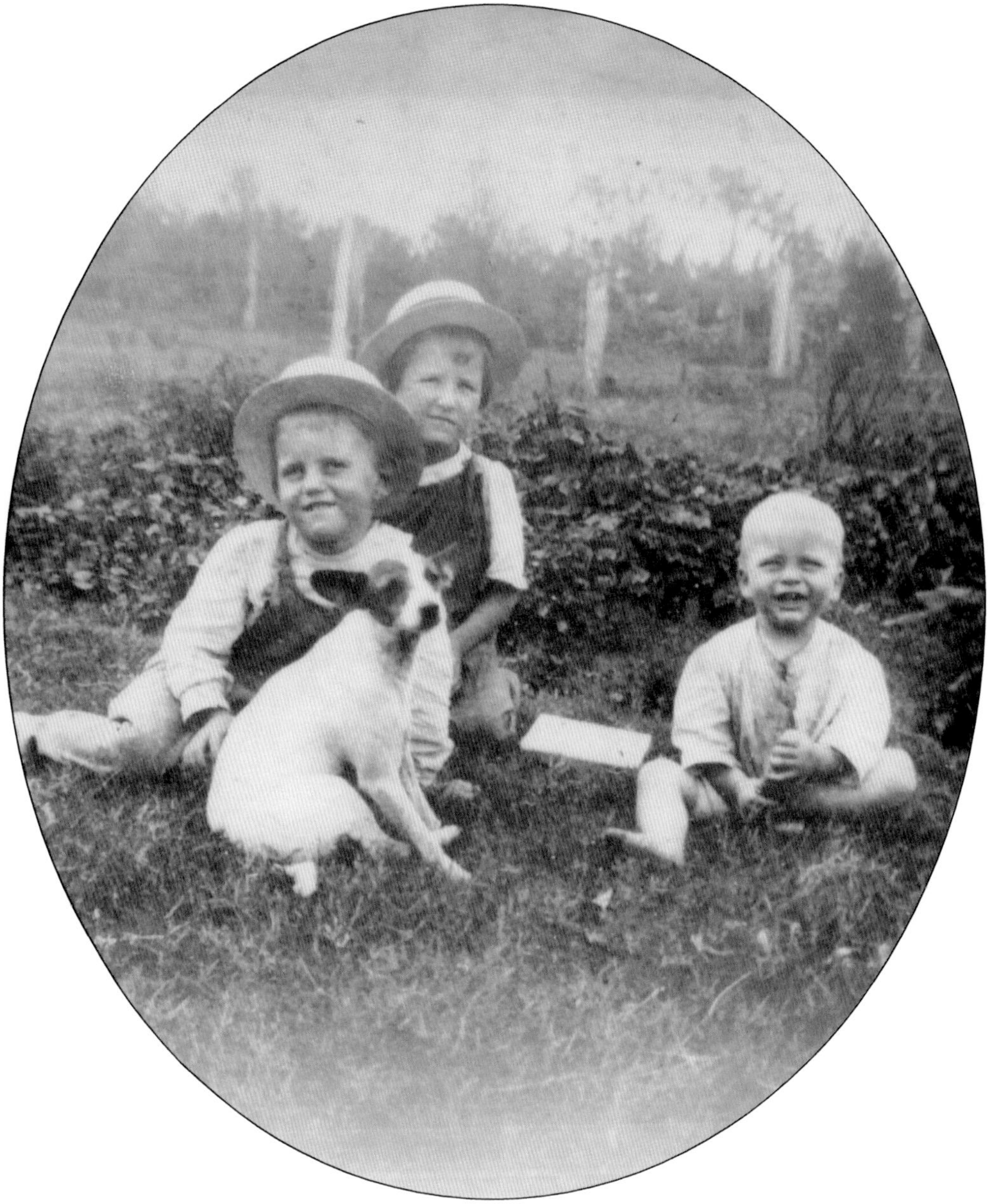

Members of the Gowen family pose in this photograph from 1900. William Gowen, a licensed preacher, arrived in Bartlett in the late 1860s. In 1890, his son Clarence Gowen built a home on Court Street across from the Nicholas Gotten house.

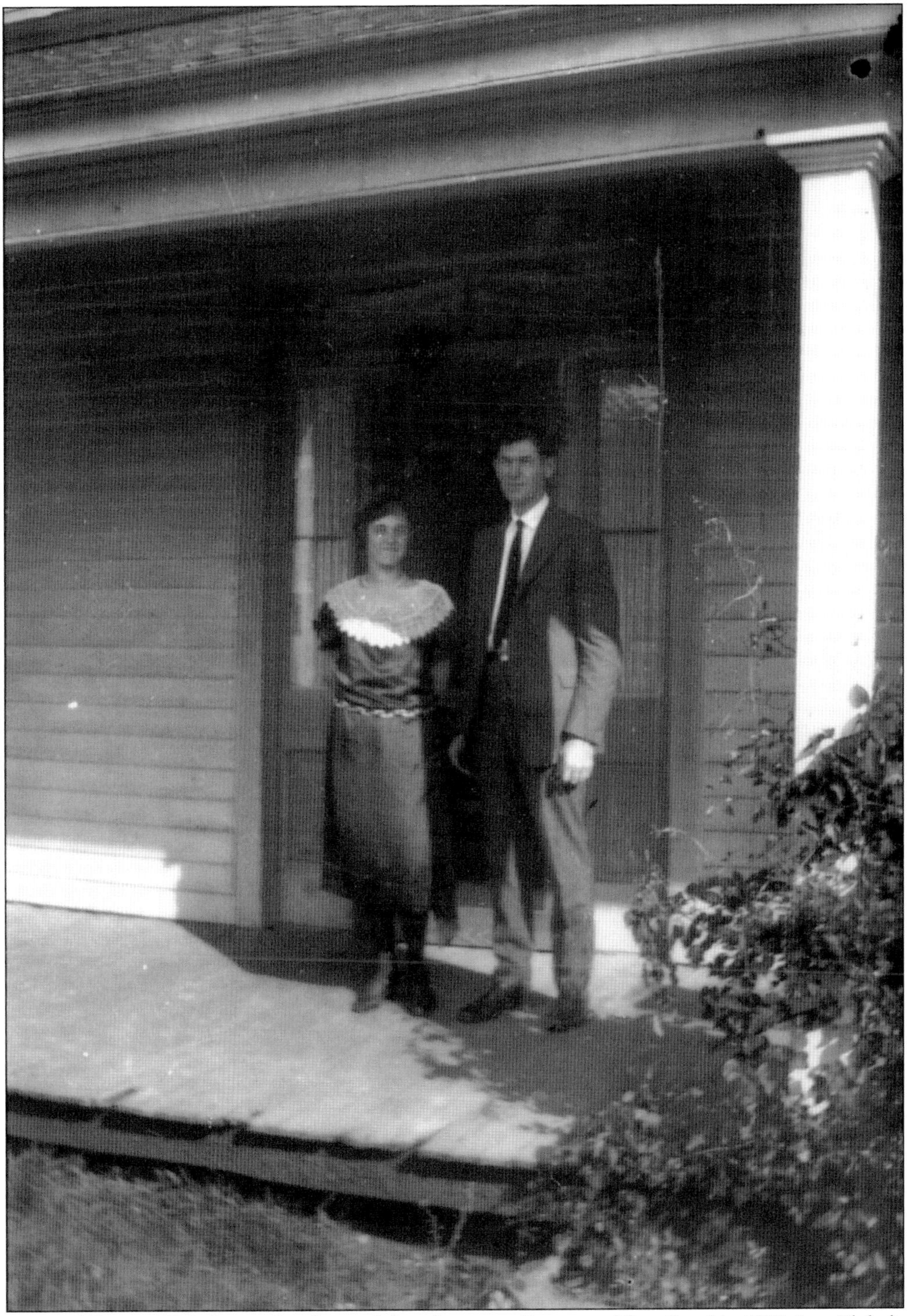

Lou and Francis Blakely stand in front of their home on Sycamore View Road in 1920. Lou Blakely was active in the Bartlett Baptist Church for many years.

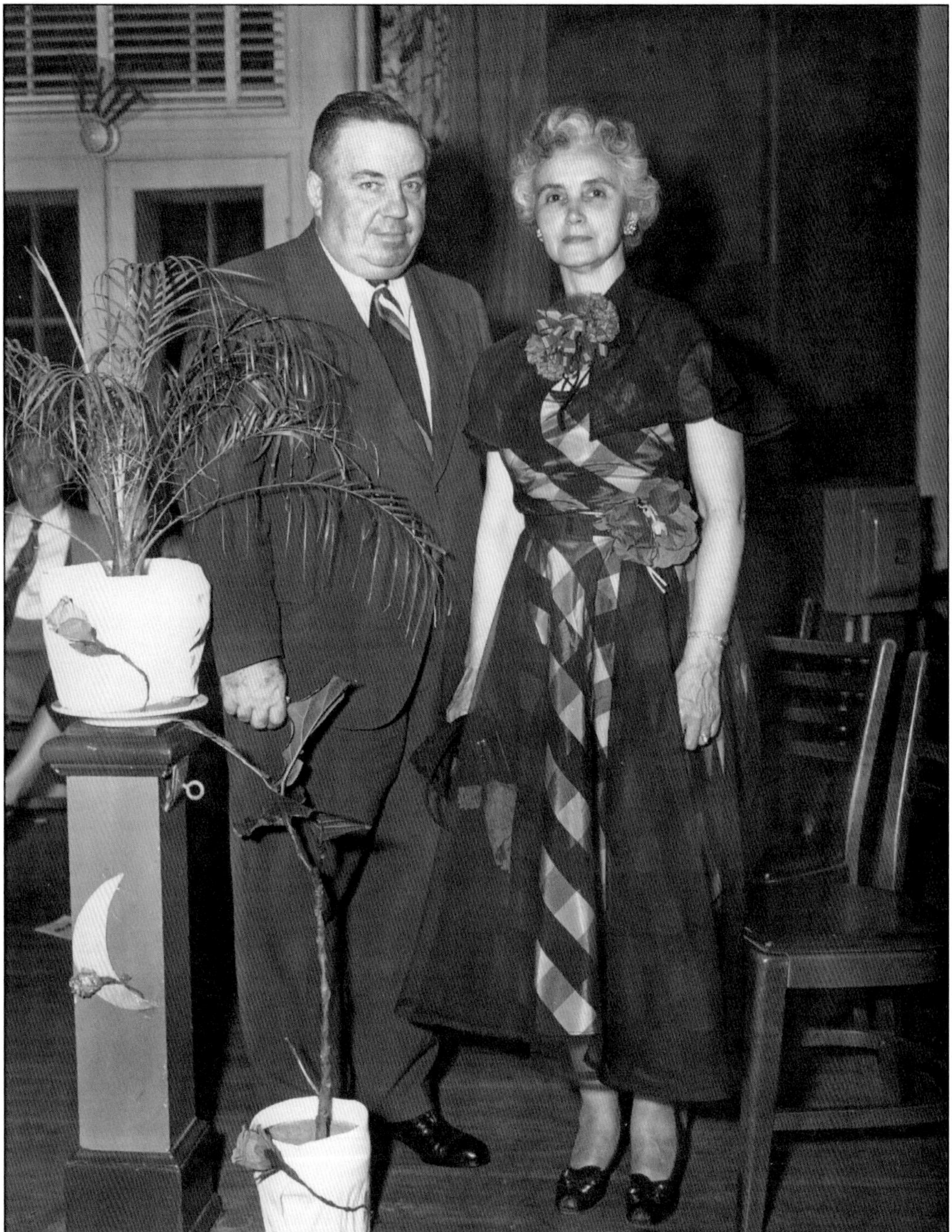

John Herald George, shown here with his wife, Virginia, at a high school dance, was principal of Bartlett High School from 1922 to 1940. In 1925, the school was accredited by the Southern Association of High Schools for its high academic standards.

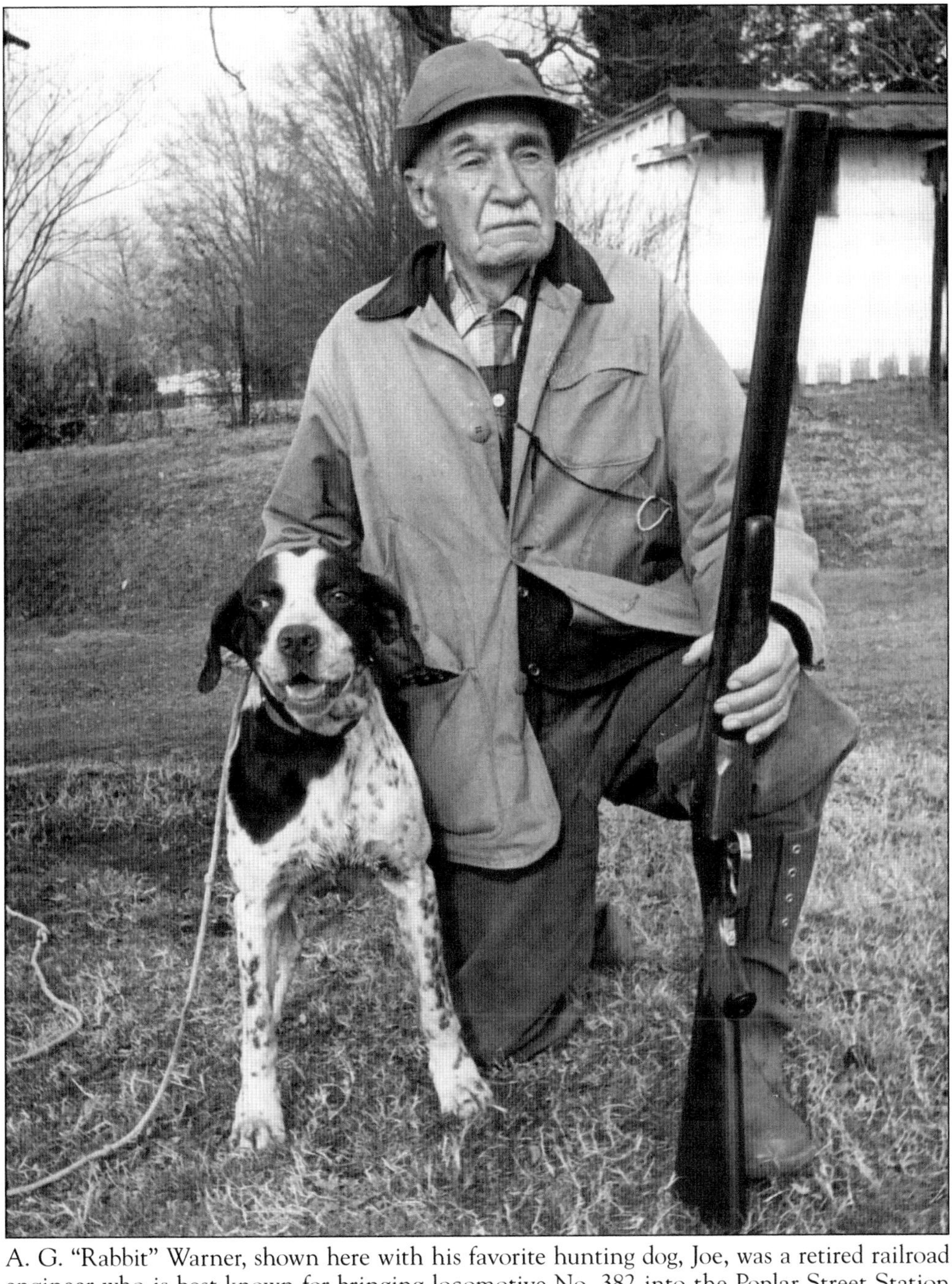

A. G. "Rabbit" Warner, shown here with his favorite hunting dog, Joe, was a retired railroad engineer who is best known for bringing locomotive No. 382 into the Poplar Street Station in Memphis on April 29, 1900. Casey Jones, who was filling in for an engineer who was sick, relieved him to continue the train journey south. Casey died that night in a tragic train accident at Canton, Mississippi.

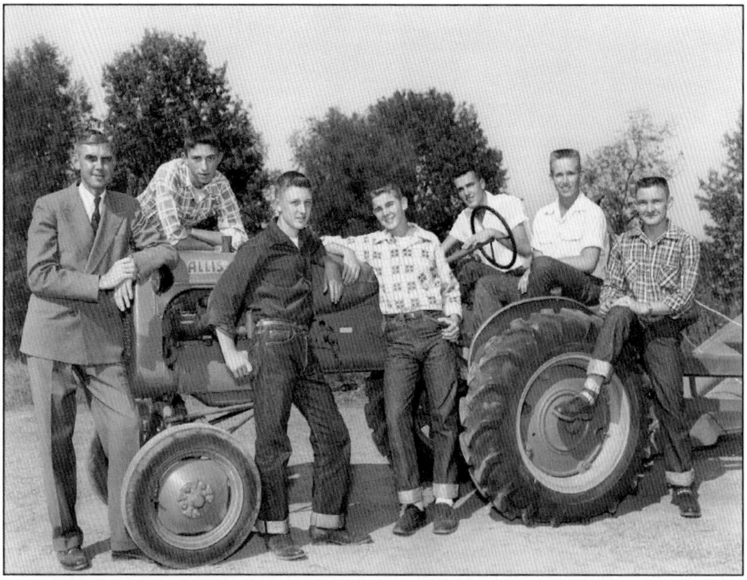

The Future Farmers of America, under the guidance of David McPherson, routinely won state and regional awards for excellence in their promotion of agriculture during the 1940s and 1950s. David McPherson moved to Bartlett in the 1930s, living for many years on Sycamore View Road with his wife, Ethyl Elam McPherson.

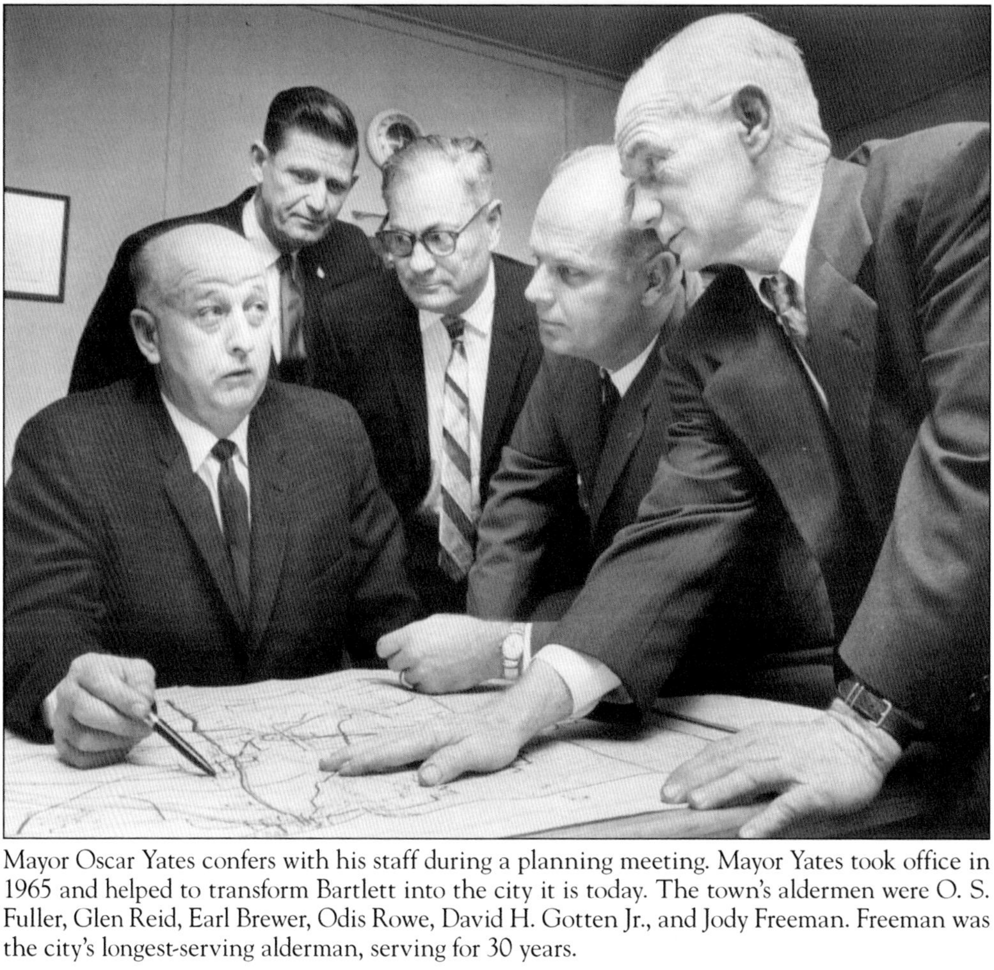

Mayor Oscar Yates confers with his staff during a planning meeting. Mayor Yates took office in 1965 and helped to transform Bartlett into the city it is today. The town's aldermen were O. S. Fuller, Glen Reid, Earl Brewer, Odis Rowe, David H. Gotten Jr., and Jody Freeman. Freeman was the city's longest-serving alderman, serving for 30 years.

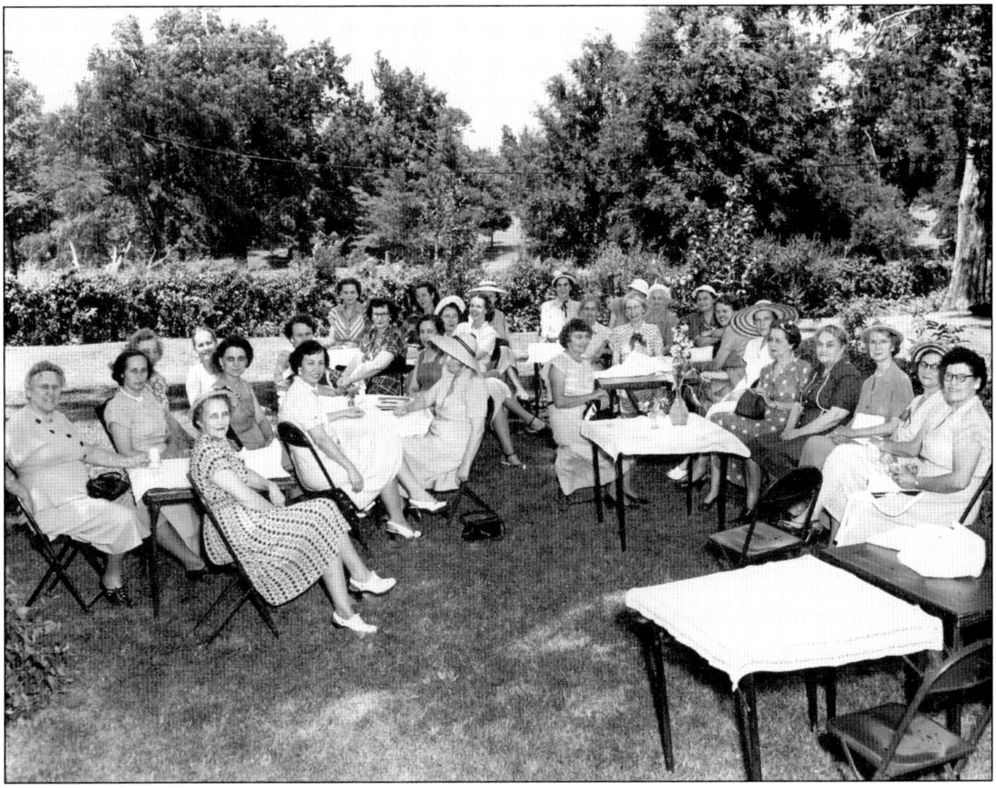

Organized in 1931, the Bartlett Garden Club is one of the town's oldest civic organizations. Shown here celebrating its 25th anniversary in 1956, the garden club is still active today.

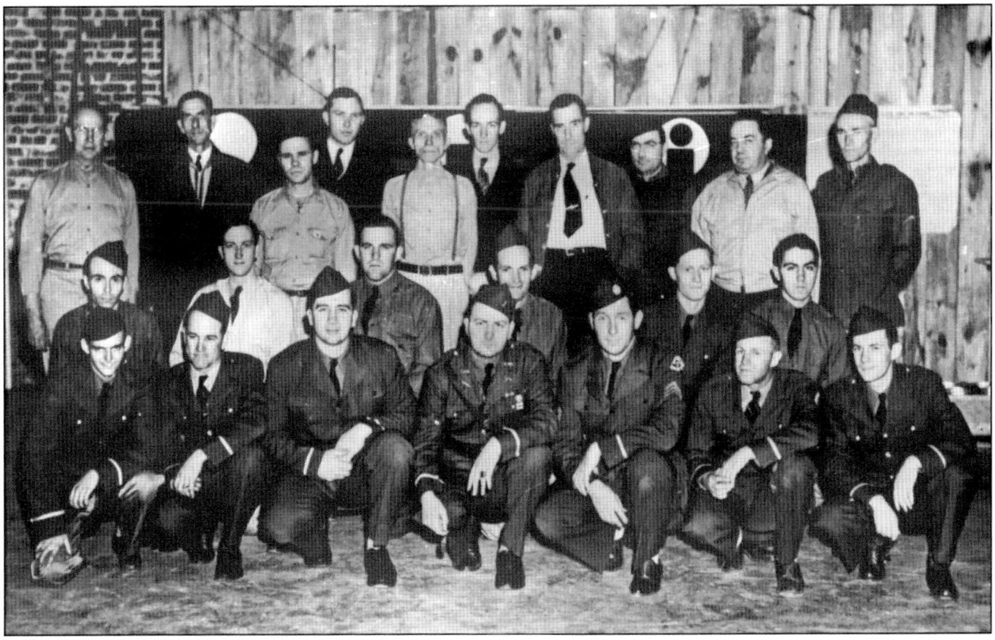

Members of the Tennessee State Reserve in Bartlett in 1948 included Evans Warr, Joseph Freeman, Red Fuller, and John George.

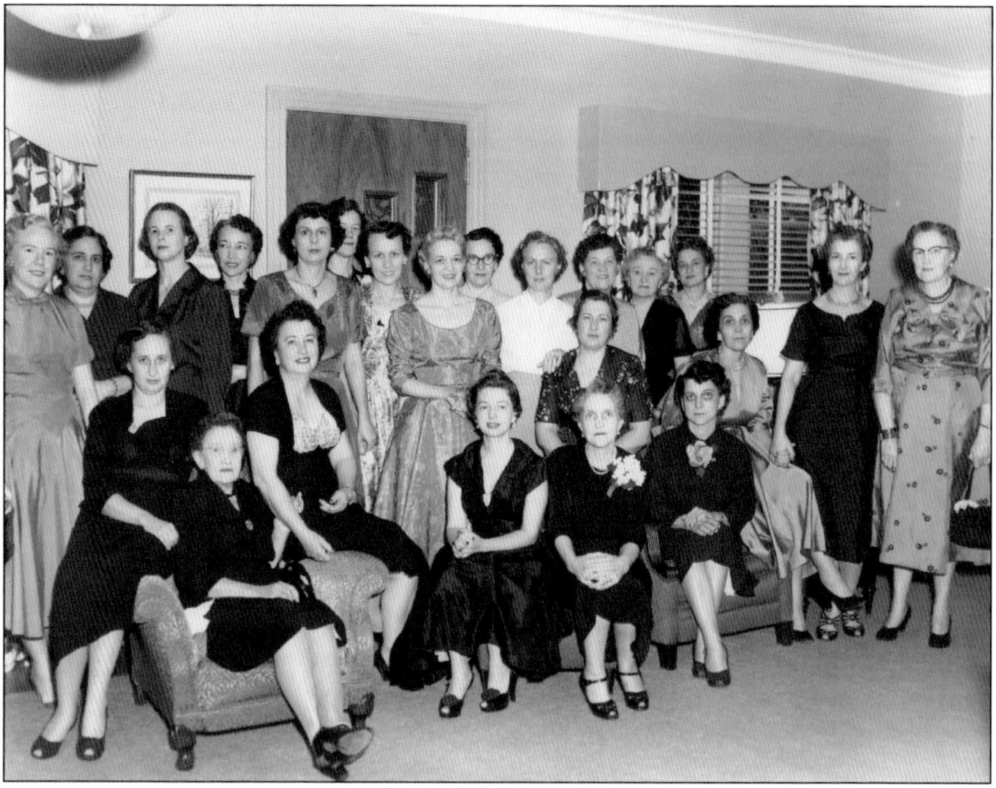

The Bartlett Garden Club was organized by Mabel Richmond in 1939 and met once at month at the various members' houses. Members would start preparing for the event weeks in advance, pulling out all the stops to make their meeting better than the previous one.

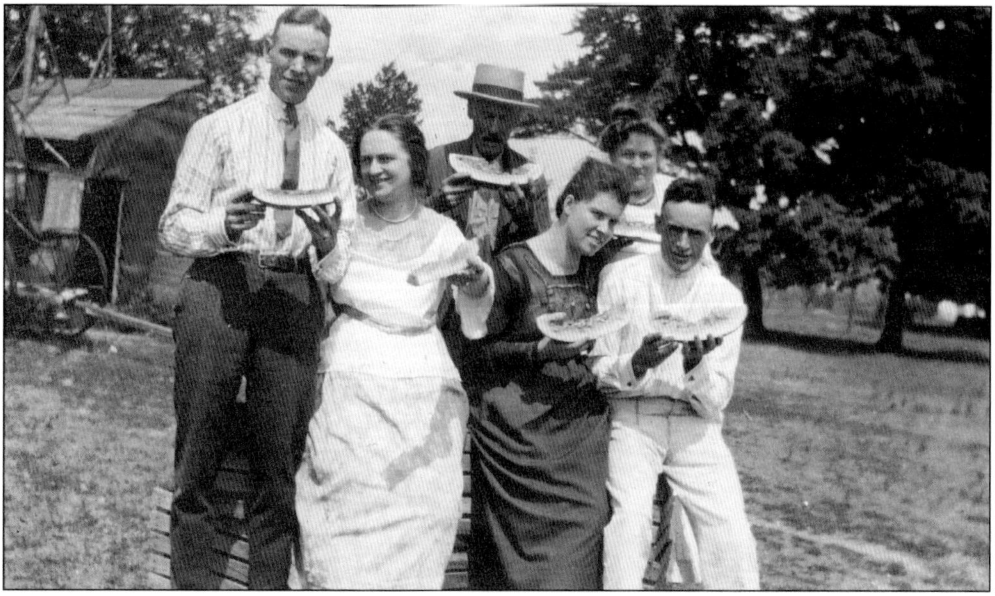

Neighbors enjoy a watermelon social on Sycamore View Road in 1922. From left to right are (first row) Lou Blakely, Francis Dye Blakely, Zola Dye, and Jesse Dye.

John George, principal of Nicholas Blackwell High School from 1922 until 1940, sells Mary Ann Freeman of Bartlett a broom during a fund-raiser for the Lions Club in 1953.

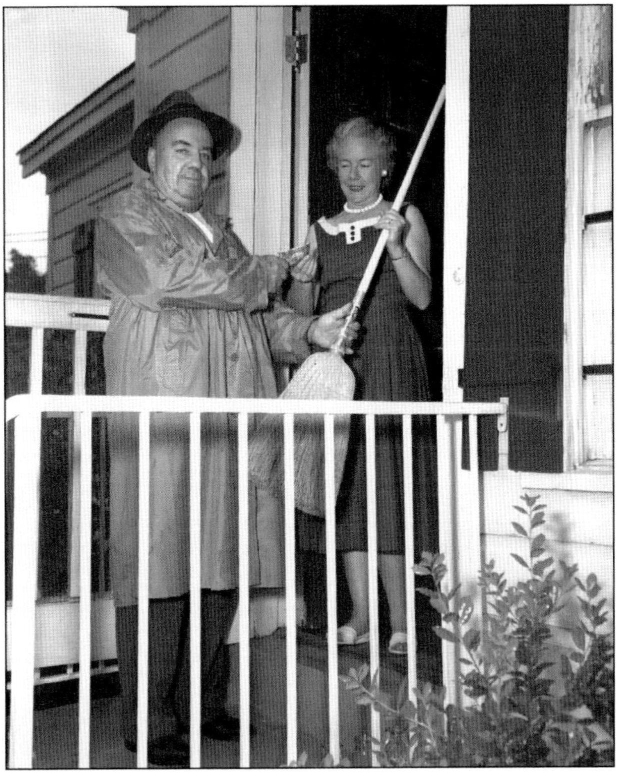

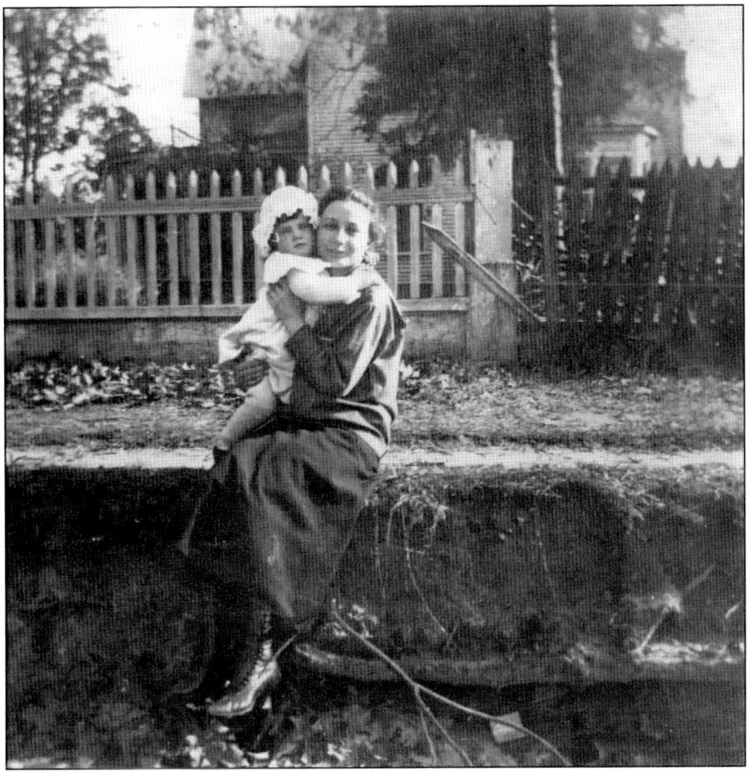

Louise Miller, shown here with her niece Betty Miller, was the granddaughter of Nicholas Blackwell. Louise, born in 1893, lived in the Blackwell house her entire life.

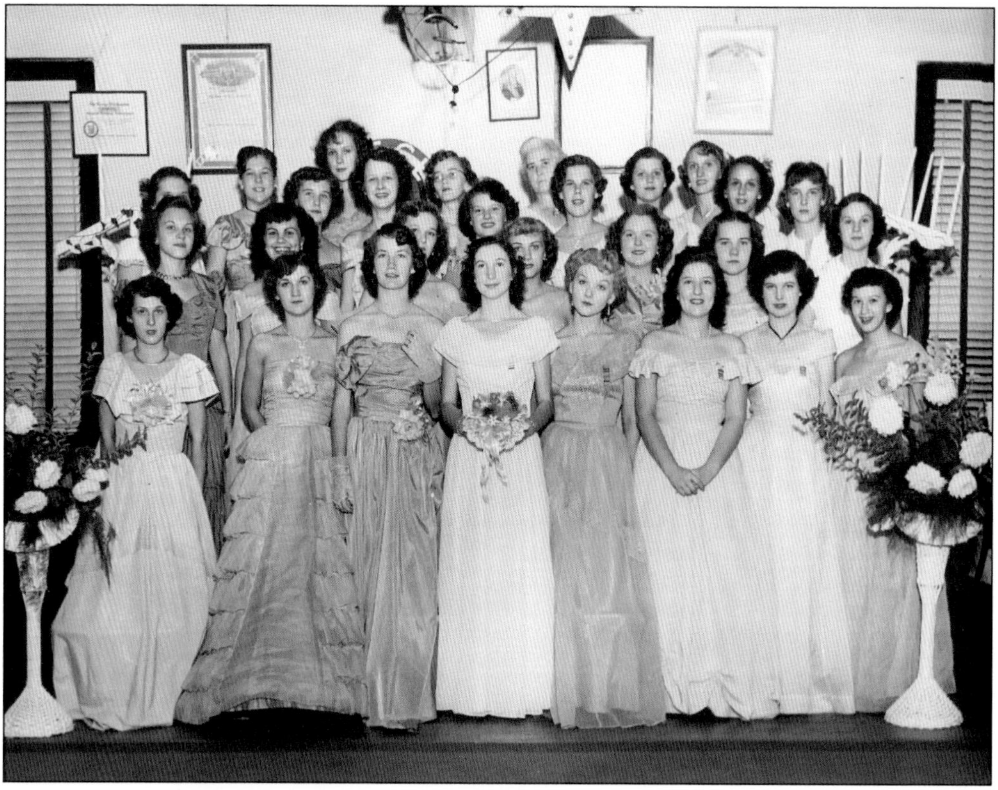

For many years, the Eastern Star met in the upper floor of the Appling building, located on Stage Road between Court Street and Sycamore View Road.

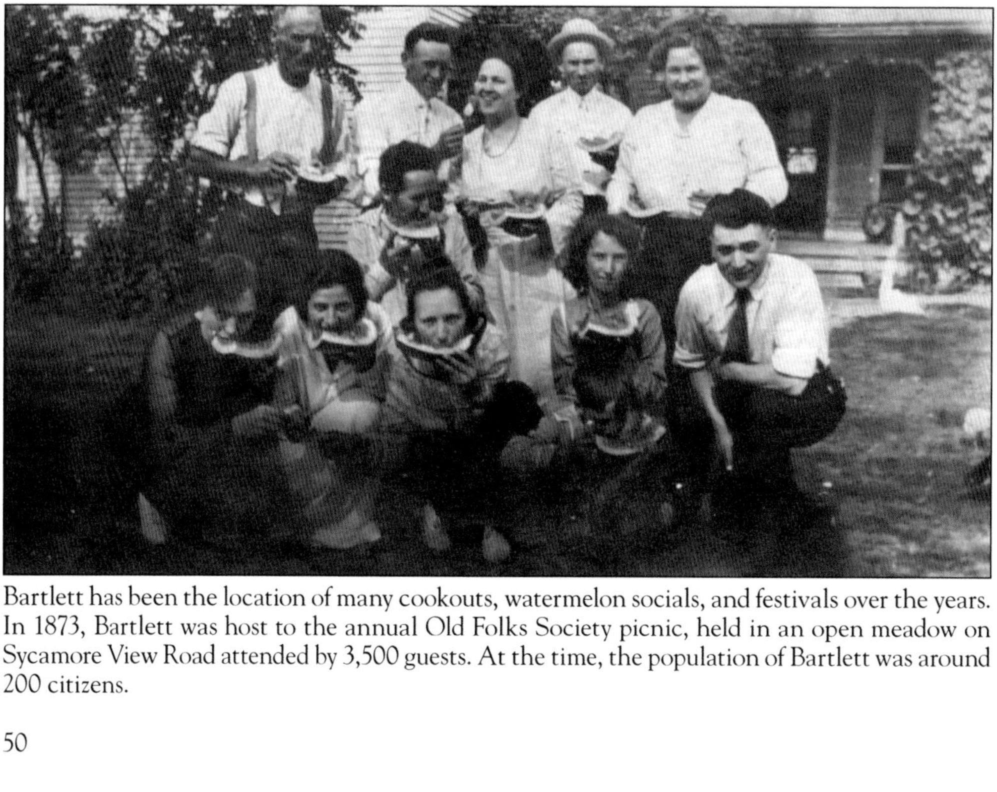

Bartlett has been the location of many cookouts, watermelon socials, and festivals over the years. In 1873, Bartlett was host to the annual Old Folks Society picnic, held in an open meadow on Sycamore View Road attended by 3,500 guests. At the time, the population of Bartlett was around 200 citizens.

Many Bartlett citizens worked in downtown Memphis, often taking the train to work each day. Among those who worked downtown were Gabriel Bartlett, Lou Blakely, and John Lilly. The Lilly Carriage Company was located on Second Street in Memphis and produced buggies and carriages beginning in 1870.

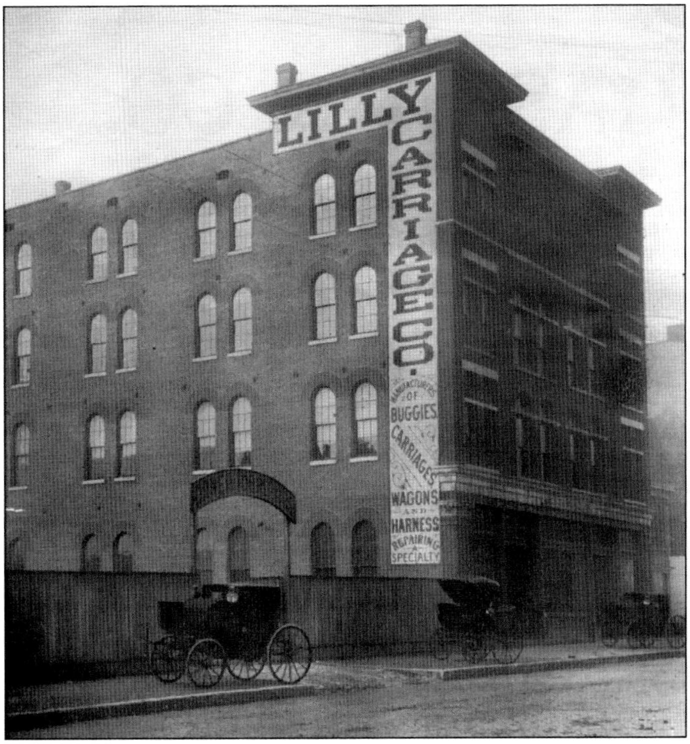

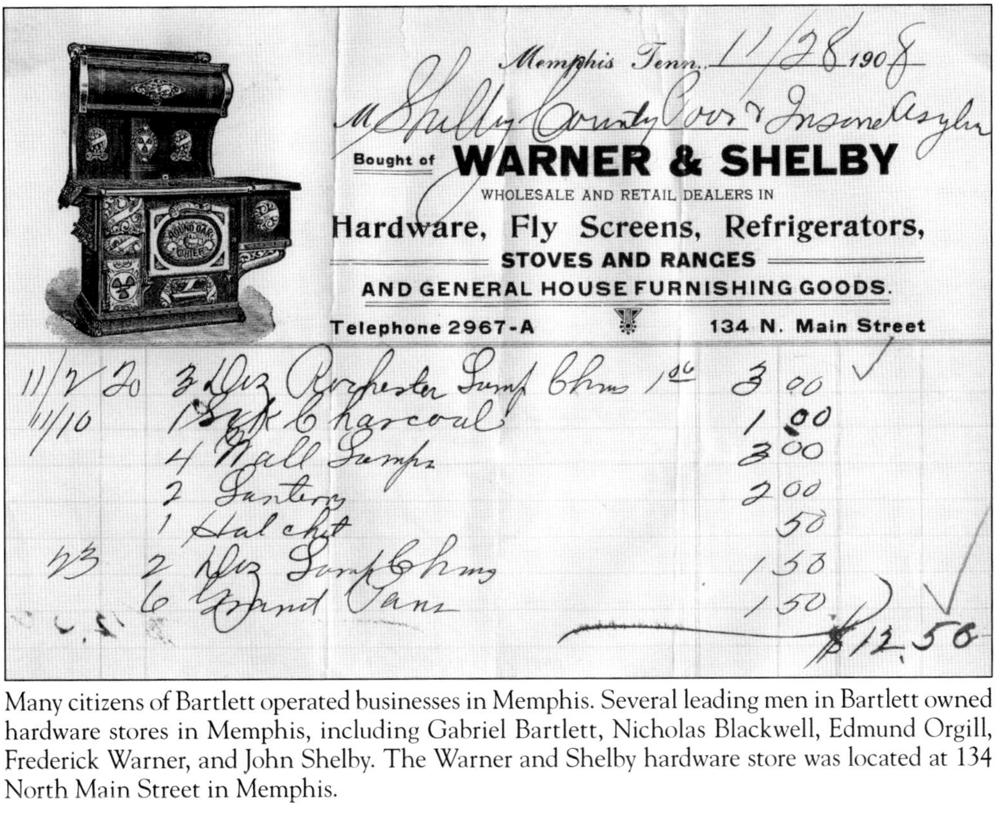

Memphis Tenn. 11/28 1908

M Shelby County Poor & Insane Asylum

Bought of **WARNER & SHELBY**

WHOLESALE AND RETAIL DEALERS IN

Hardware, Fly Screens, Refrigerators,

STOVES AND RANGES

AND GENERAL HOUSE FURNISHING GOODS.

Telephone 2967-A 134 N. Main Street

11/2 20	3 Doz Rochester Lamp Chms 1.00	3 00
11/10	1 Bx Charcoal	1 00
	4 Wall Lamps	3 00
	2 Lantern	2 00
	1 Hatchet	50
23	2 Doz Lamp Chms	1 50
	6 Grand Pans	1 50
		$12.50

Many citizens of Bartlett operated businesses in Memphis. Several leading men in Bartlett owned hardware stores in Memphis, including Gabriel Bartlett, Nicholas Blackwell, Edmund Orgill, Frederick Warner, and John Shelby. The Warner and Shelby hardware store was located at 134 North Main Street in Memphis.

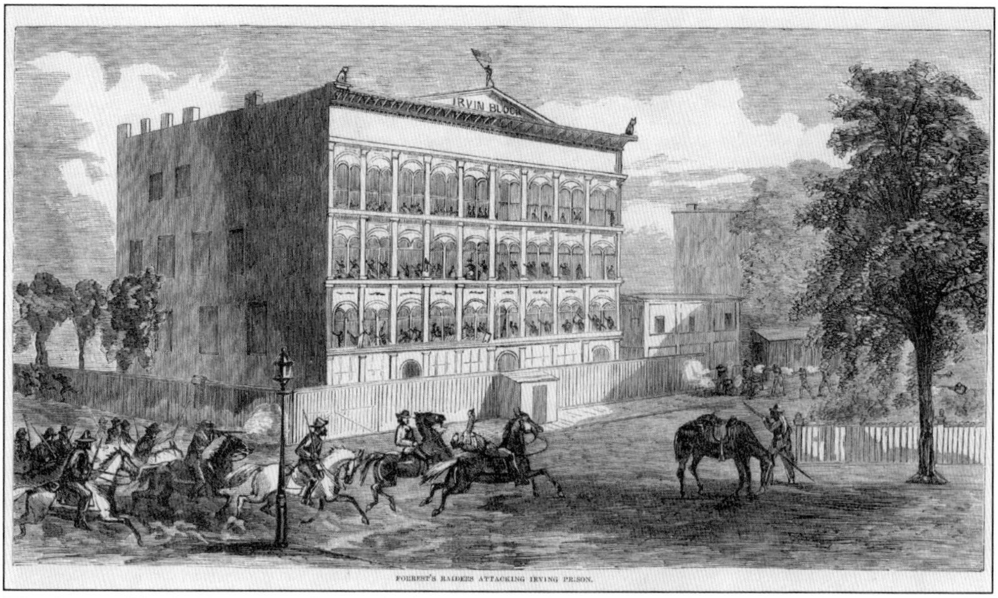

The Irving Block Prison was located adjacent to Court Square in downtown Memphis. It was here that Nicholas Gotten was held as a prisoner during the Civil War. Gotten was a Confederate cavalryman under Nathan Bedford Forrest during much of the Civil War.

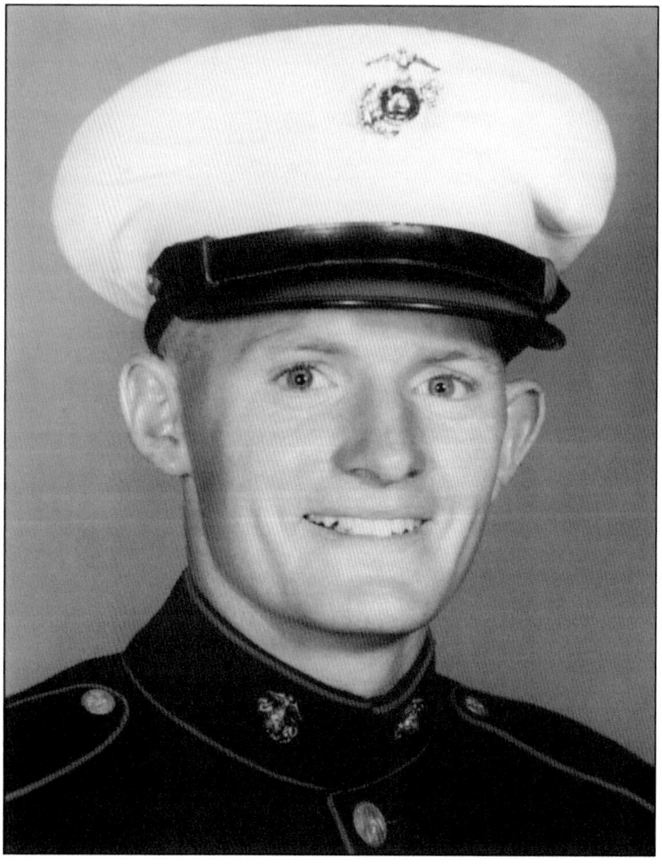

Sgt. Walter Singleton was posthumously awarded the Medal of Honor for his "conspicuous gallantry and intrepidity at the risk of his life above and beyond the call of duty" in Vietnam. The Bartlett High School graduate was killed in action trying to save the lives of those around him.

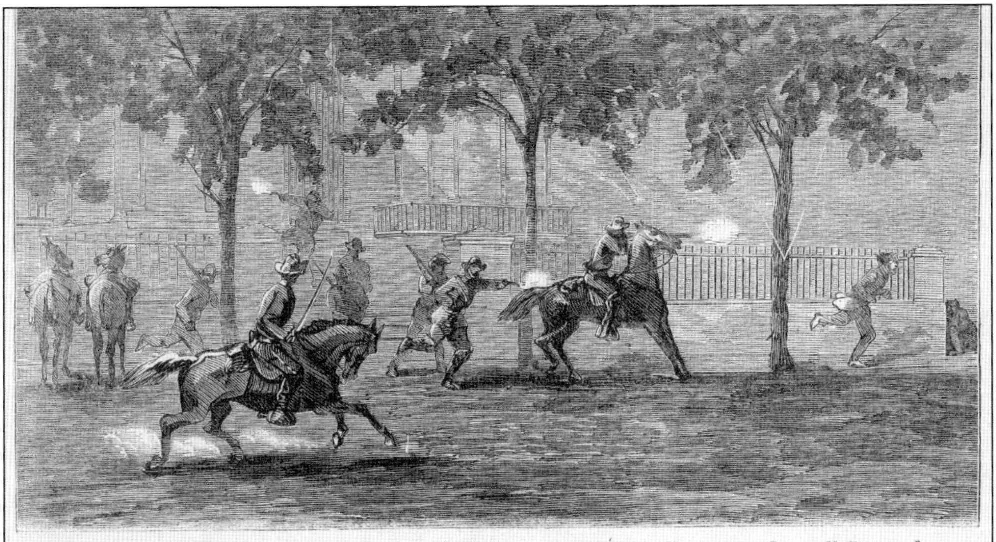
FORREST'S RAID INTO MEMPHIS—ESCAPE OF GENERAL WASHBÚRNE.—[SKETCHED BY GEORGE H. ELLSBURY.]

Nathan Bedford Forrest was always a thorn in the Union army's side. His guerilla tactics were hard to anticipate, and he could easily hide in the neighboring villages with the help of loyal citizens. Bartlett resident Nicholas Gotten was the blacksmith for General Forrest's cavalry.

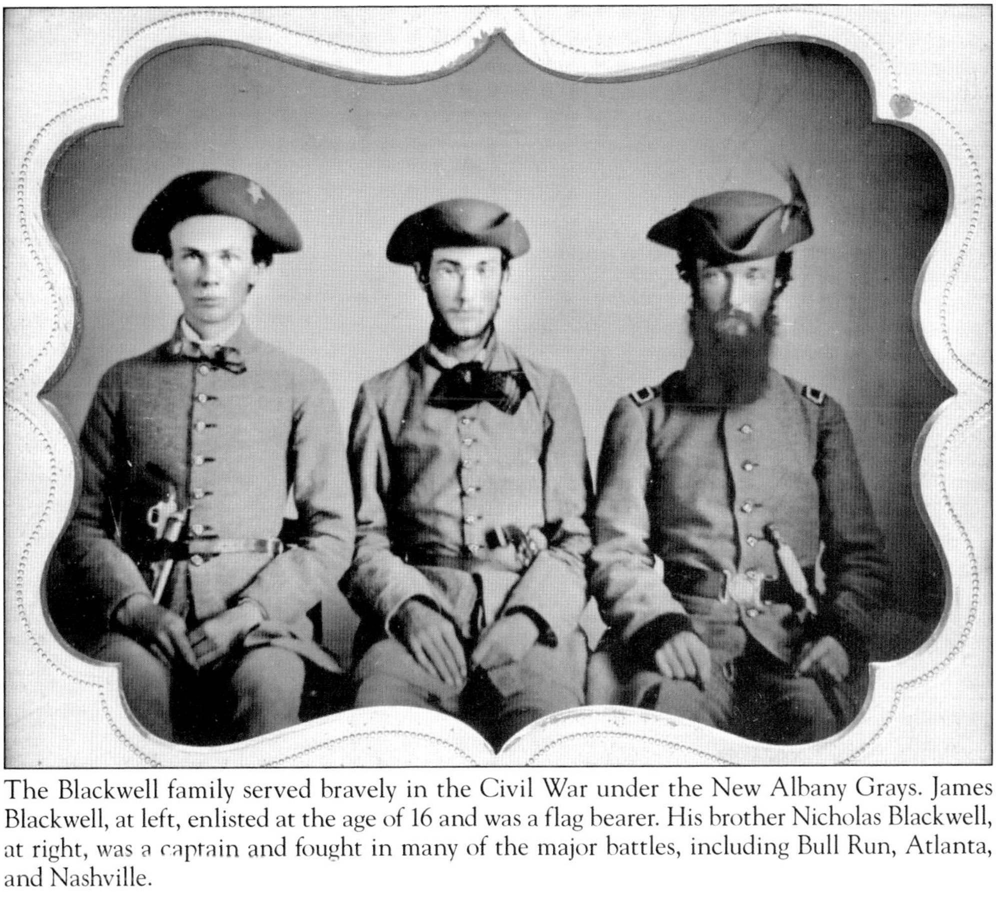

The Blackwell family served bravely in the Civil War under the New Albany Grays. James Blackwell, at left, enlisted at the age of 16 and was a flag bearer. His brother Nicholas Blackwell, at right, was a captain and fought in many of the major battles, including Bull Run, Atlanta, and Nashville.

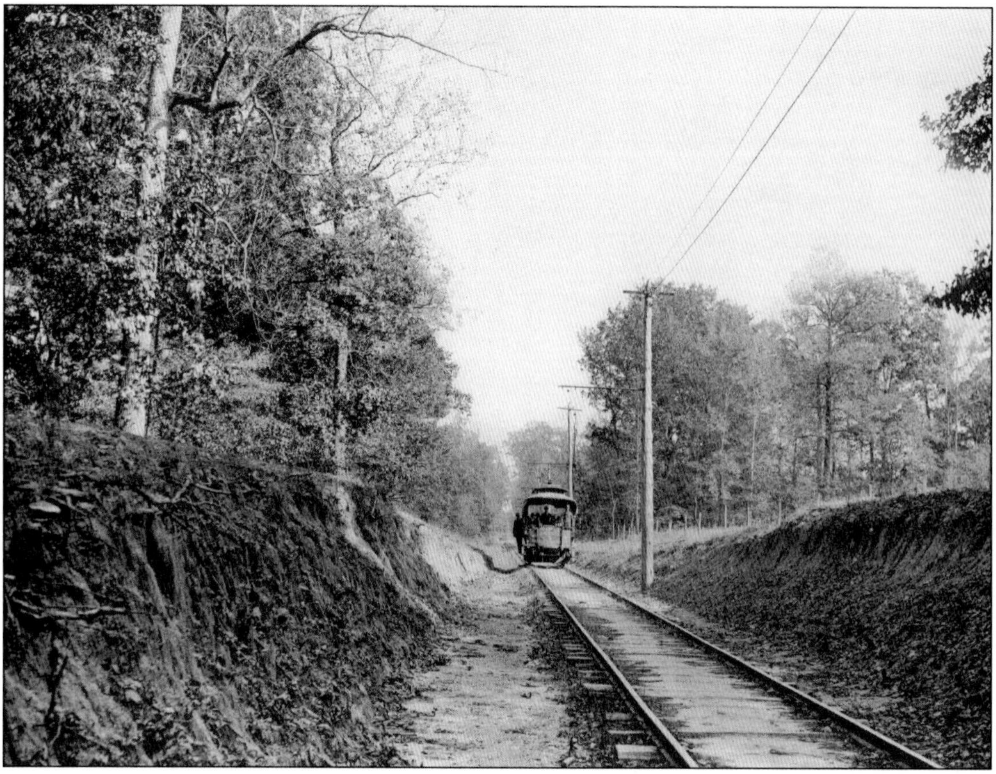

The first railroad in Shelby County was the LaGrange and Memphis Railroad, running along Poplar Avenue toward Collierville in 1842. In 1853, the Memphis and Ohio Railroad was completed through the Bartlett area, heading toward Paris, Tennessee. Through mergers and acquisitions, the line was purchased in 1983 and is today run as part of the CSX Railroad.

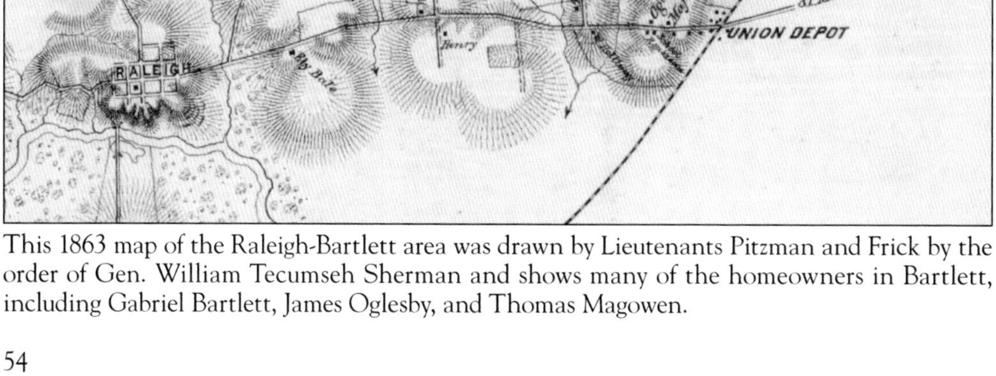

This 1863 map of the Raleigh-Bartlett area was drawn by Lieutenants Pitzman and Frick by the order of Gen. William Tecumseh Sherman and shows many of the homeowners in Bartlett, including Gabriel Bartlett, James Oglesby, and Thomas Magowen.

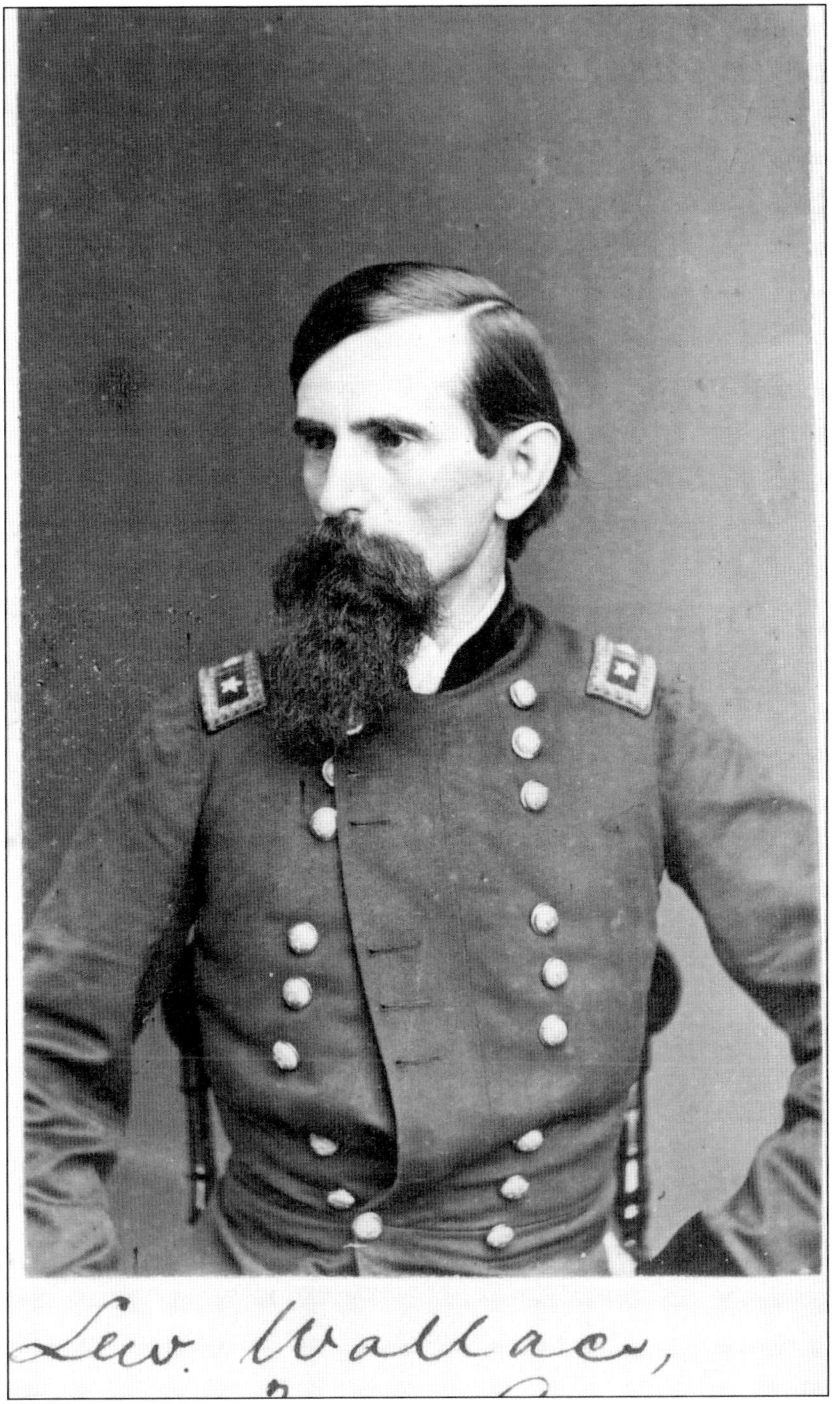

Lew Wallace was the Union general who used Bartlett as a command post during the Civil War. He secured Gabriel Bartlett's home as a headquarters and was there on orders to fight the rebel guerillas—including Nathan Bedford Forrest—who were causing the North great problems by interrupting the rail lines. In 1880, Wallace wrote *Ben Hur*, which was later made into a movie and won 11 academy awards.

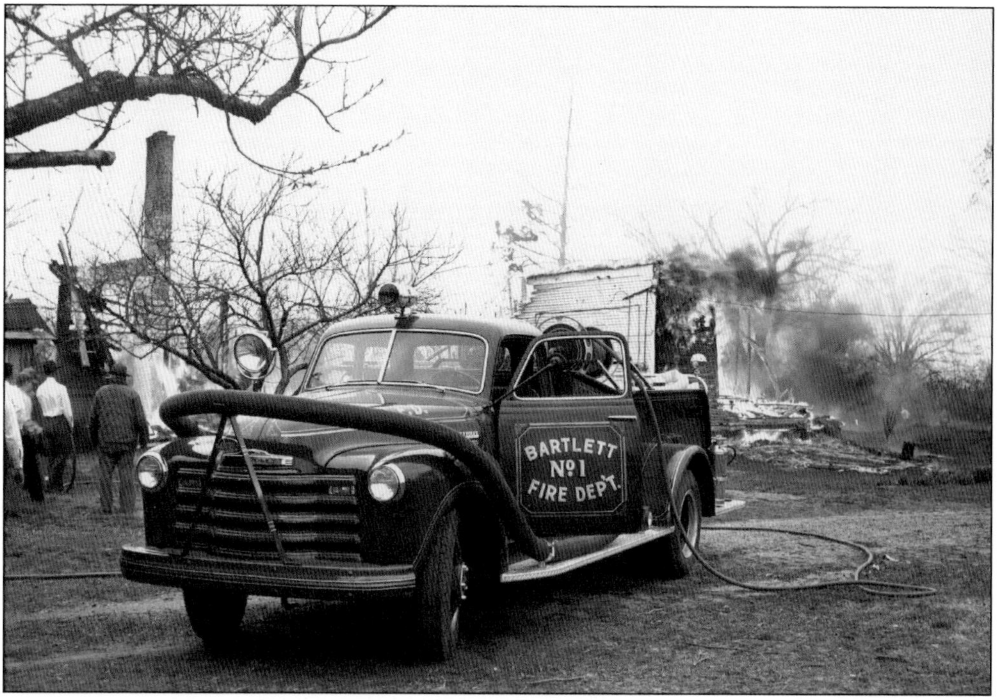

Like many small towns, Bartlett relied on a volunteer fire department. Led by Red Fuller, the fire department was alerted by Mabel Richmond, a bedridden volunteer who, after receiving the telephone call for help, would ring a bell located next to her home on Court Street. Shown here is the first fire truck for Bartlett in 1949.

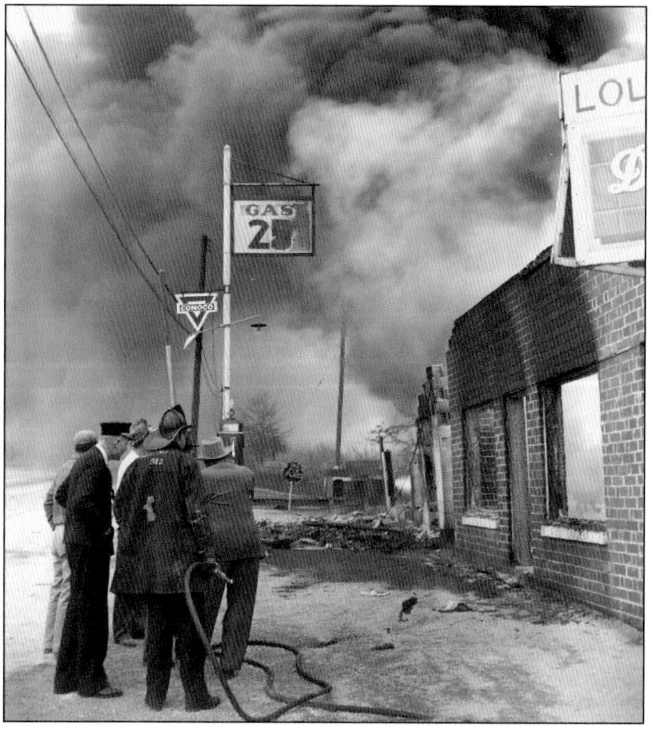

The Bartlett volunteer fire department is seen here helping to put out a fire at Canale Grocery on Highway 70 in 1951. Many high school students volunteered for the fire department, as the fire station was across the street from the high school. Fighting a fire was better than geometry class any day.

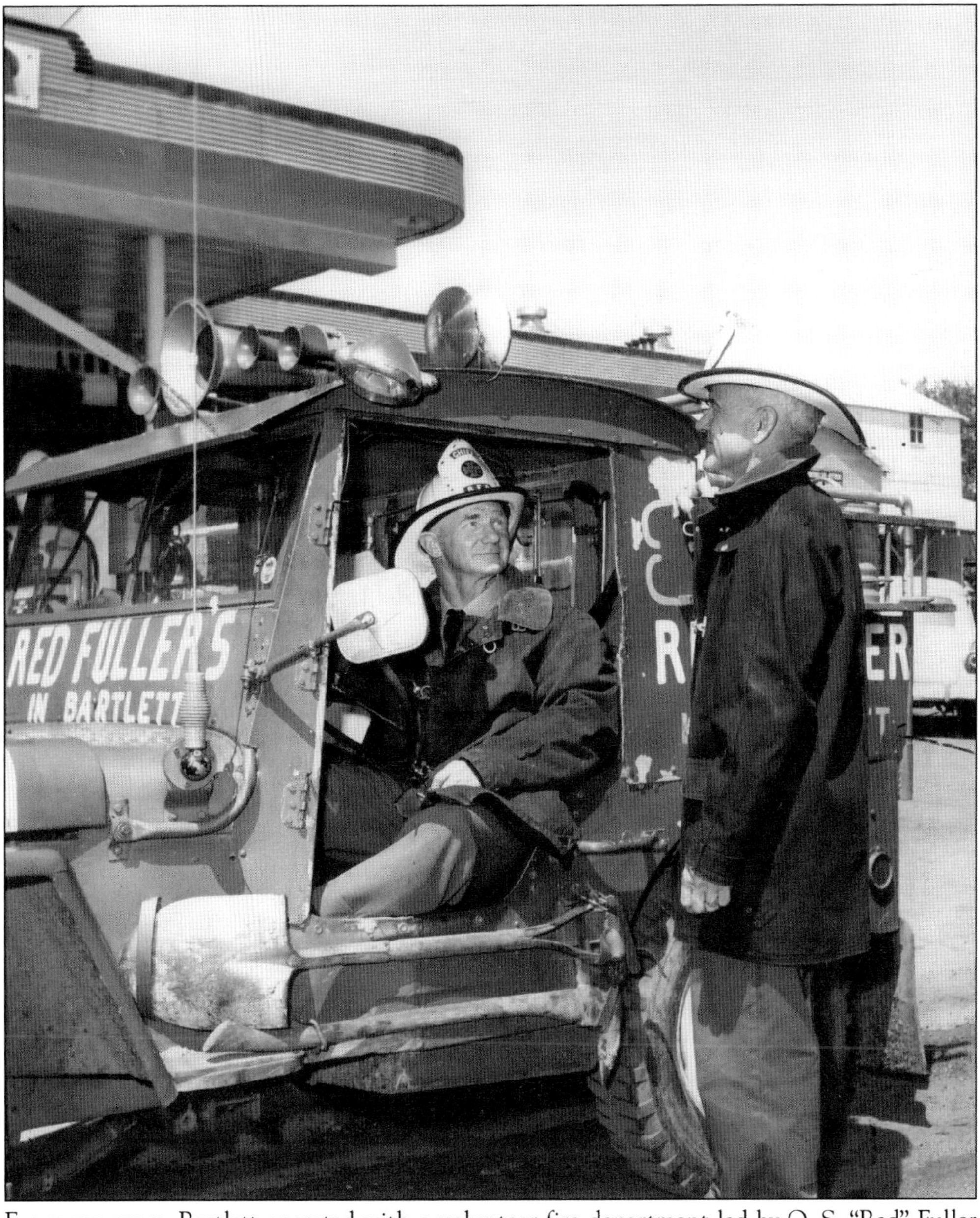

For many years, Bartlett operated with a volunteer fire department led by O. S. "Red" Fuller out of his Sinclair gas station on Stage Road near Court Street. Red Fuller retired in 1968 after 20 years as a volunteer fireman. It was estimated that he extinguished over 800 fires during his career in the Bartlett area.

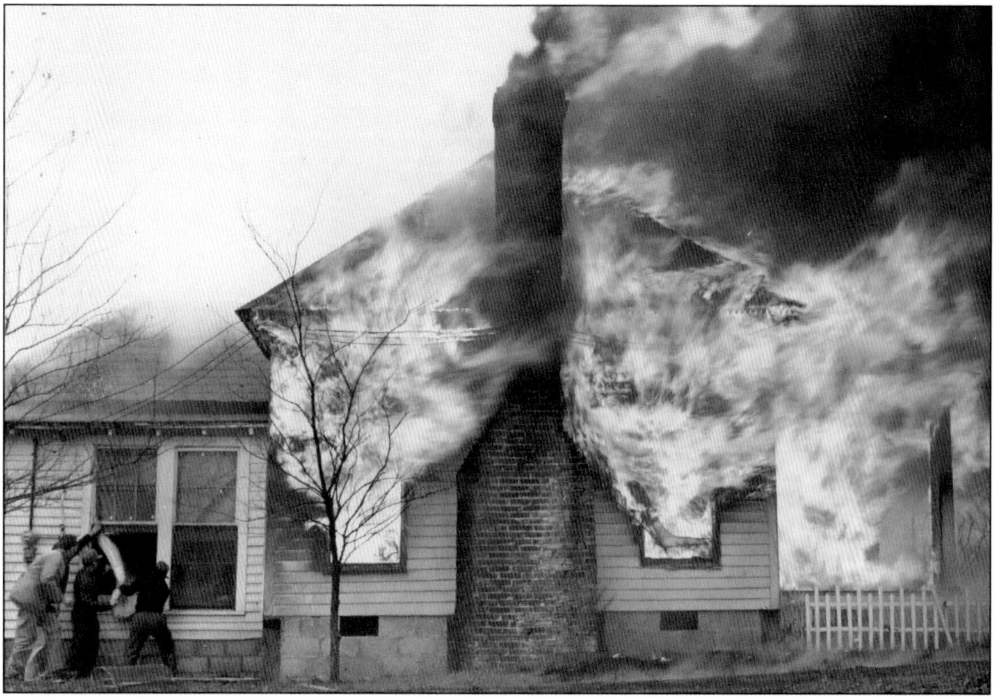

On December 25, 1956, a fire broke out in the home of Mr. and Mrs. B. L. Jones, located south of Bartlett on Raleigh LaGrange Road. The house was totally destroyed, but neighbors pitched in to buy food for the family and even Christmas presents for the children.

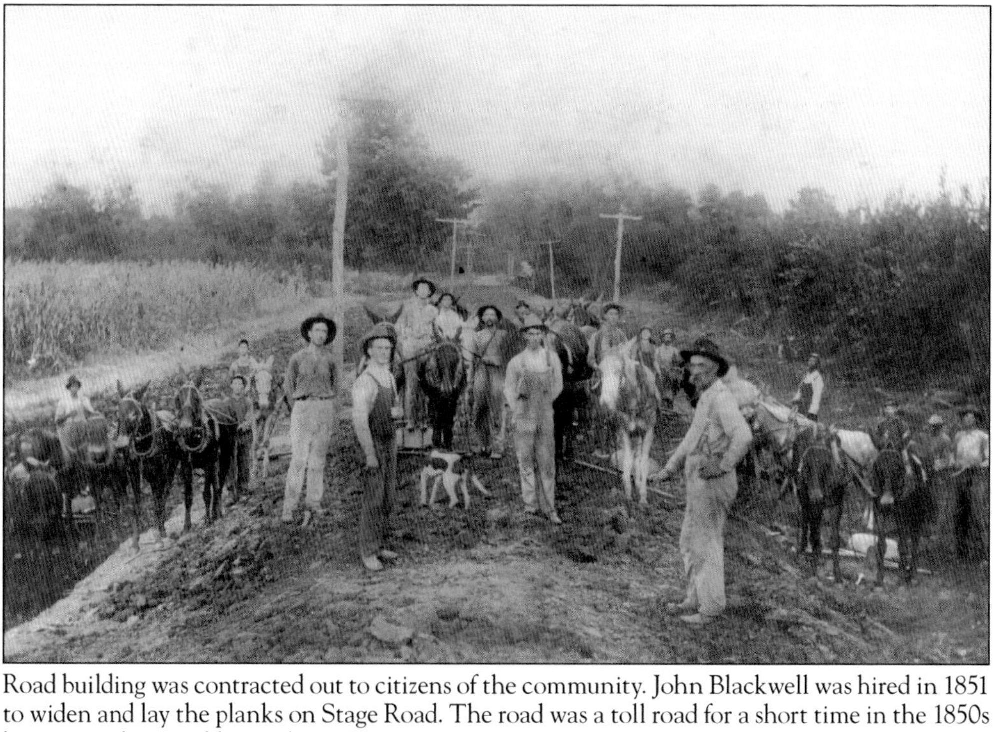

Road building was contracted out to citizens of the community. John Blackwell was hired in 1851 to widen and lay the planks on Stage Road. The road was a toll road for a short time in the 1850s but reverted to a public road in 1855.

Three

Houses

The earliest homes in the Bartlett area were usually log cabins made from local hardwood trees. Two good examples of such structures are the Davies Manor home and the Moser home. Davies Manor was built in the 1830s near the Morning Sun community in eastern Bartlett. The Davies family, who arrived in 1838, occupied the home for over 150 years. In 1931, the property was willed to Ellen Davies-Rogers, who became the first Shelby County historian. The home today is operated as a museum and cultural center. The Moser home is located on Sycamore View Road. Master carpenter James Oglesby moved to Bartlett after the Civil War and was responsible for building many of the homes in the Bartlett Historic District, including the homes of Nicholas Gotten, William Ward, Nicholas Blackwell, John Shelton, and John Priddy. His style of home varied from a large Gothic Revival for Nicholas Blackwell to a traditional New England saltbox style for Nicholas Gotten and a Victorian piano-box style for William Ward.

Today there are three homes in Bartlett listed on the National Register of Historic Places: the Nicholas Gotten home, Cedar Hall, and Davies Manor. Each of these represent a very different building style, just as their owners came from diverse backgrounds. Gotten was a Prussian immigrant who brought his skill of blacksmithing to Bartlett and went on to apply for, and receive, a U.S. patent for his work in the field of cotton machinery. Samuel Bond, who built Cedar Hall, then known as Avenue, in 1845, was educated at the University of Nashville and was a practicing doctor before becoming a skilled farmer. In 1851, Dr. Bond was awarded a medal at the World's Fair in London for his superior cotton. Davies Manor was built in the 1830s, and in the 1850s, it was occupied by Logan and James Davies. The property was willed to Julius and William Davies, sons of James, who were both doctors. The property was a working plantation with a library, post office, and its own general store. Each of these three families had in common a keen sense of ingenuity, a strong will to work, and an interest in the community. When one looks back on the old records showing community involvement in Bartlett, the names Gotten, Bond, and Davies are always there. They ran for public office, established churches, were members of the PTA and Masonic lodges, and sat on numerous committees. They did what so many in Bartlett have done over the years; they gave back to a community that gave them the opportunity to succeed.

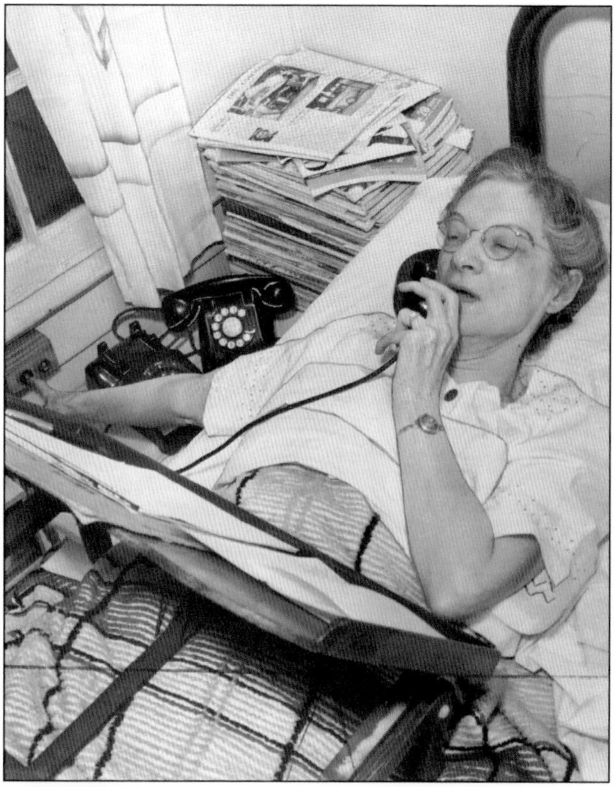

Mabel Richmond served as a schoolteacher in Bartlett for many years. In later years, she was confined to her bed but still acted as the operator who received all calls for the Bartlett volunteer fire department. As the calls came in, she would push a button beside her bed that activated a siren outside her house, alerting the firemen.

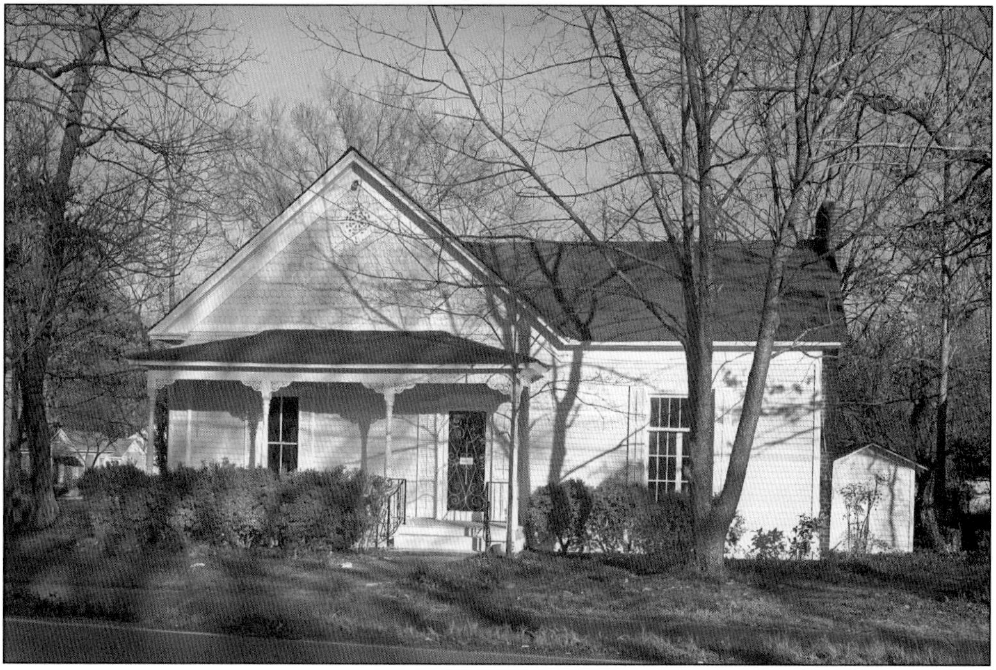

The Mabel Richmond house is located at the southeast corner of Court Street and Woodlawn Street. The house was built in 1884 for the Shelby family. It was from this house that Richmond worked from her bed as an operator for the Bartlett volunteer fire department.

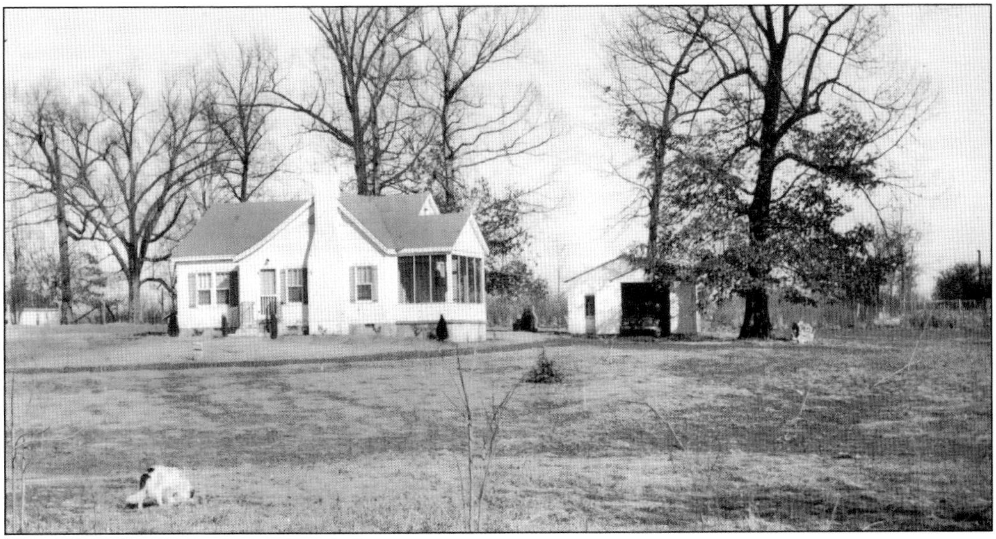

Joseph Freeman built his new home on the northeast corner of Court Street and Blackwell Street in 1939. His grandmother, Sarah Elizabeth Williford, had moved to Bartlett in 1853 from North Carolina, residing near Old Brownsville Road. Jody, as he was known, was born on Sycamore View Road and lived his entire life in what would become the Bartlett Historic District.

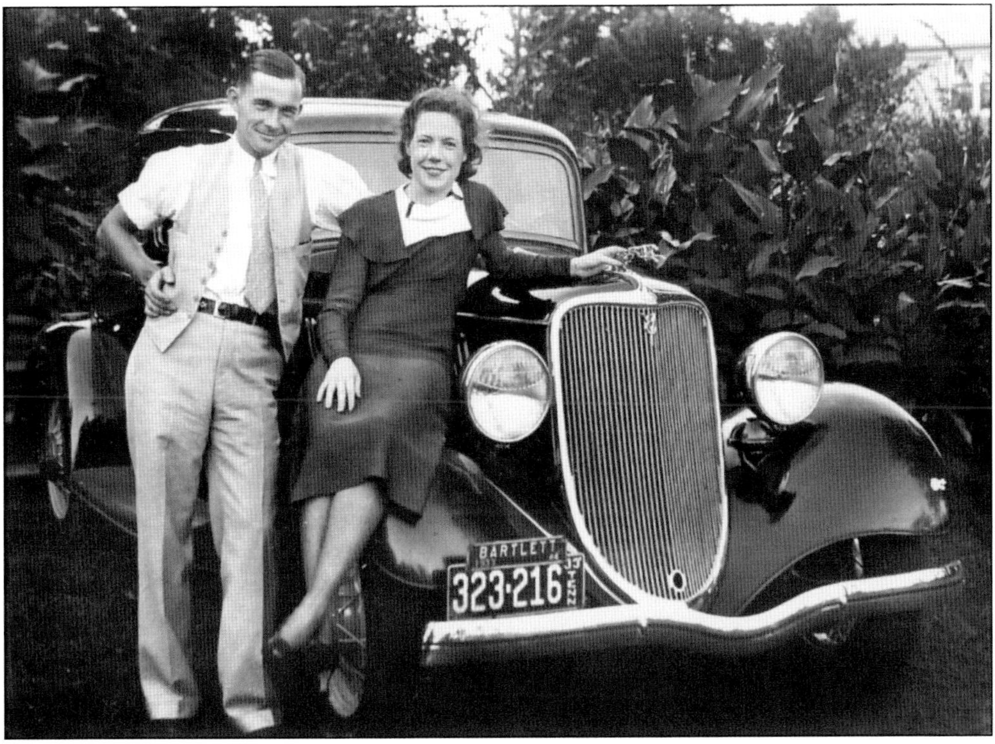

Jody Freeman had known Mary Ann Blakely since childhood, as they were neighbors while growing up in Bartlett. They married in 1935, built a home on Court Street, and raised two girls, Jo Ann and Ginger. W. J. Freeman Park in Bartlett is named in Jody's honor. From 1957 until 1992, he was a Bartlett alderman, helping to guide the city during it years of greatest growth. It is because of citizens like Jody Freeman that Bartlett is known as a great place to live and raise a family.

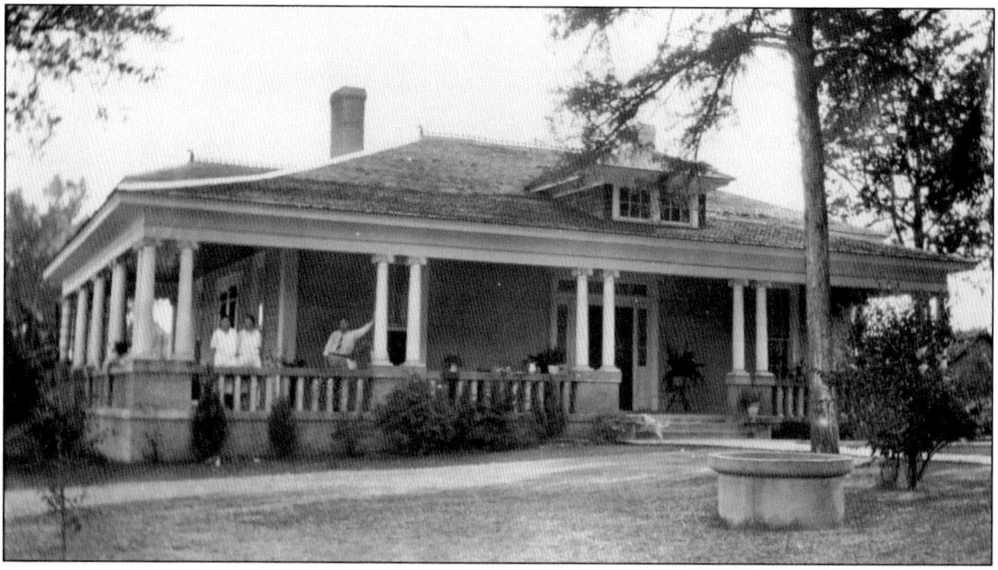

Dave Gotten, son of Nicholas Gotten, purchased the home shown above in 1910. The house, located on Stage Road across from Court Street, was built in the 1880s for the Elmore family. Tragically, in 1917, Dave Gotten was accidentally killed by another security guard while keeping night watch for a burglar in a local business.

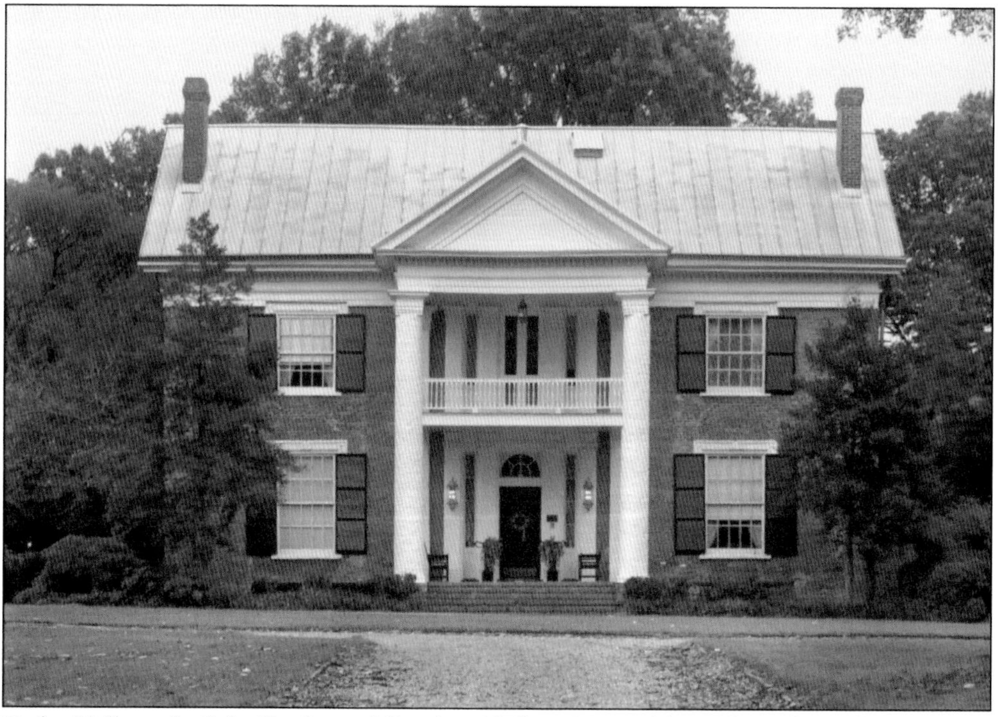

Cedar Hall was built by Dr. Samuel Bond in 1845 and was sold to Edmund Orgill in 1862 for $23,672. The Orgills lived there for many years, until Edmund's death in 1905, when the land was sold to a real estate developer. Cedar Hall was purchased in 1977 by Jasper and Jeanette Rainey, who lived in the home for many years. The home was placed on the National Register of Historic Places in 1994.

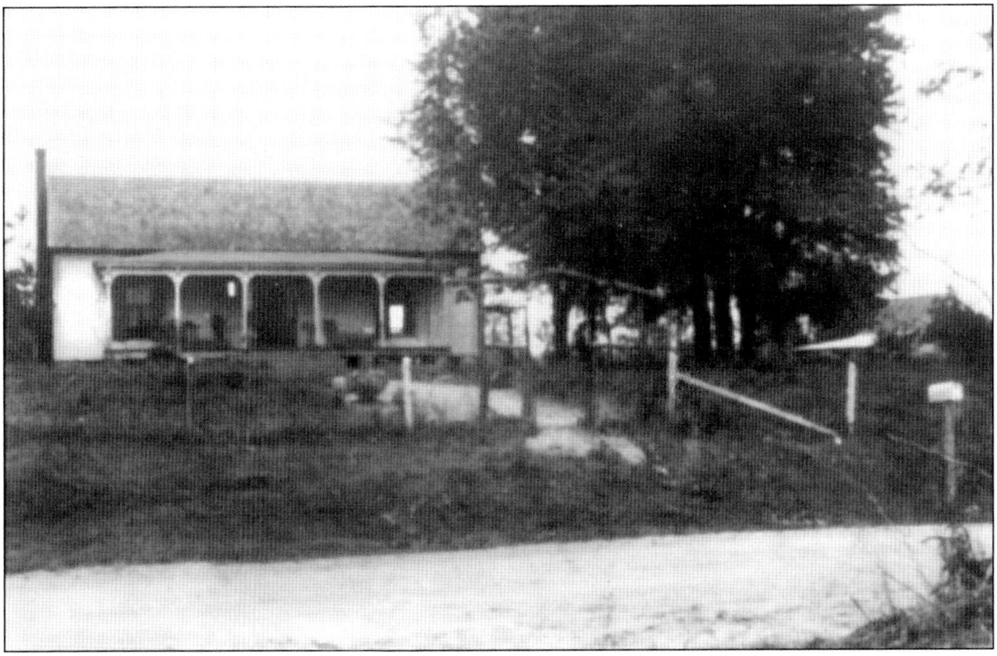

The William Bond house was built in 1883 on land deeded to him from his mother, who had married Harvey Williams after the death of his father, Dr. Samuel Bond. The home, located at Kate Bond Road and Stage Road, was passed down to their daughter, Kate Bond, who lived there here entire live, raising flowers.

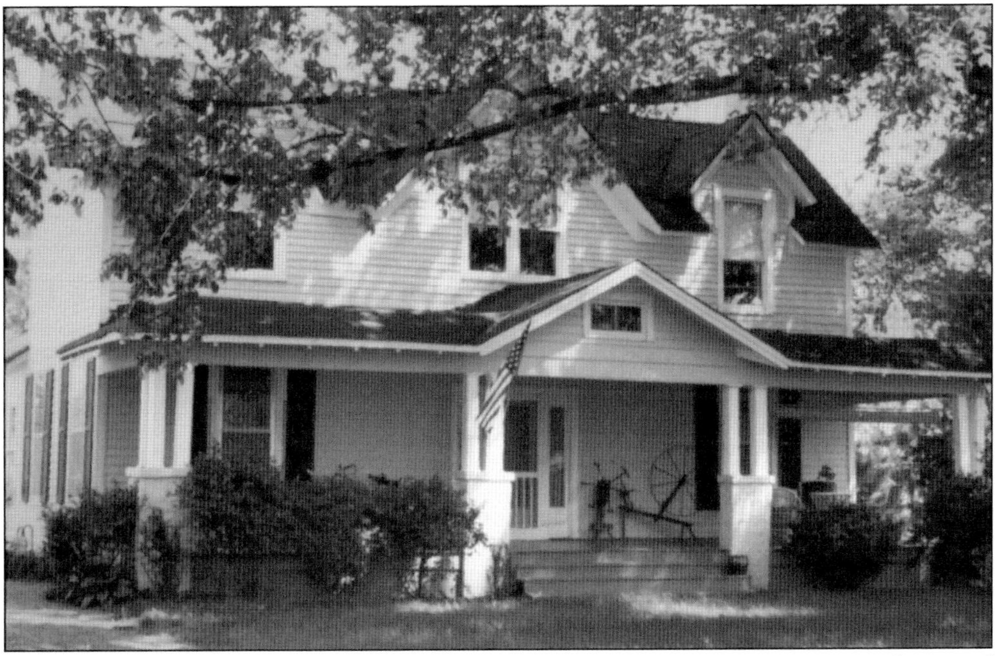

The Williams house, located on the corner of Court and North Streets, is unique in its architectural design. Many of the longtime Bartlett families lived in the home, including the Bledsoes, Williamses, and Graveses. Its most recent owners, Jae and Zeke Graves, have worked hard to restore the home and make it one of the jewels of the historic district.

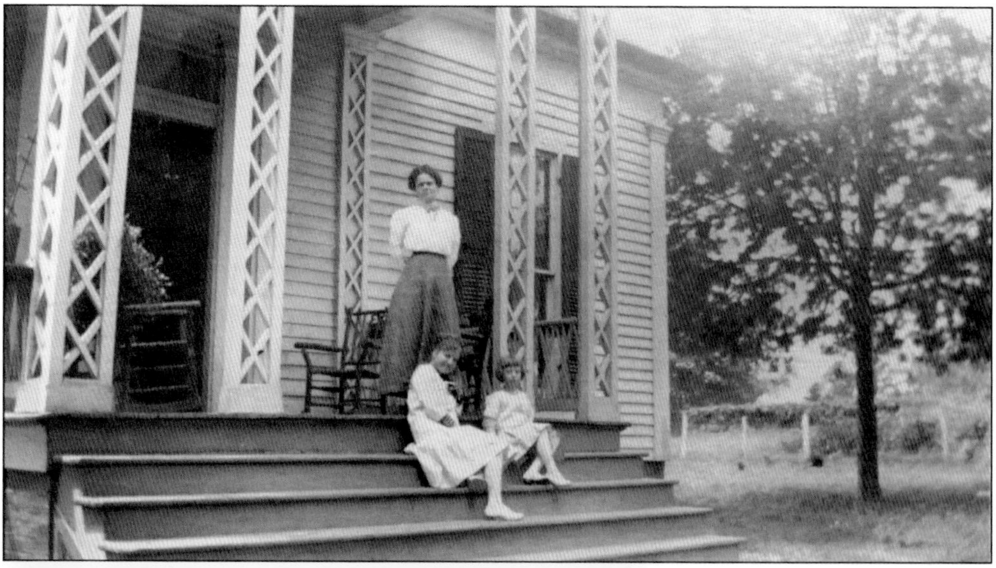

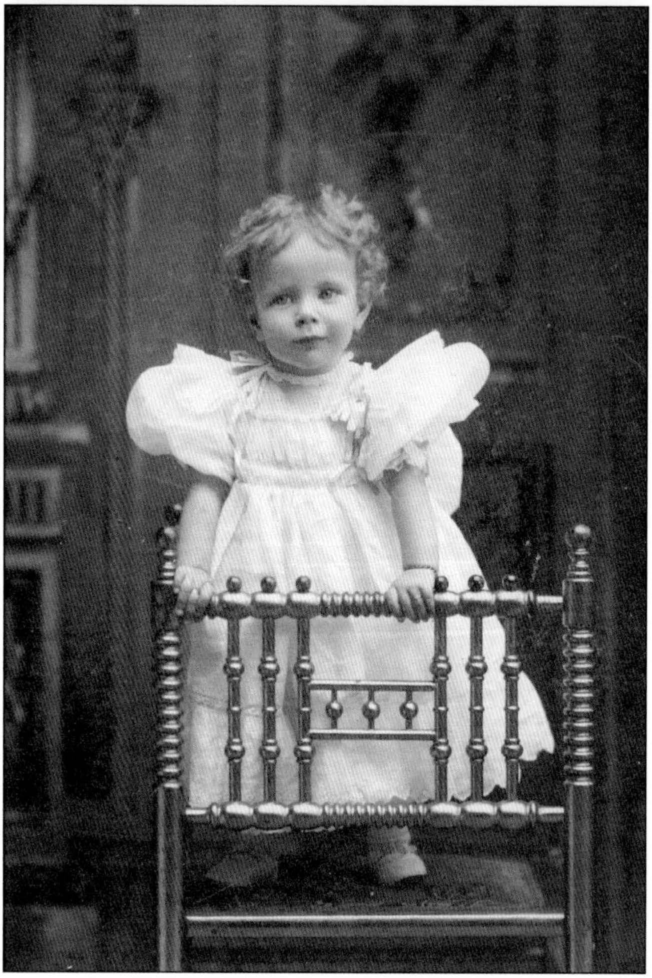

Built in the late 1850s, the Shelton house is the oldest remaining home in the Bartlett historic district. Rev. John Shelton was a schoolteacher during the Civil War in Bartlett, then known as Union Depot. Nicholas Blackwell and his wife, Virginia, lived there in the late 1860s while their home was being constructed next door. Their only child, Willie Bugg Blackwell, was born in the Shelton house.

Polly Smith lived in the Shelton house on Sycamore View Road from 1907 until the 1940s.

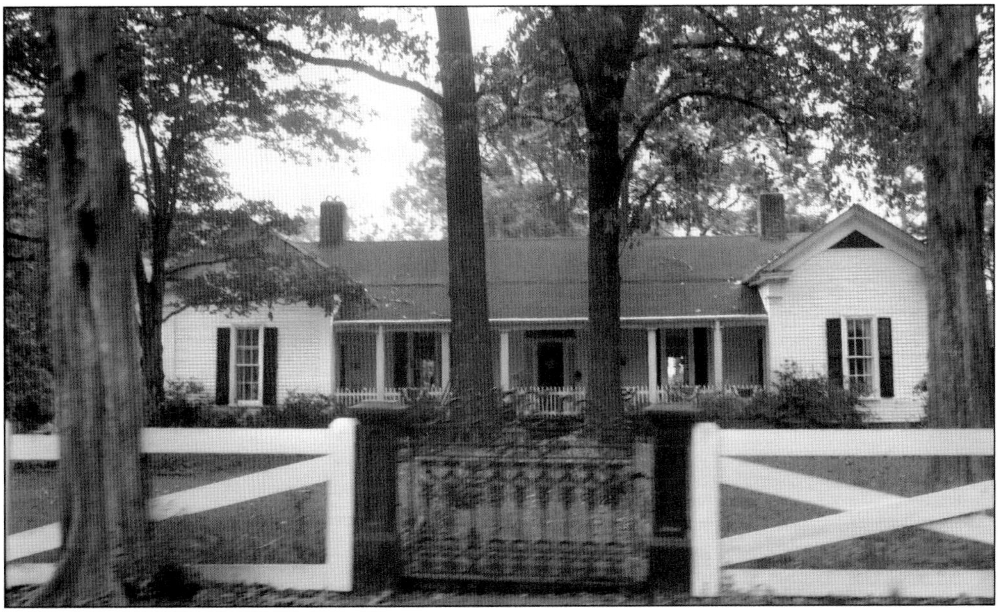

William Ward built this piano-style home in 1871 on Sycamore View Road on land his family had owned for many years. The Ward family's 300-acre tract of land stretched from Sycamore View Road to Alturia Road along Stage Road.

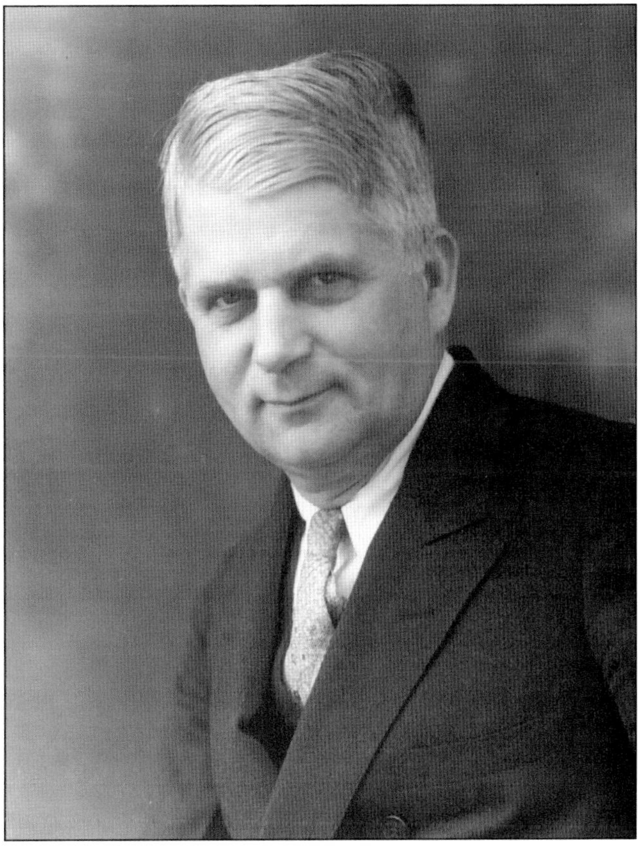

In 1952, the Ward house was purchased by Clarence Saunders, who gained fame by creating the first self-serve grocery store, Piggly Wiggly, in 1916. His original home in Memphis, known as the Pink Palace, was sold in 1927 to pay off debts before he could move in and is now a museum. Saunders died in his Bartlett home in October 1953.

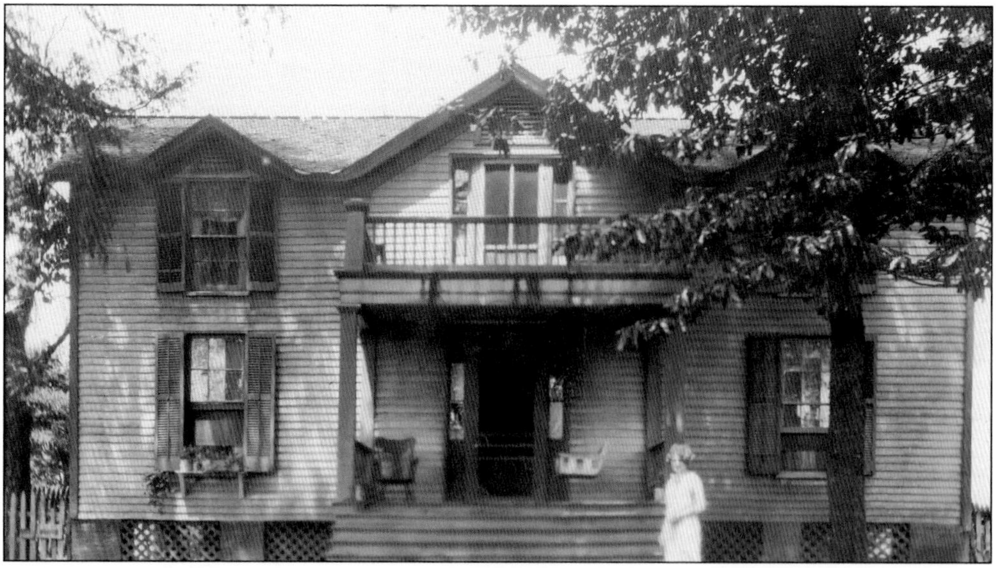

Nicholas Gotten, a Prussian immigrant who fought with Nathan Bedford Forrest in the Civil War, moved to Bartlett in 1860. Gotten was the town's first constable and also a blacksmith and ginner. He was granted a patent for an improved cotton feeder in 1879. Today the house, located on Court Street, is home to the Bartlett Historical Society and is listed on the National Register of Historic Places.

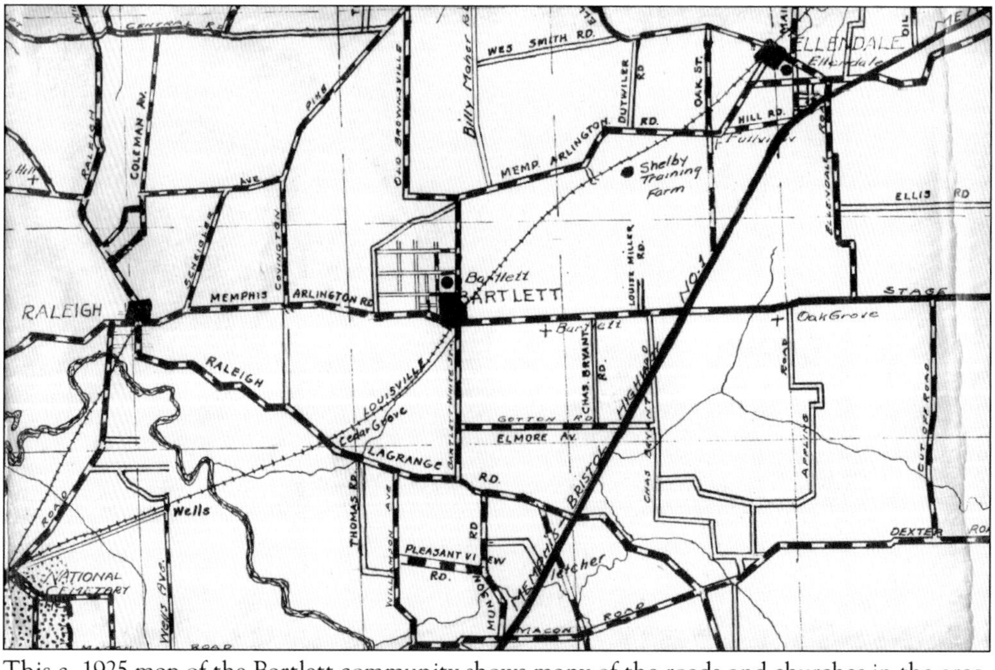

This *c.* 1925 map of the Bartlett community shows many of the roads and churches in the area. Bartlett Boulevard was known as the Bartlett–White Station Road, and Bartlett Road south of Raleigh LaGrange Road was called Williamson Avenue.

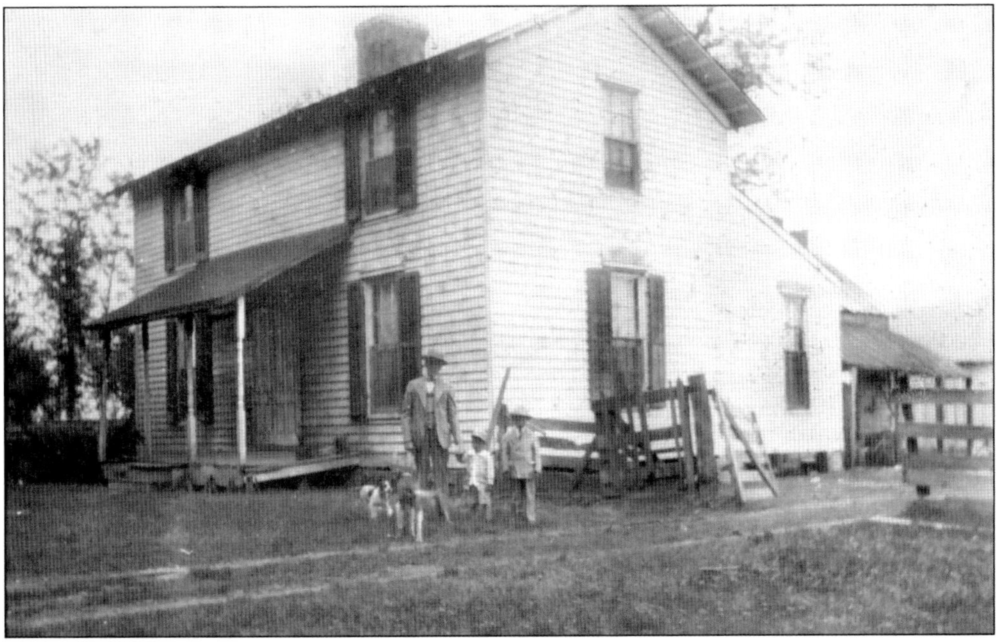

One of the earliest settlers in the area was Benjamin Williamson, who moved to Raleigh LaGrange Road in 1829. His son W. W. Williamson built the house shown above in 1870 on Bartlett Road. In 1925, the house was purchased by Jesse Dye, shown here with his two sons, Robert and Lorell. The house burned on Christmas Eve, 1927.

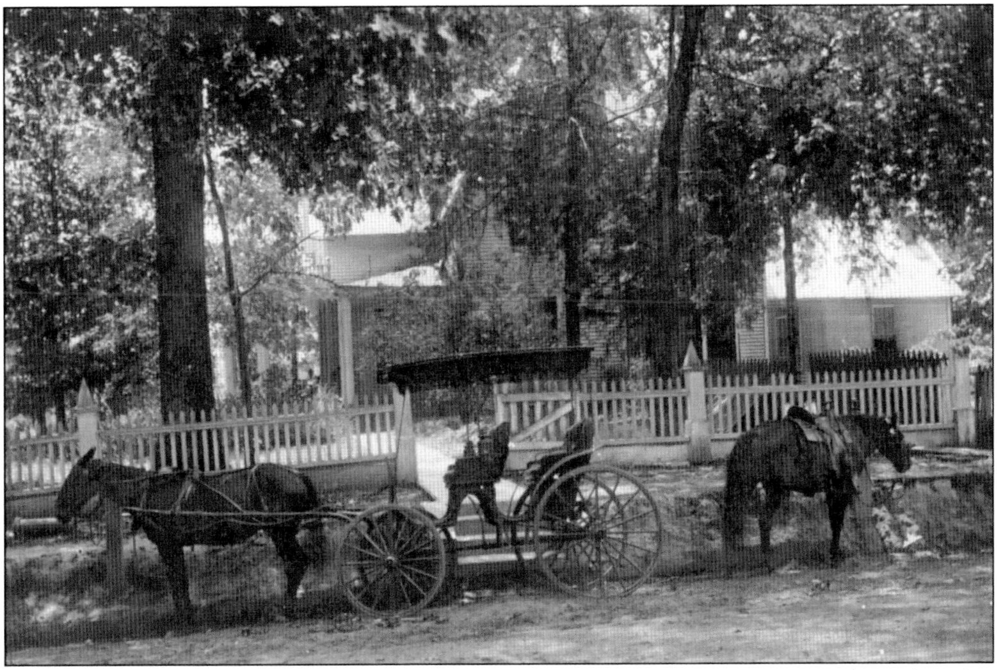

Dr. Nicholas Blackwell would make his medical rounds in a horse-drawn carriage throughout his career in Bartlett. During the yellow fever epidemic of 1878, he stayed in Bartlett and cared far the sick, being written up in the Memphis papers for his self-sacrificing ethic. Here his carriage is shown beside his home, located at Sycamore View Road and Blackwell Street, in 1900.

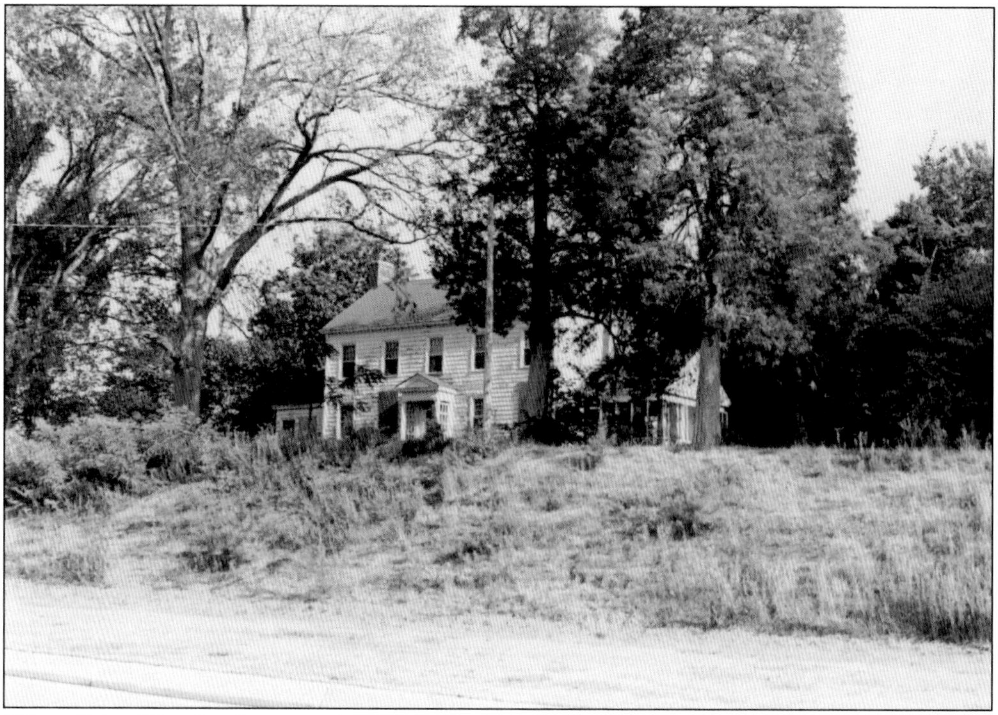

When Gabriel Bartlett first moved to Bartlett in 1847, he lived in a large two-story home surrounded by 425 acres he farmed on Stage Road. The area was then known as Green Bottom and was located between what are today Highway 70 and Kate Bond Road. The home passed through many owners over the years and was eventually torn down in the 1990s. Today it is the site of a Captain D's restaurant.

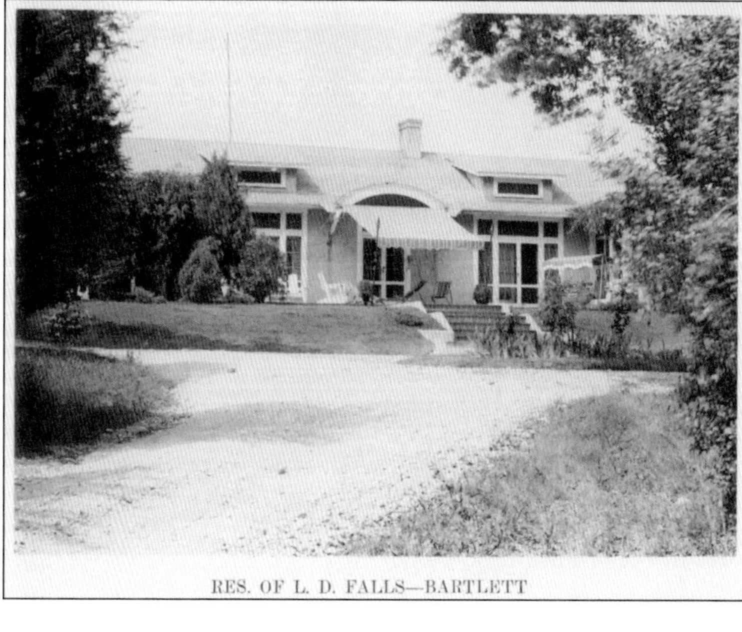

RES. OF L. D. FALLS—BARTLETT

The Falls house, shown here in 1924, was located on Stage Road just west of Bartlett United Methodist Church. The site was originally home to Mary Blackwell, who moved there from her Goodwood plantation after the Civil War. During the 1950s, the Guillarys called the tranquil lot home.

John Blackwell was born in South Carolina and moved to middle Tennessee in 1819 with the Bartlett family, who were relatives. John Blackwell and Gabriel Bartlett were first cousins. It was John Blackwell who first settled in Bartlett in 1843, soon to be followed by Gabriel Bartlett in 1847.

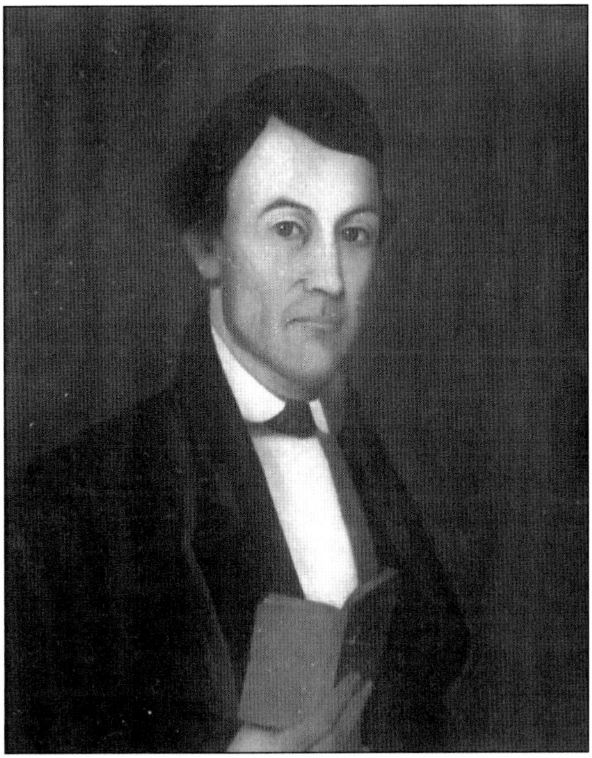

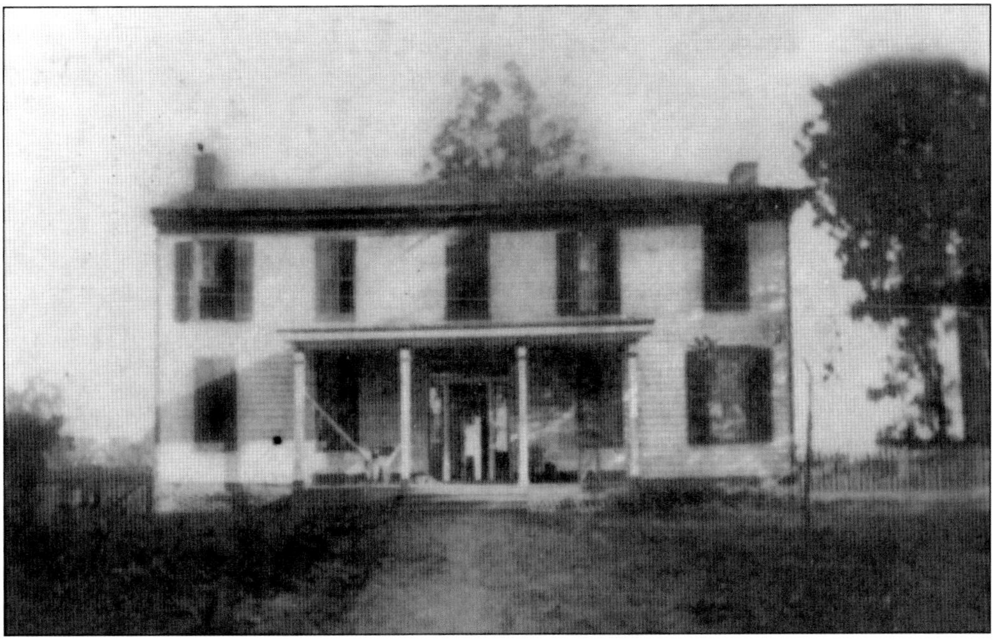

Originally owned by Joseph Cotton in the 1830s, Goodwood was one of Bartlett's few actual plantations. The 971-acre plantation was sold to John Blackwell in the 1840s for $16,000. Consisting of a main house, 12 slave houses containing 72 slaves, and vast fields of cotton and corn, Goodwood prospered until the death of John Blackwell in 1860, after which it was divided and sold at auction.

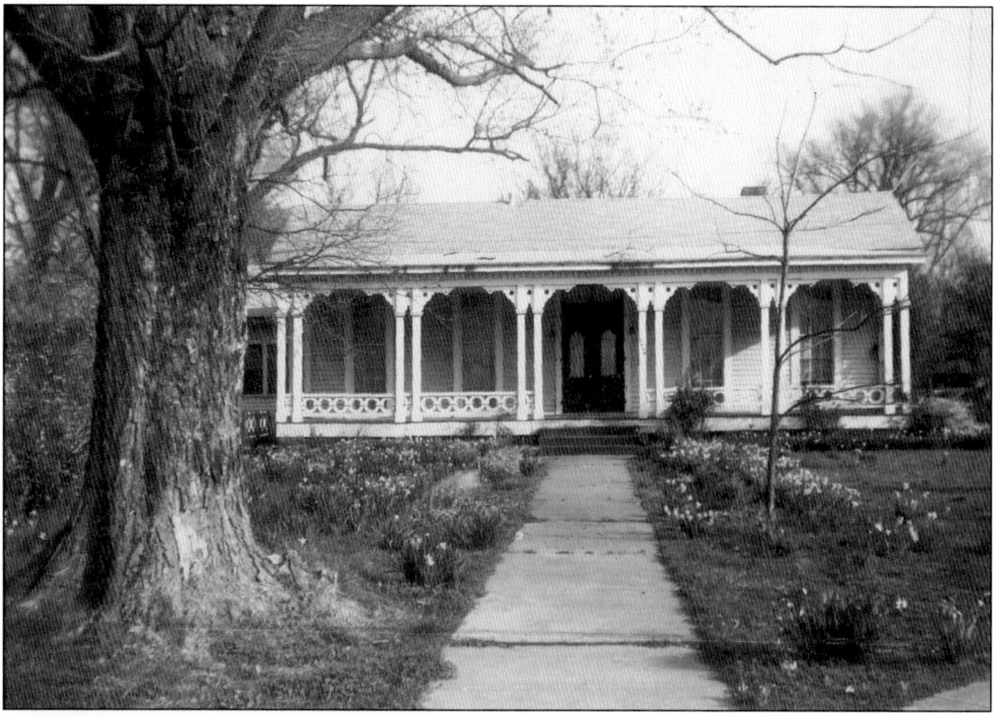

The Carter house stood for many years at the northwest corner of Sycamore View Road and Stage Road.

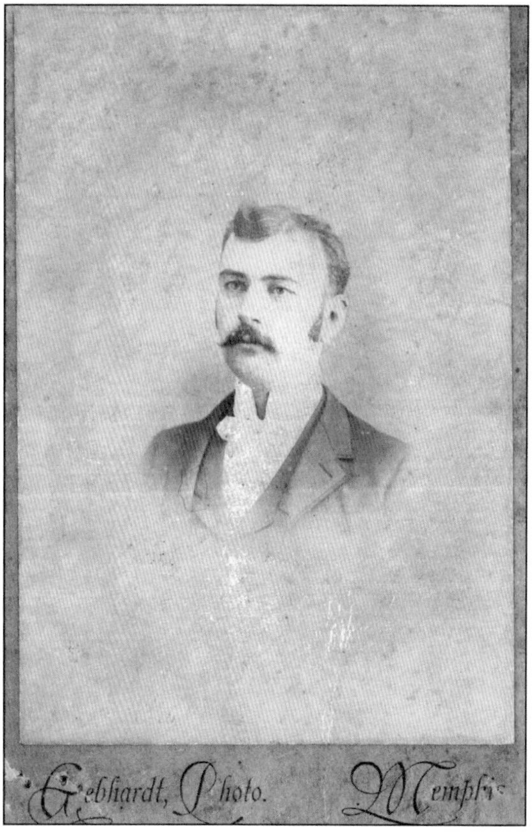

Dr. Walter B. Carter, shown here in 1890, lived for many years in Bartlett, operating a medical practice out of his home at Sycamore View Road and Stage Road. The mortality rate in the South was double that of the North, due to infectious diseases that spread easily in the warm climate. Medicines such as Groves Tasteless Chill Tonic, cod liver oil, and Dr. Rush's Bilious Pills were popular in the 1800s.

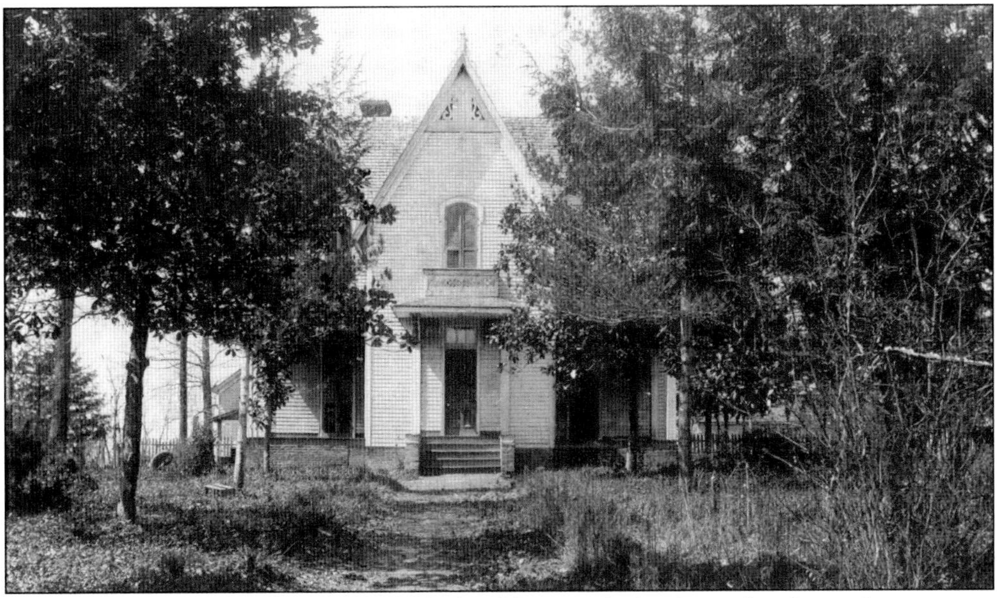

In 1869, James Oglesby constructed the Blackwell house, which is located at the southwest corner of Sycamore View Road and Blackwell Street. Dr. Nicholas Blackwell lived in the home until his death in 1910. Dr. Blackwell was noted for his selfless work during the yellow fever epidemics of the late 1870s.

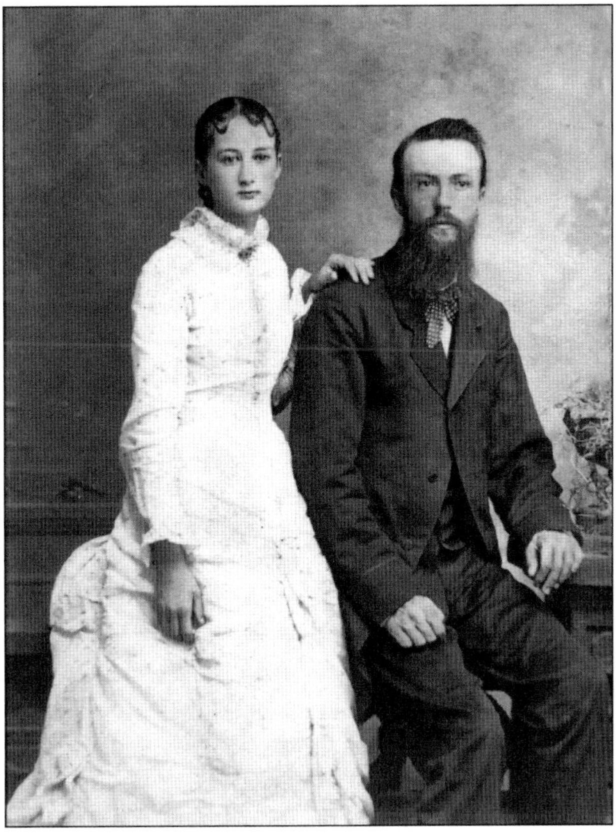

Amanda Duncan, seen here with her uncle Nicholas Blackwell in 1875, helped to care for his only daughter, Willie Bugg, after the death of his wife. Amanda was from Pontotoc, Mississippi, and lived in the Blackwell home until 1890, when she married and moved to Arkansas.

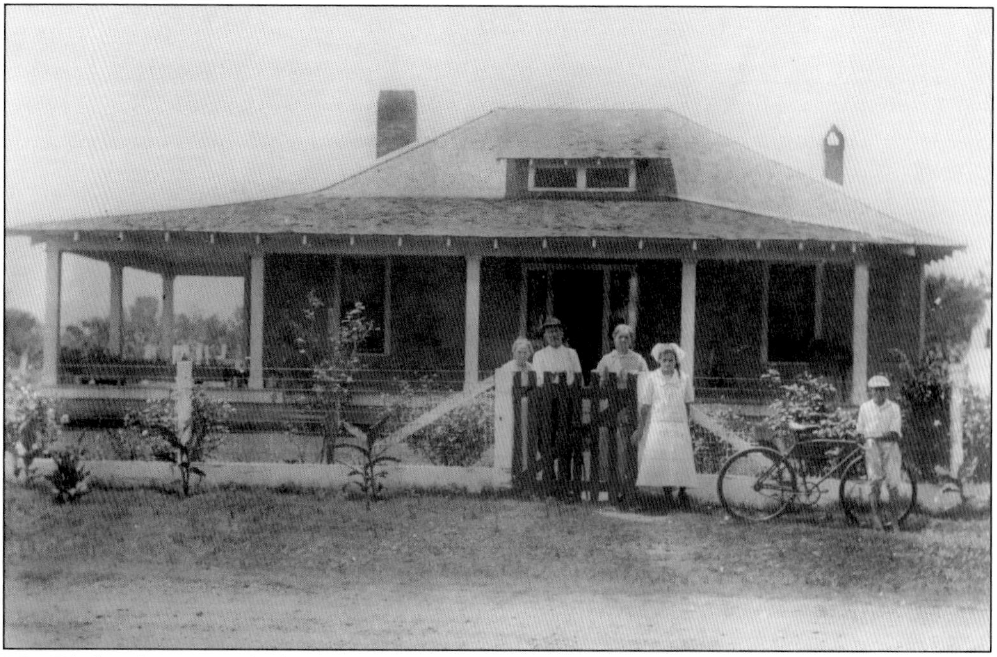

The Bledsoe house was built in 1905 and is located at the southwest corner of Court Street and North Street. In 1931, Robert Bledsoe, the small boy pictured with the bicycle, married Elva Talbot and moved into his parents' home. Elva Bledsoe, a longtime Bartlett historian, was the founder of the Bartlett Historical Society.

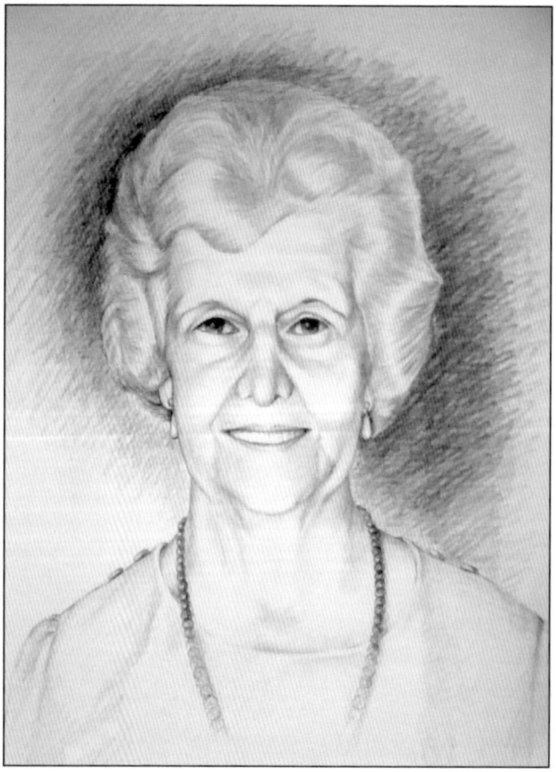

Elva Talbot Bledsoe was born in 1913, and in 1931, she married Robert Bledsoe, moving to Bartlett soon afterward. Her love of Bartlett and of its history has been a blessing to the community. When there was talk of tearing down the Nicholas Gotten house, she stepped in and brokered a deal with the city to operate the Bartlett Museum out of the historic home.

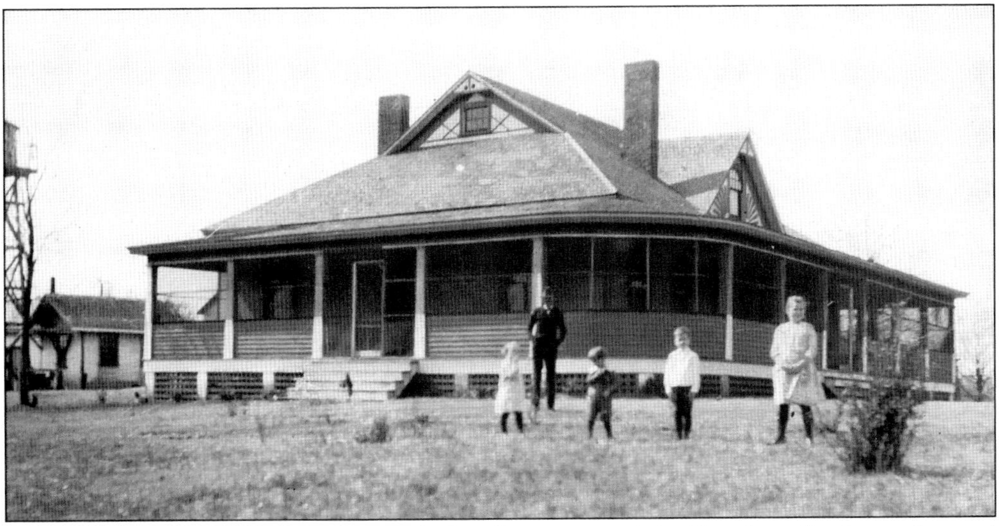

Built in 1905, the Wilfong house at Cedar Grove was originally a boardinghouse located next to the Louisville and Nashville train platform on Raleigh LaGrange Road. In 1916, the Wilfong family purchased the house and established Cedar Gove Dairy, one of the area's largest processing dairies.

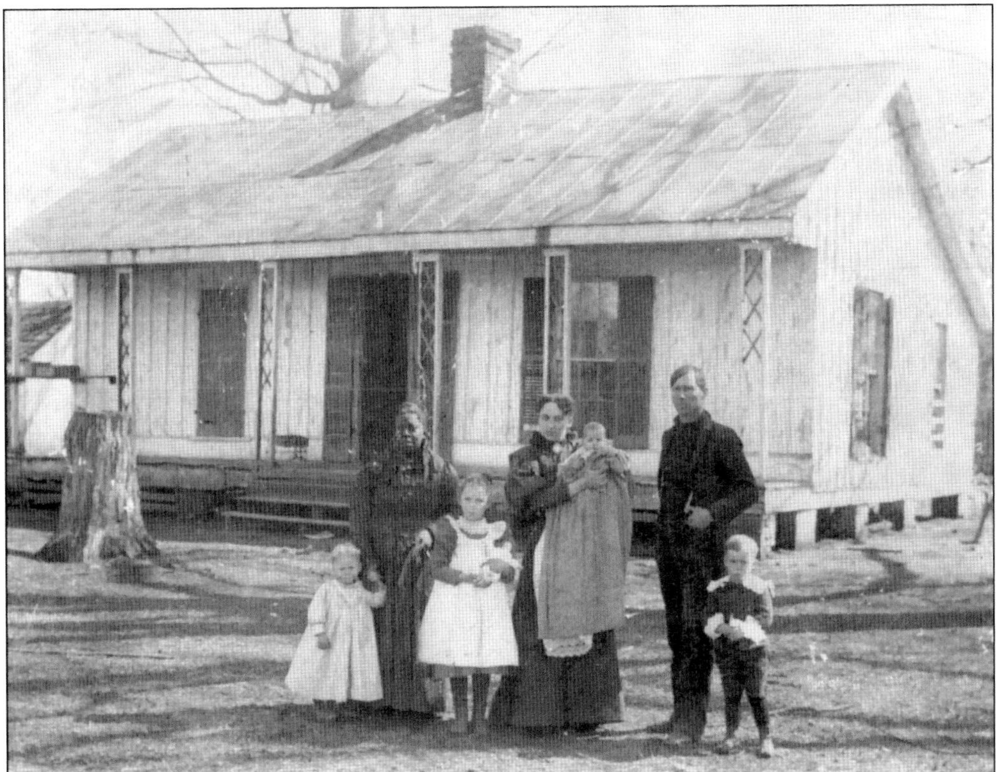

The Isham M. Davis home, built in the 1880s, was located at the southeast corner of Stage and Bartlett Roads, across from the train depot. The town post office was next door, and for many years, Davis operated a steam gin and mill behind his residence.

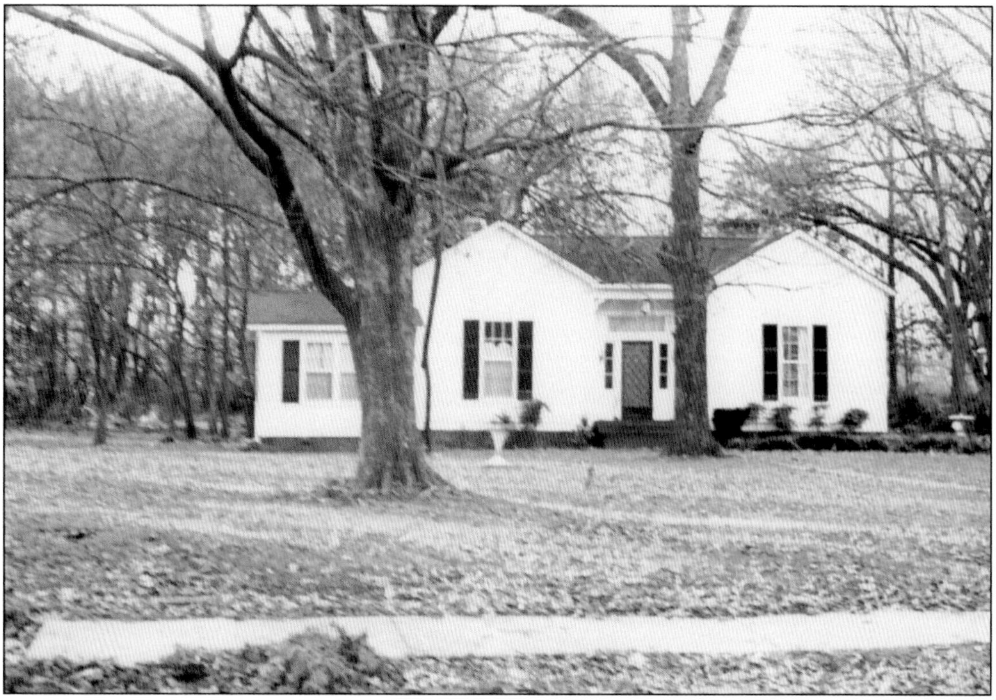

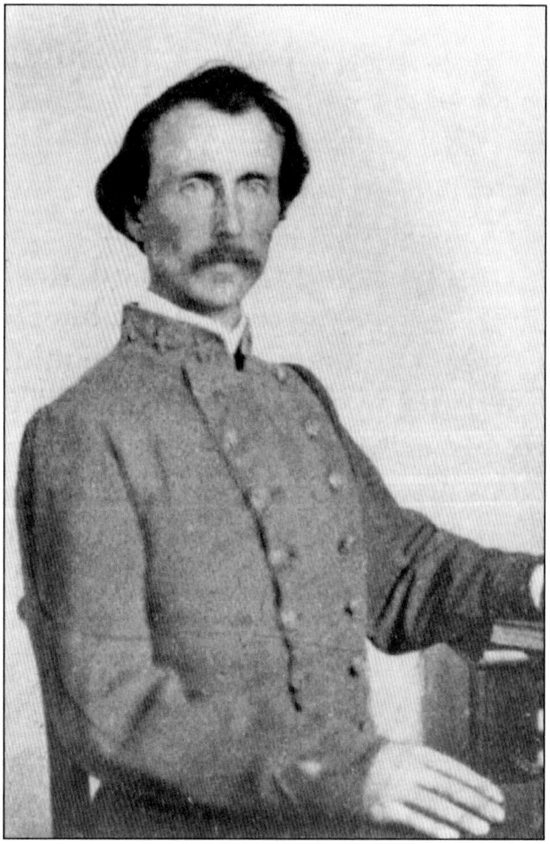

The Barteau house on Sycamore View Road was home to Clark Russell Barteau, a Civil War veteran and lawyer. The home was sold in 1905 to James Dickey for $600. Today it has been restored to its former glory.

Col. Clark Russell Barteau was born in 1835 and arrived in Bartlett in 1868. He became a lieutenant colonel of the 2nd Tennessee Cavalry, better known as the 22nd Tennessee. For many years, he and his wife, Zura, kept a school in their home.

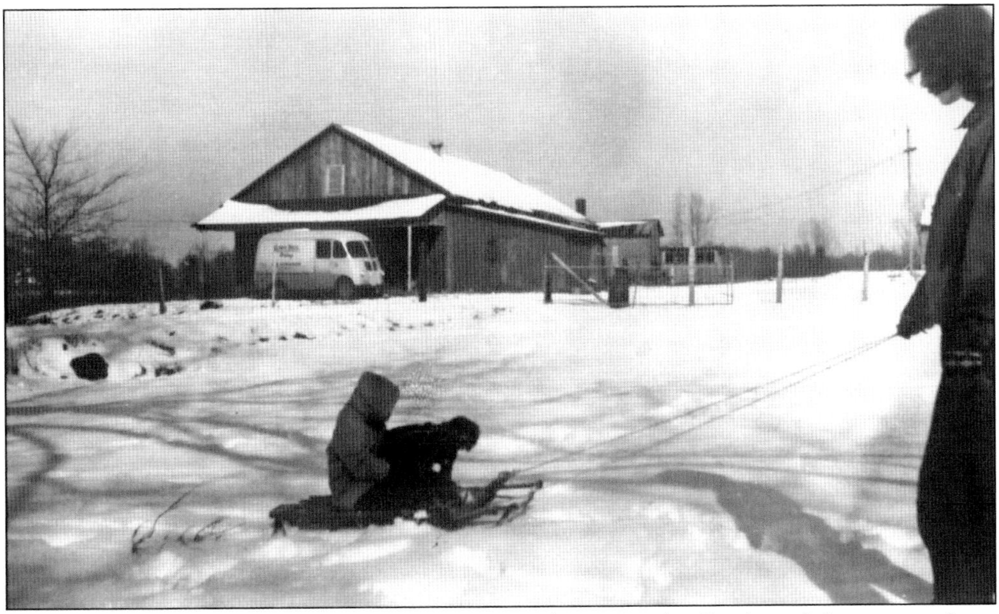

The E. E. Norwood Dairy was located on Stage Road near Bartlett Boulevard. It was one of two Norwood dairies in Bartlett. The other, run by J. D. Norwood, was on Bartlett Boulevard where Freeman Park is today.

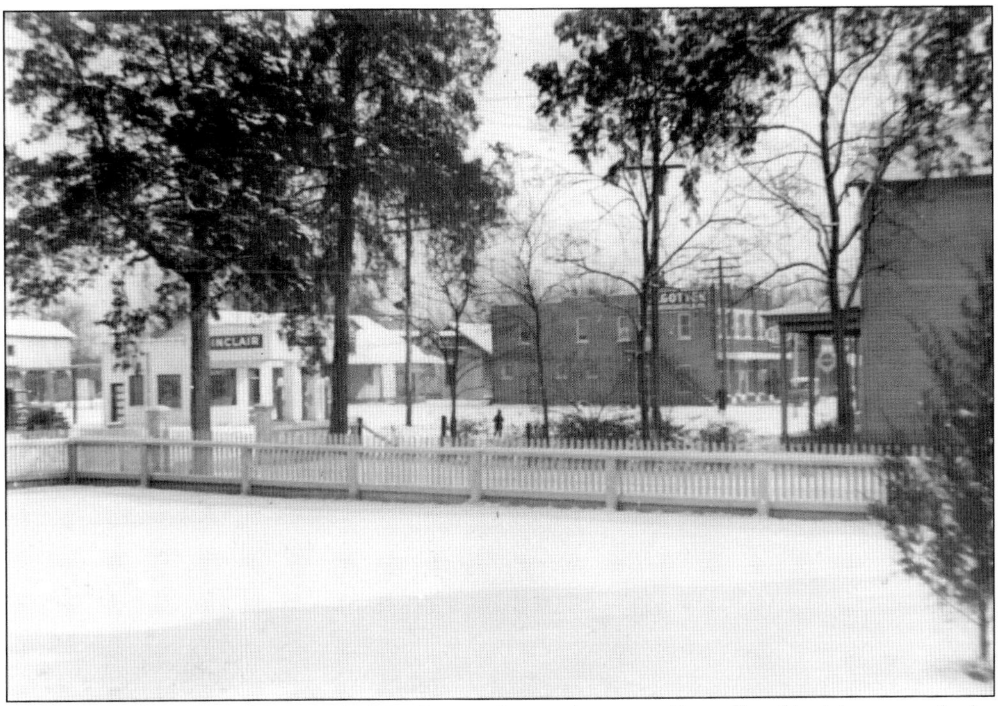

This is a view from the front yard of the Leona Gotten home on Stage Road looking towards the Red Fuller gas station around 1930.

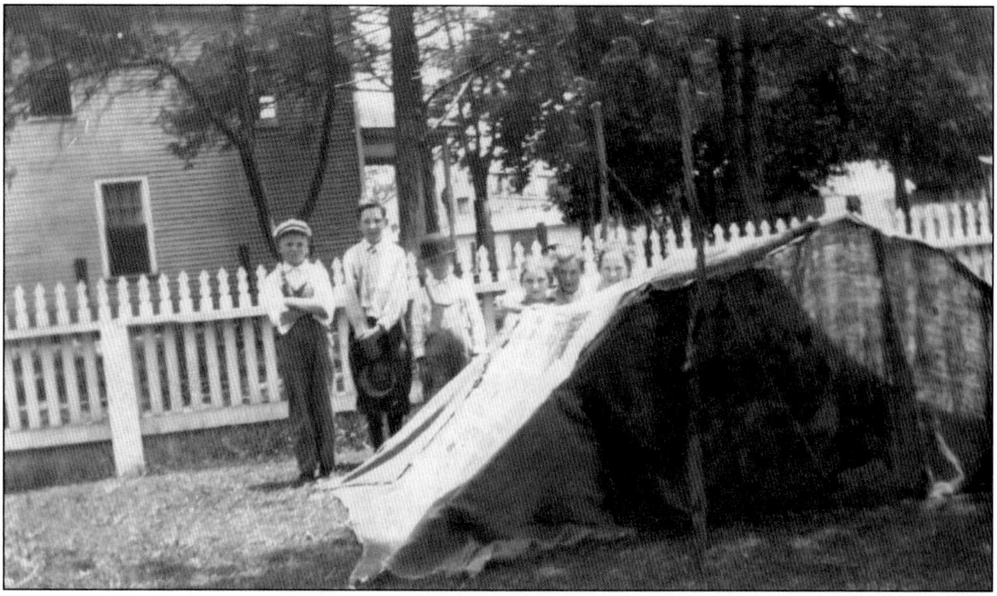

Two young boys camp out beside the Nicholas Gotten house around 1930. The home was built in 1871 and was the home of the Gotten family for many years.

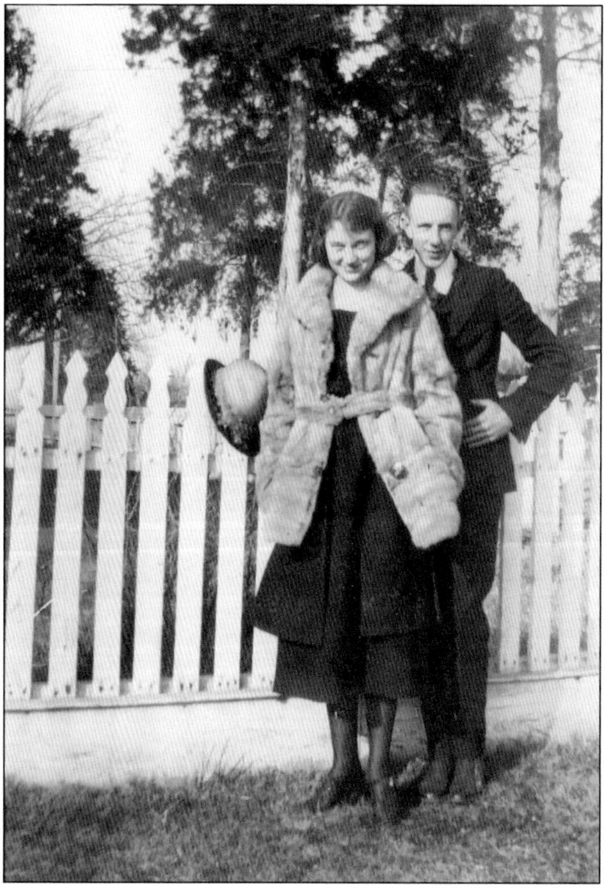

Francis Gotten was born in 1903 and was the daughter of David and Leona Gotten. The Gotten house stood on the south side of Stage Road across from Court Street. Dora Gholson and Mabel Richmond were boarders at the Gotten house while they taught at the Bartlett Courthouse School.

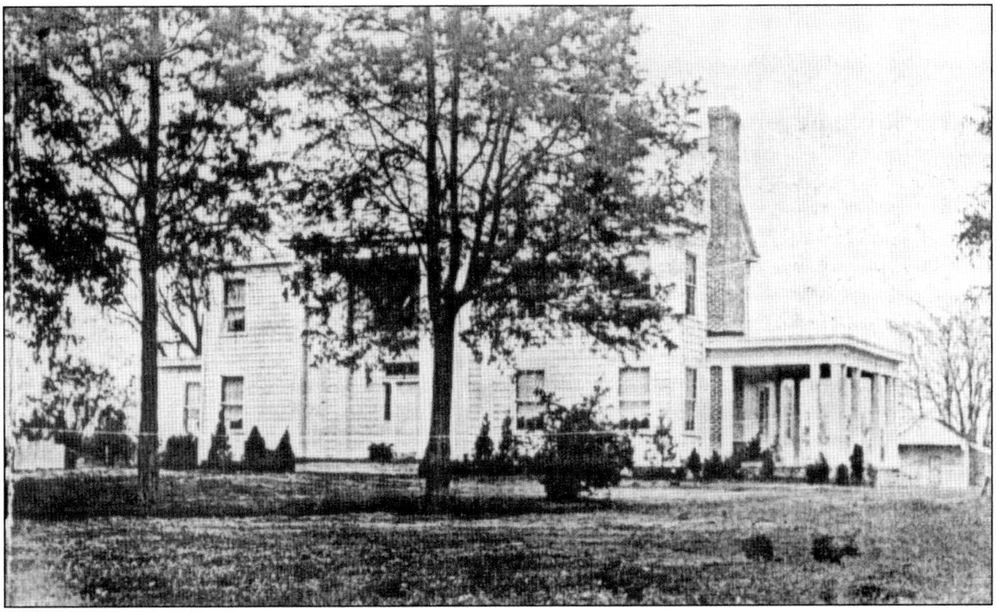

The Schwam house, on Stage Road, was built in 1926 on the foundation of the Gabriel Bartlett home. The house was a focal point in Bartlett for many years until the land was sold for commercial development in 1965.

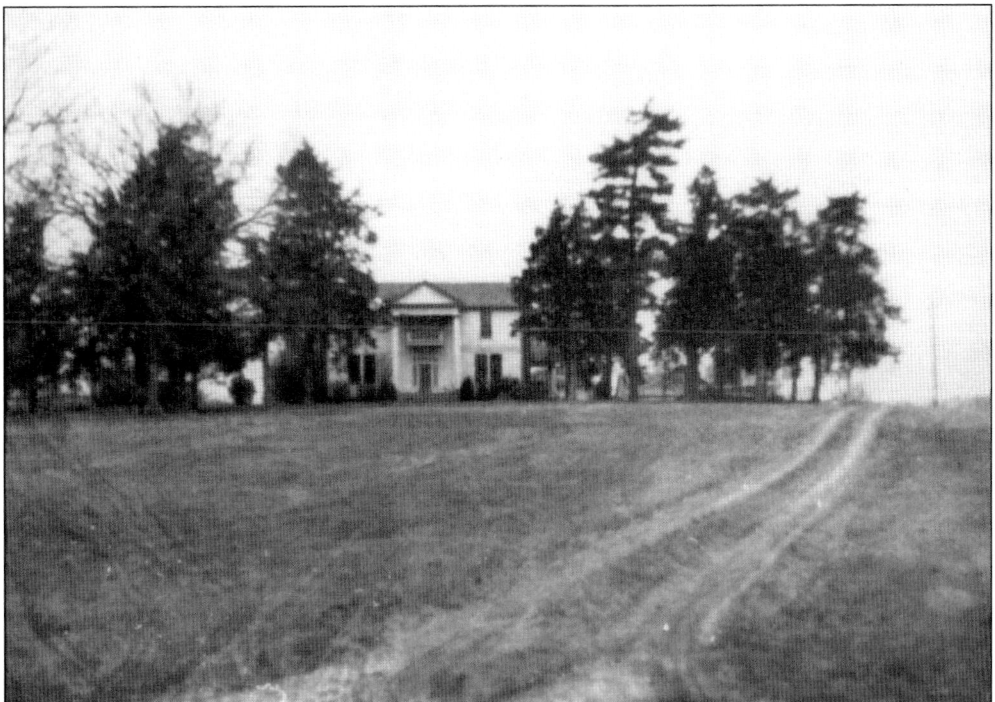

Henry Detwiller, a native of France, purchased the Starkey Redditt property in Ellendale in 1895 and for many years ran a dairy farm. There were over 30 dairies in the Bartlett area in the early 1930s.

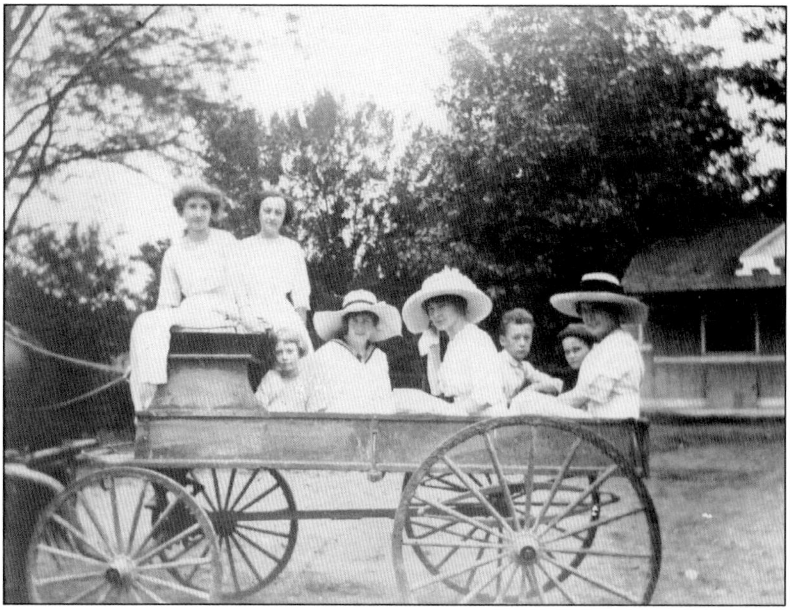

Taking a ride in 1910 meant hitching up the horses to a wagon and traveling over dirt roads a 10 miles per hour. Many citizens would routinely ride to Memphis in wagons or on horseback in the late 1800s.

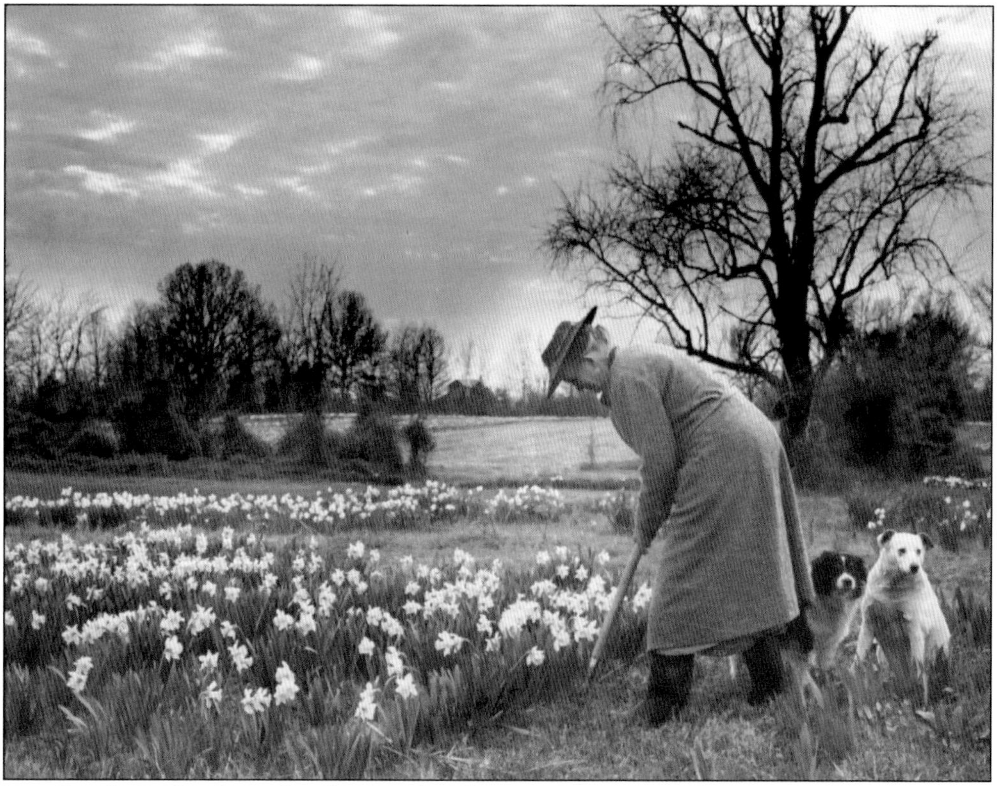

Kate Bond, the daughter of William and Hallie Bond, was born in 1886 in Bartlett. Kate lived for many years in the 1883 homestead built by her parents at the southwest corner of Stage and Kate Bond Roads. It was there that she grew her fields of flowers that she sold at the Curb Market in Memphis.

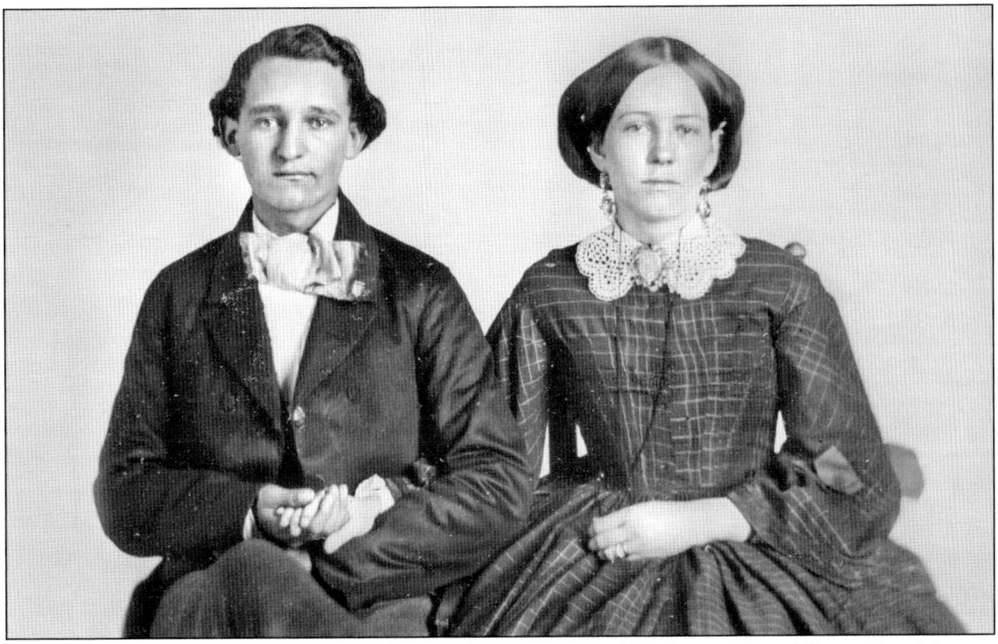

James and Emma Blackwell lived at the northeast corner of Highway 70 and Stage Road. James was the brother of Nicholas Blackwell and a veteran of the Civil War. In 1930, their only daughter, Mamie Blackwell Rock, donated the land for the Baptist Children's Home, located across the street from their home.

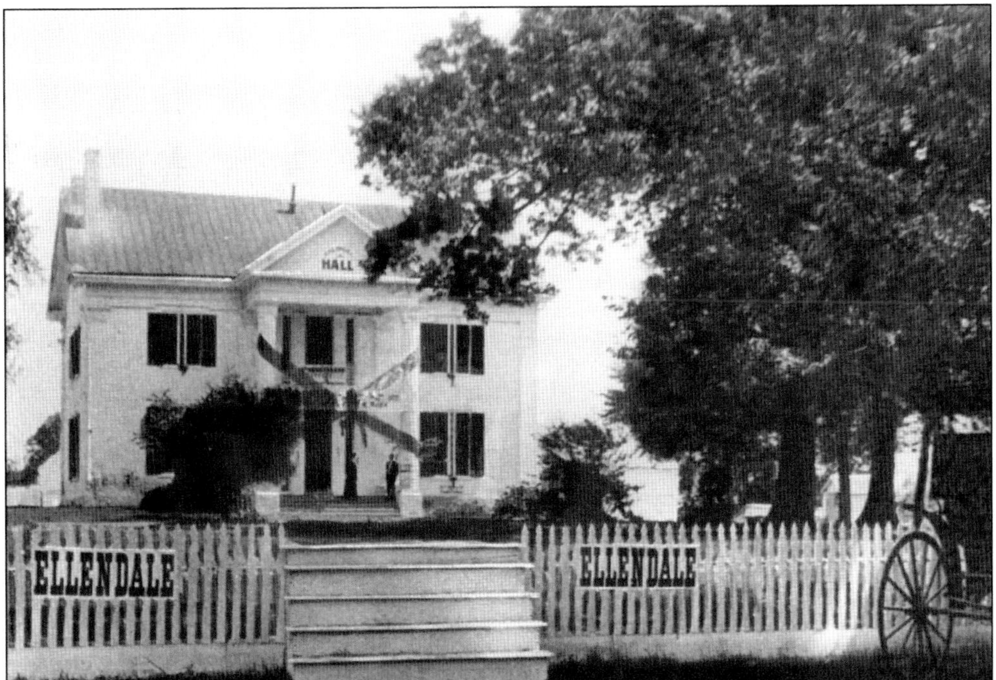

In 1847, the Whig party of Tennessee endorsed Dr. Samuel Bond, the owner of Cedar Hall—then known simply as Avenue—to be a state representative in Nashville. He won the election and represented the Bartlett area from 1847 to 1848.

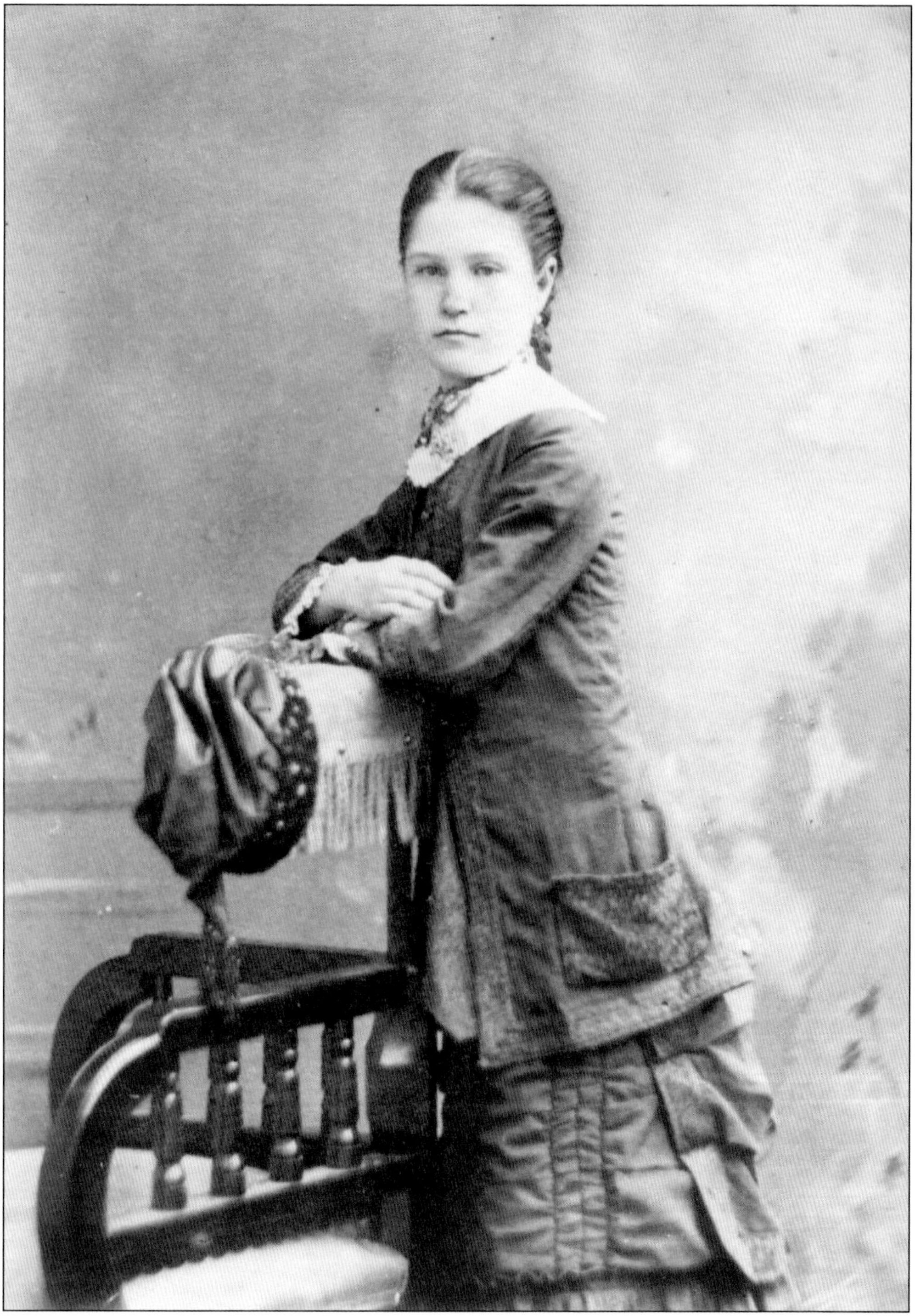

Amanda Duncan arrived in Bartlett in 1872 to care for the daughter of her uncle Nicholas Blackwell. Amanda helped raise Willie Bugg, whose mother had died suddenly the same year. Nicholas would often take Amanda to Memphis to have her portrait taken in one of the photography studios located on Main Street.

Willie Bugg Blackwell was born in the Shelton house on Sycamore View Road in 1869. Her middle name, Bugg, was the last name of a neighbor of her father, Nicholas Blackwell, when he lived in Pontotoc, Mississippi. Growing up, Willie Bugg attended the Clara Conaway School on Poplar Avenue in downtown Memphis.

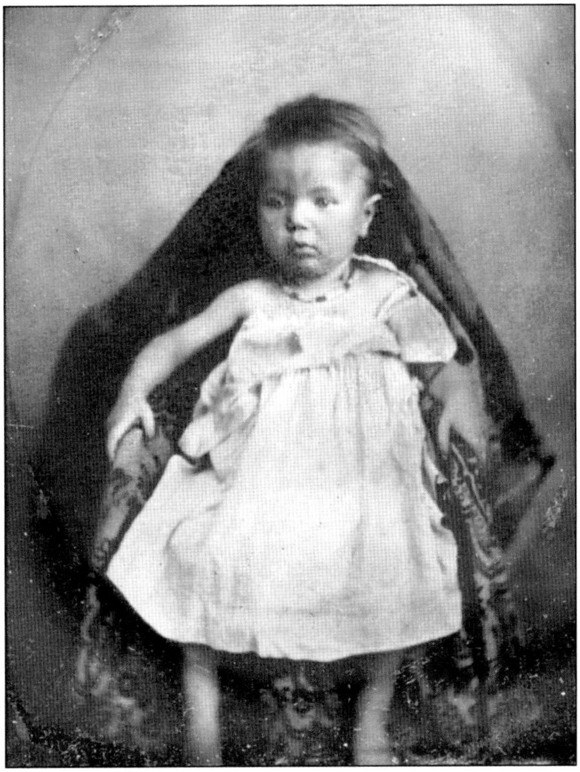

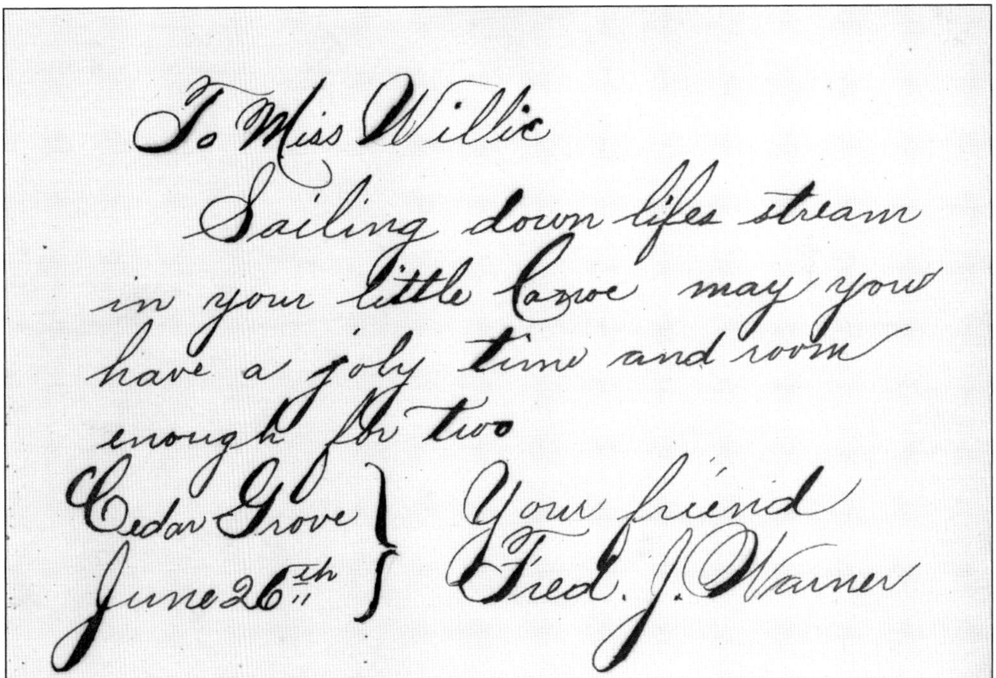

To Miss Willie
Sailing down lifes stream
in your little Canoe may you
have a joly time and room
enough for two

Cedar Grove }
June 26th }

Your friend
Fred. J. Warner

A note given to Willie Bugg Blackwell from Frederick Warner for her high school graduation in 1888 is shown here.

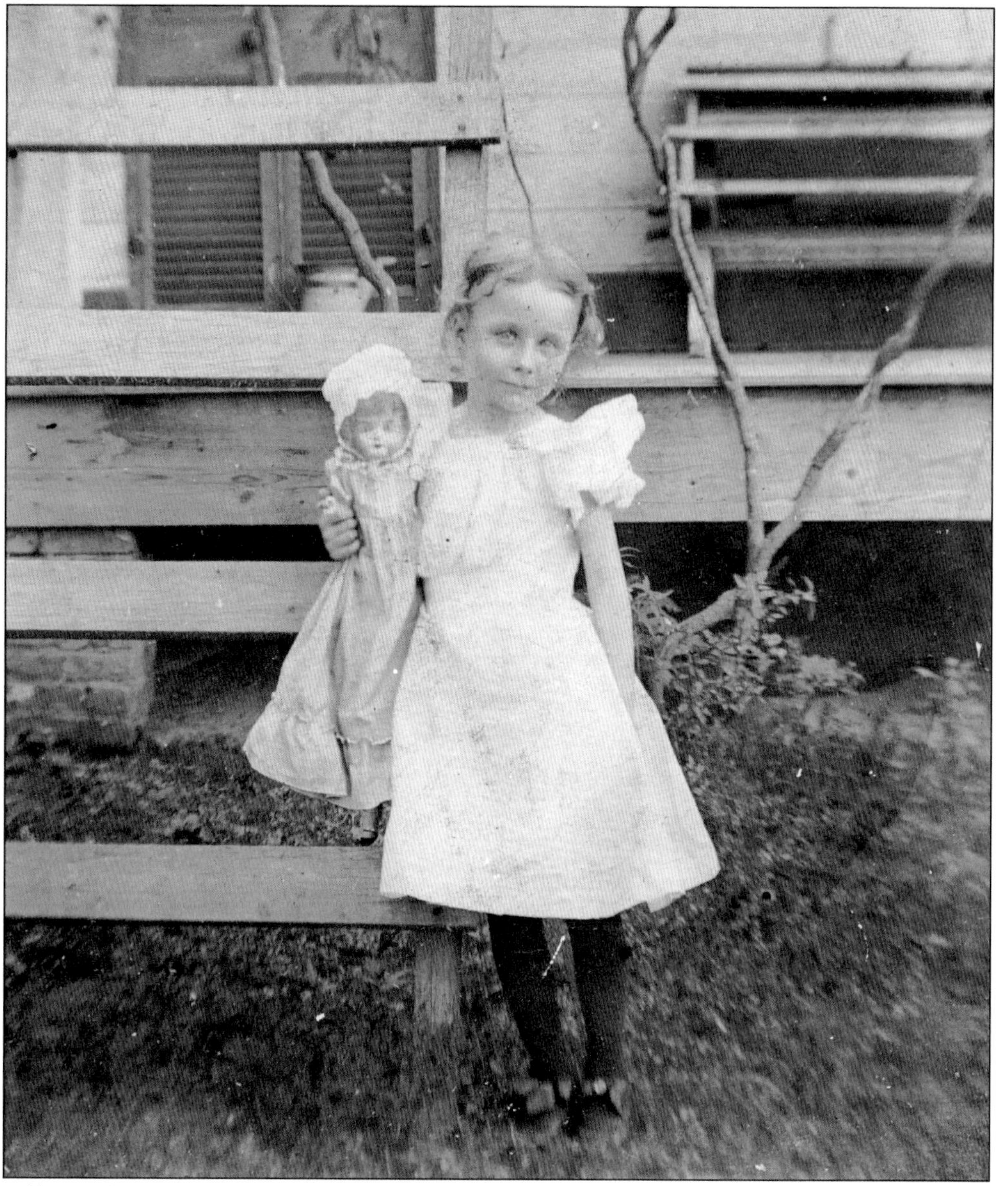

Polly Smith is shown outside the Shelton house on Sycamore View Road around 1910. Her mother, Jennie Reeves, purchased the home in 1907 and lived there with her sister and their children. The Reeves called their home place Algarina.

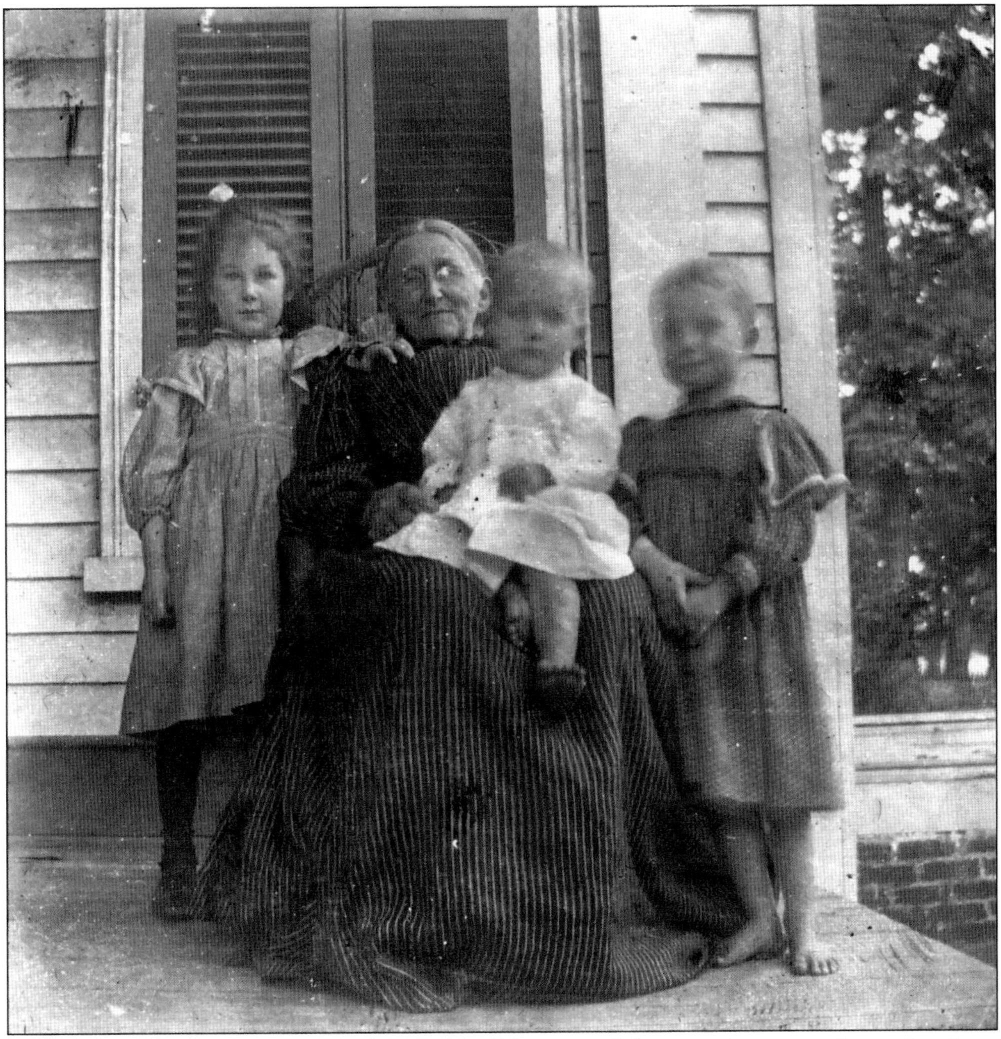

Sara Blackwell is seen in 1900 at the Blackwell house with her grandnieces and grandnephew, Louise, Nicholas, and Katherine Miller. In 1889, Willie Bugg Blackwell married Benjamin Miller, president of the Bartlett Saving Bank.

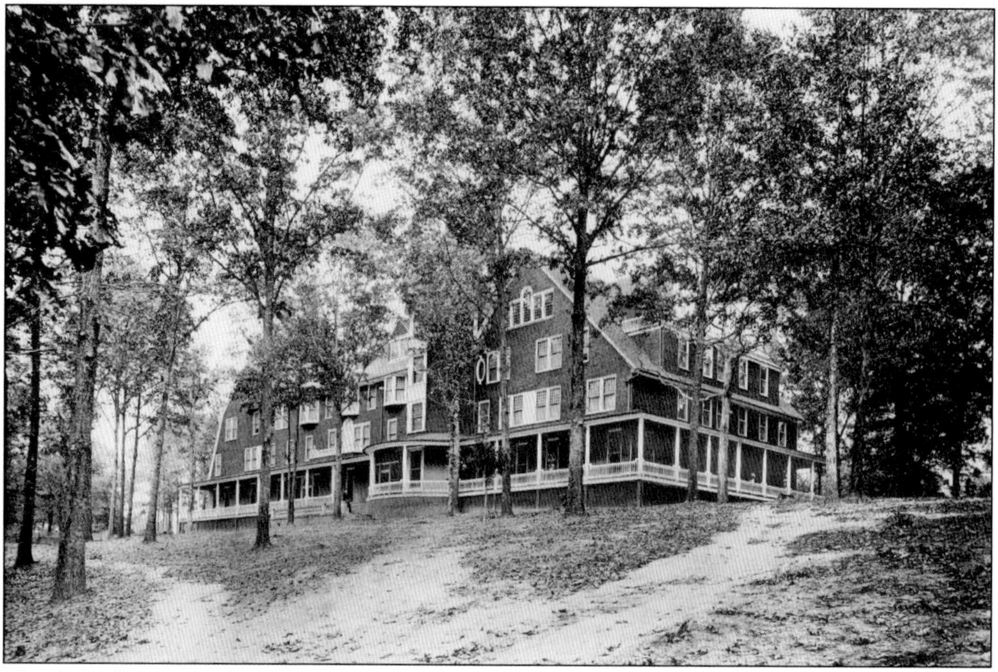

The Raleigh Inn was built in 1873 and updated in 1892 by B. I. Duke of North Carolina. People came for the natural springs, which were reported to have great health benefits. The inn prospered, hosting band concerts, grand balls, and military drills by the Chickasaw Guards until closing in 1903. The inn was briefly the Maddox School for Girls before becoming the James Sanitarium. The inn burned in 1912.

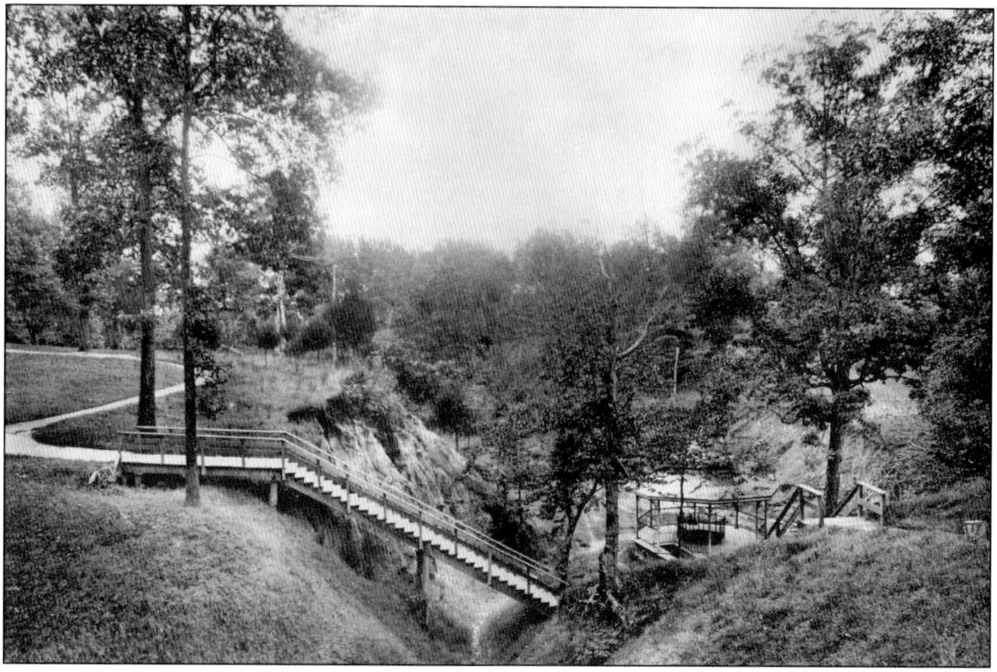

As far back as 1842, each spring at Raleigh advertised a specific name and chemical composition. Where one spring was believed to be good for gout or arthritis, another may help colicky babies.

Four

Churches

With any new community, one of the first orders of business is to set up a meetinghouse for religious services. In 1840, Egypt Baptist Church was organized in Raleigh, located just west of Bartlett and at the time the county seat for Shelby County. In 1849, thirty-six members of this church chose to form their own congregation, located near present-day Billy Maher Road and Old Brownsville Road. The members, including John Blackwell, James Pruden, and James Wood, called the new congregation Prosperity and built a small meetinghouse, which was also used as a school. In 1851, with a growing congregation, they purchased land on Stage Road from Joseph Ward and built a new meetinghouse, which stood until 1870, when they built a larger Gothic-style sanctuary. This building, bricked over in 1932, still stands today on Stage Road, just east of the railroad. In 1896, the name was officially changed to Bartlett Baptist Church. Over the years, a new larger sanctuary was built and Sunday school classes were added, and it is now the oldest public building in Bartlett. In 1837, the Greenbottom Cumberland Presbyterian Church was organized, and in 1839, a small log meetinghouse was built on 2 acres just west of present-day Kate Bond Road and Stage Road. Some of its earliest members included Dr. Samuel Bond, John Bond, and Samuel Ecklin. The first Methodist meetinghouse built outside of Memphis was Warren Chapel, completed in 1837 in what would become Ellendale. It was named for James Warren, its first pastor. In 1851, Gabriel Bartlett, Washington Bond, and Henry Grenade—trustees for the Methodist church—purchased 3 acres of this property for $20. This land is now the Bartlett-Ellendale Cemetery, once known as the Pisgah Cemetery. Some of Bartlett's earliest families are buried there, including Bond, Bartlett, Blackwell, Warren, Locke, and Oglesby. In 1872, a white frame church was constructed on the northeast corner of Stage Road and Court Street on property donated to the local Methodist congregation of Bartlett. A disastrous fire in 1923 completely destroyed the building, despite the efforts of neighbors to put out the fire. A new sanctuary was built in 1924 on the northwest corner of Stage Road and Shelby Street, where the Bartlett Methodist Church worships today.

Fullview Baptist Church was established in 1877 on the corner of what is now Oak Road and the old Memphis-Arlington Road in the Ellendale area, where an acre of land was purchased from the Evergreen plantation. In 1890, two more acres were purchased and became their cemetery, adjacent to Pisgah Cemetery. A new building was constructed in 1910 and was used until 1977, when it was replaced by a larger sanctuary. In 1985, the congregation purchased 6 acres across the street for a Christian family life center that was completed in 1996. Rev. Walter Peggs has led this congregation for many years.

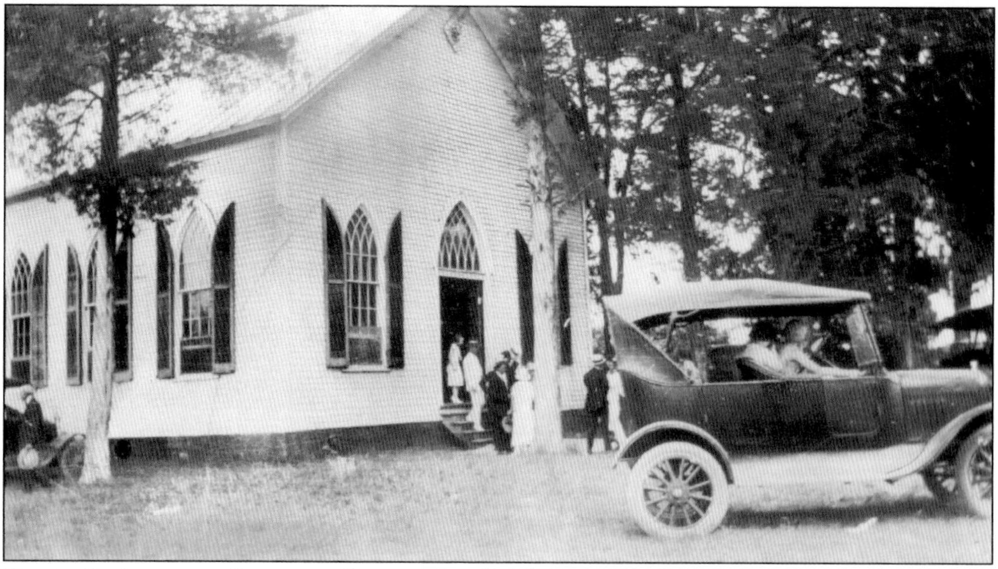

Originally known as Prosperity Baptist, Bartlett Baptist Church was organized in 1849. The congregation moved to Bartlett in 1871 and built a small frame church. The chapel was bricked over in 1932 and today is the oldest public building in Bartlett.

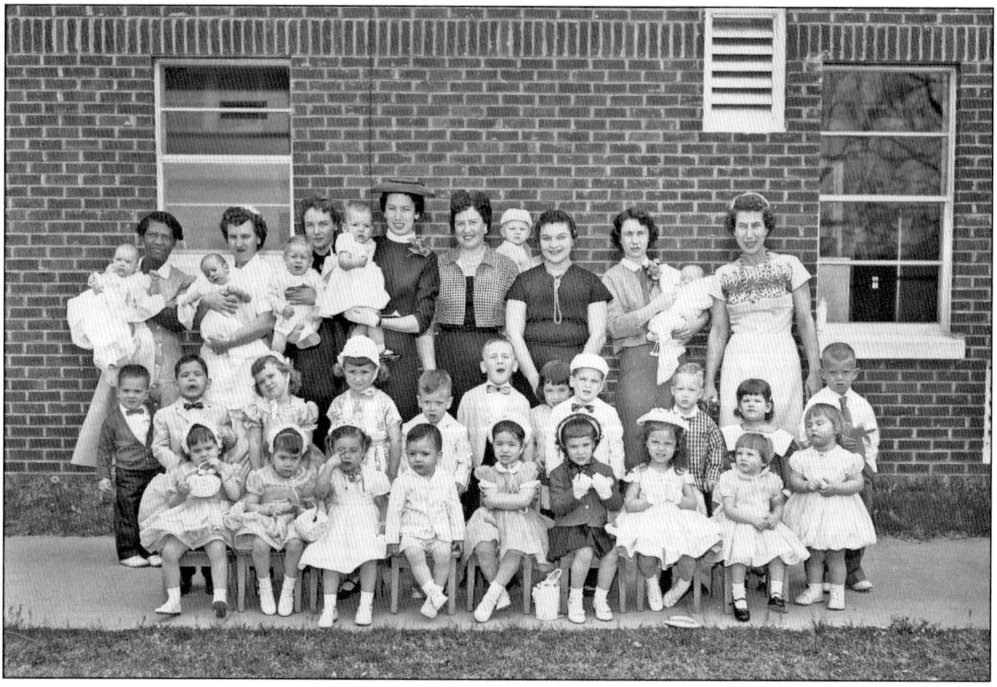

The Bartlett Baptist Church was built in 1871 on land purchased from the Ward family. Shown here is the children's nursery of the church in 1961. In 2005, the church relocated to a more modern facility on Kirby-Whitten Road.

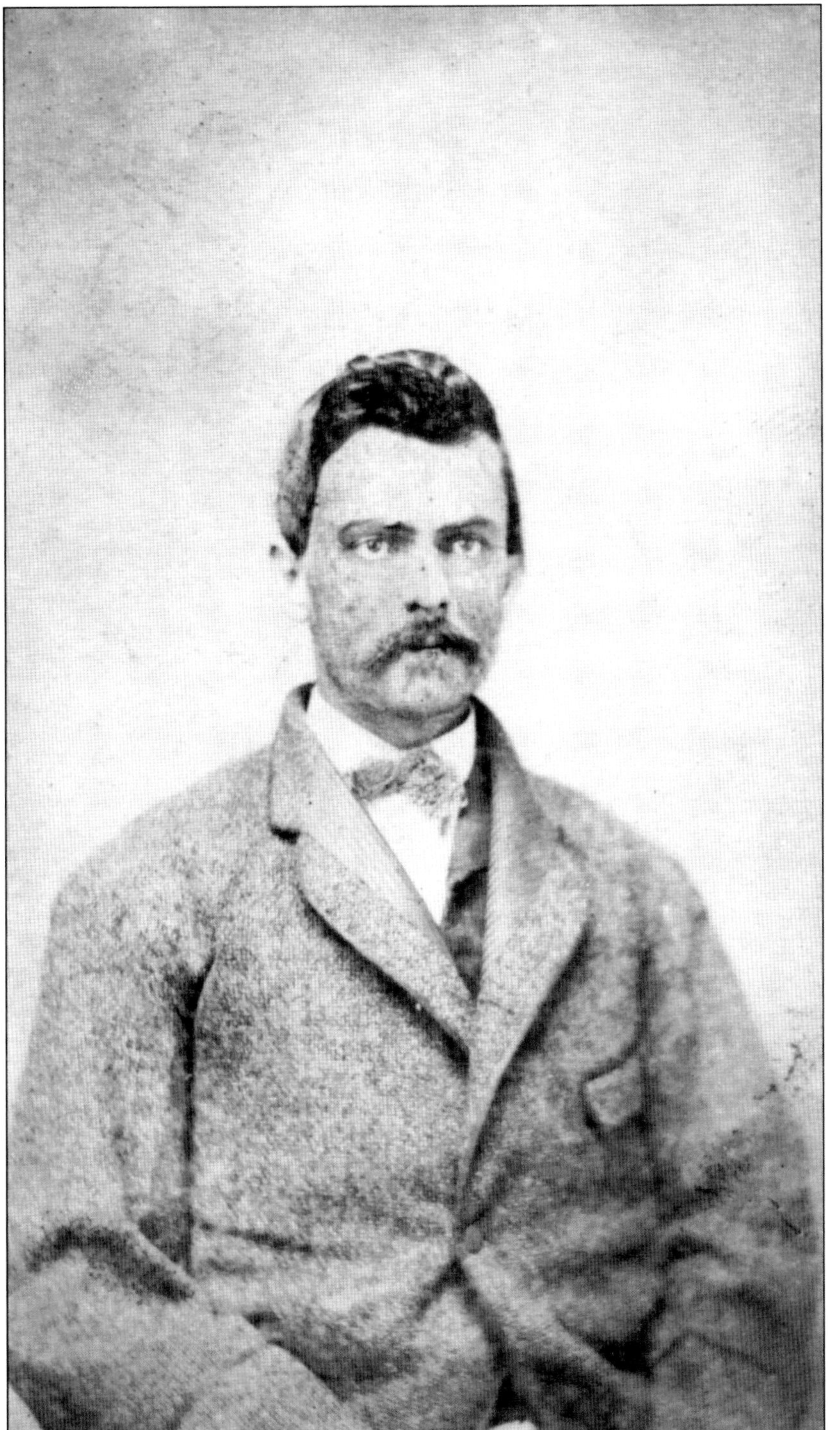

John Byron Canada was one of the first pastors for the Prosperity Baptist Church, being ordained there on August 19, 1850. For over 20 years, he was the church's pastor; he retired in 1876. The Prosperity Baptist Church is now known as Bartlett Baptist Church.

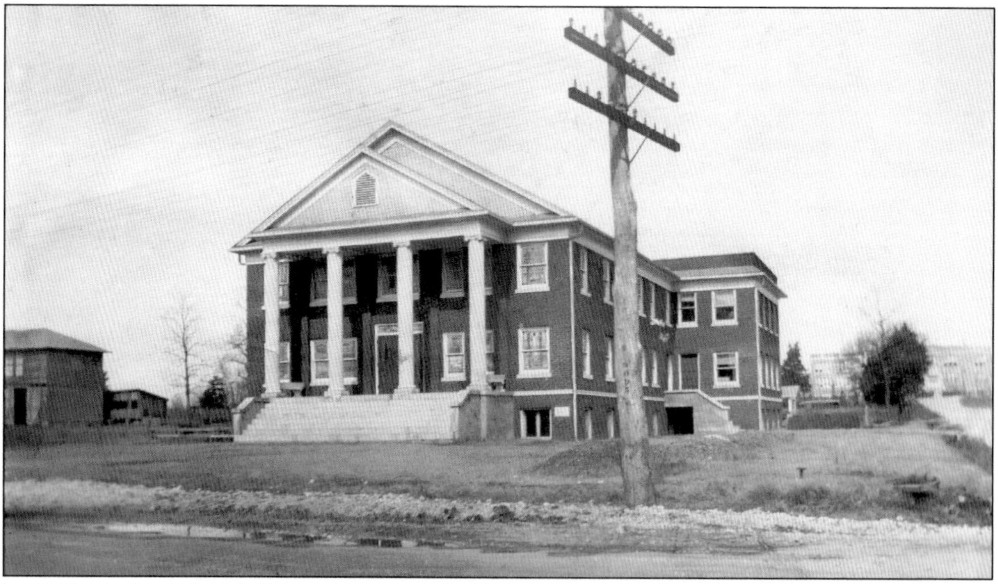

In 1871, the local Methodist congregation built a Gothic chapel on the corner of Court Street and Stage Road. This building tragically burned in 1923, and within a few years, the members rebuilt just down the street at Shelby Street and Stage Road, where they are located today. In 2002, a new, larger sanctuary was built just west of the old sanctuary.

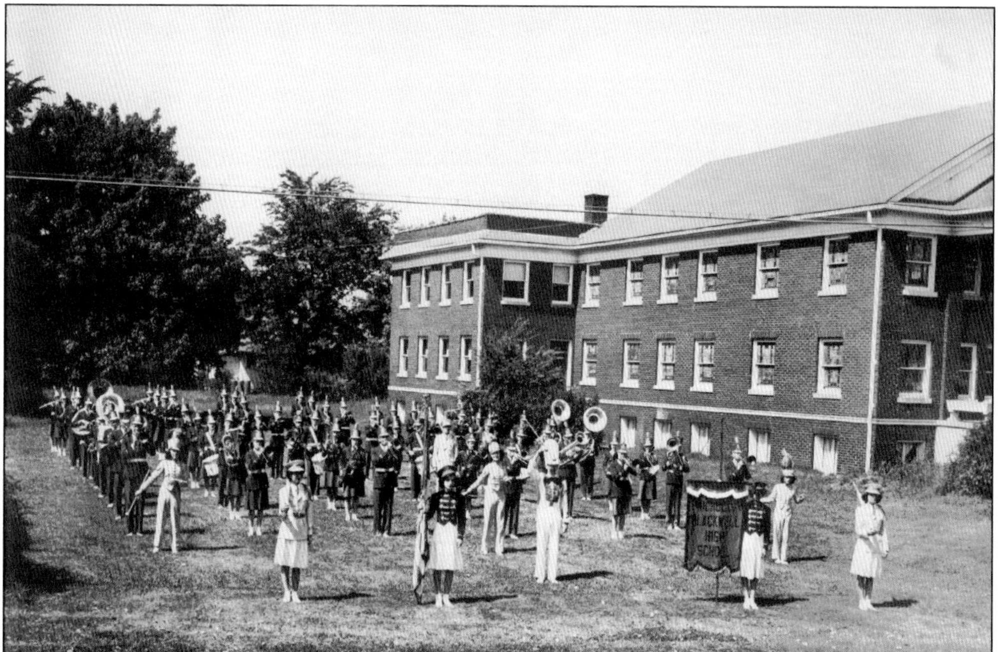

When the football team was practicing on its playing field, the Bartlett High School band used the vacant field next to the Methodist church to rehearse.

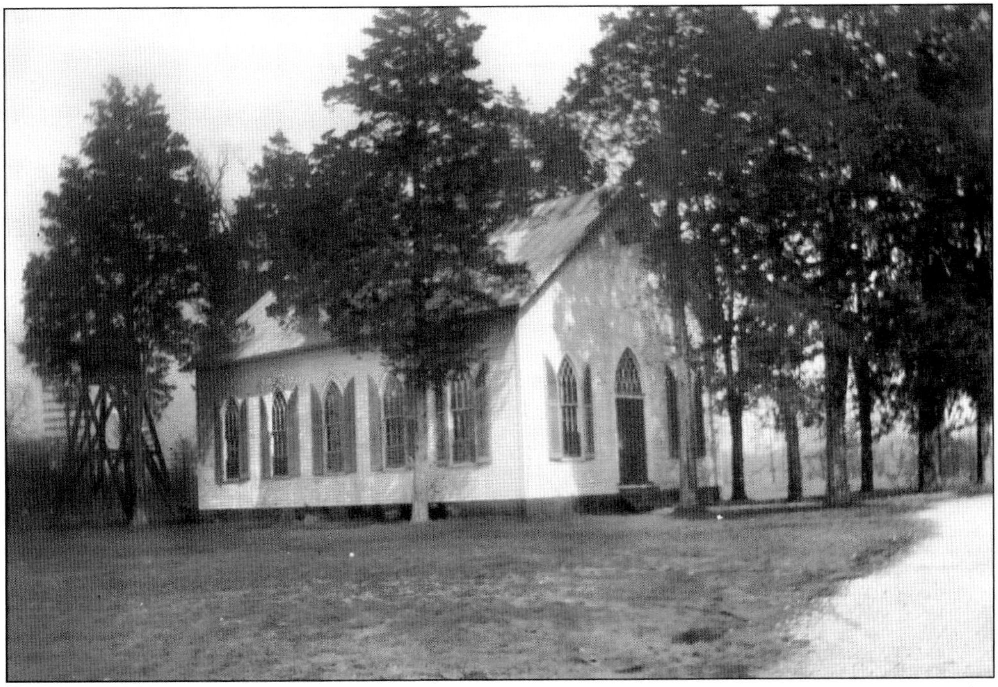

The Bartlett Baptist Church, shown here in 1920, was built in 1870 on land purchased from the Ward plantation. The building was brick veneered in 1932 and is today known as the Bartlett Station Municipal Center.

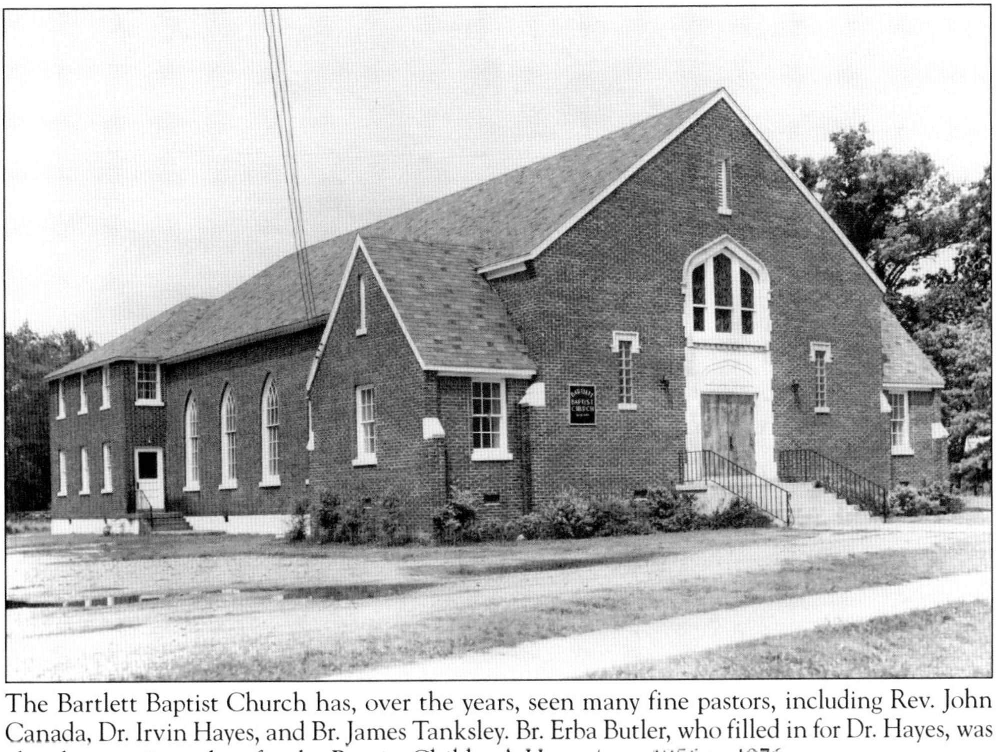

The Bartlett Baptist Church has, over the years, seen many fine pastors, including Rev. John Canada, Dr. Irvin Hayes, and Br. James Tanksley. Br. Erba Butler, who filled in for Dr. Hayes, was also the superintendent for the Baptist Children's Home from 1956 to 1976.

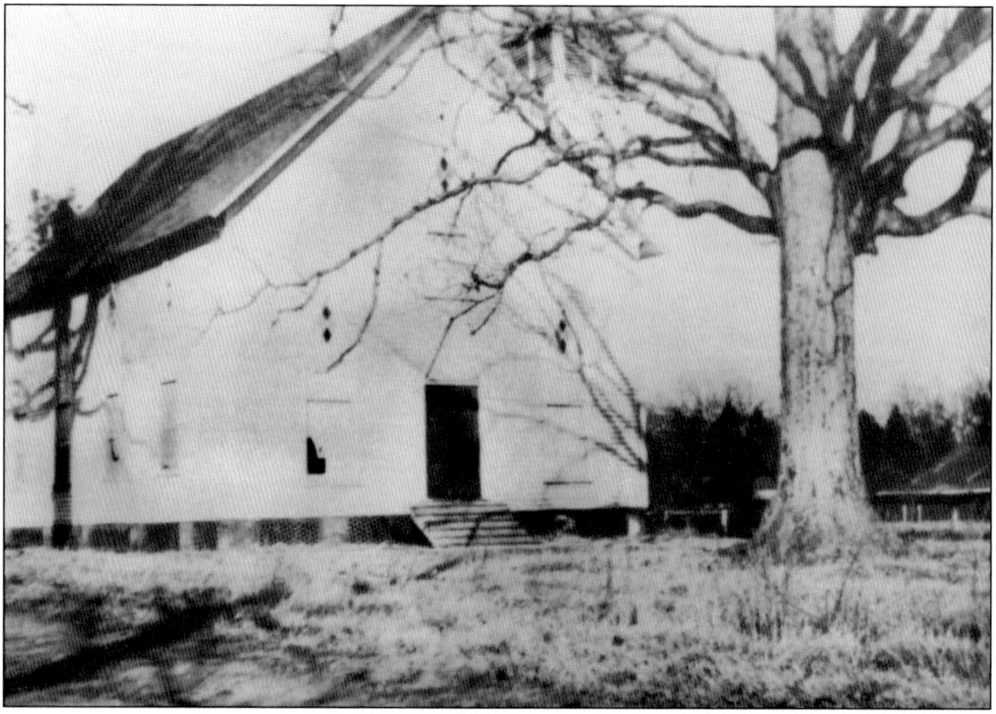

Built in 1872, the Bartlett Methodist Church was located on Court Street at Stage Road. The church burned in 1923 in a large fire, completely destroying the building and many historic artifacts.

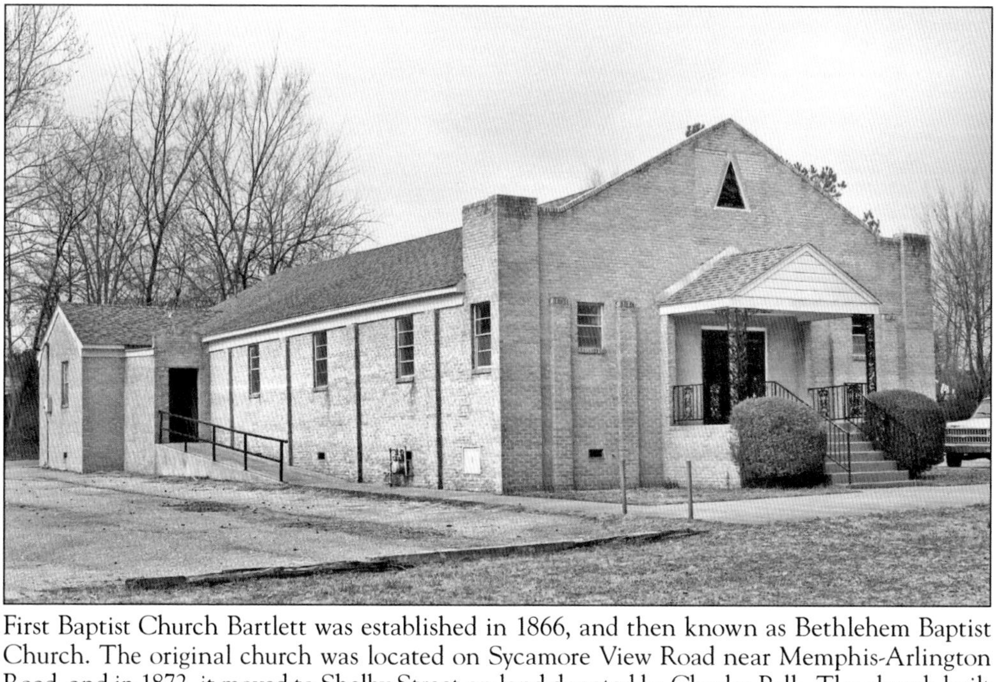

First Baptist Church Bartlett was established in 1866, and then known as Bethlehem Baptist Church. The original church was located on Sycamore View Road near Memphis-Arlington Road, and in 1872, it moved to Shelby Street on land donated by Charles Polk. The church built a new sanctuary, seen above, in 1968.

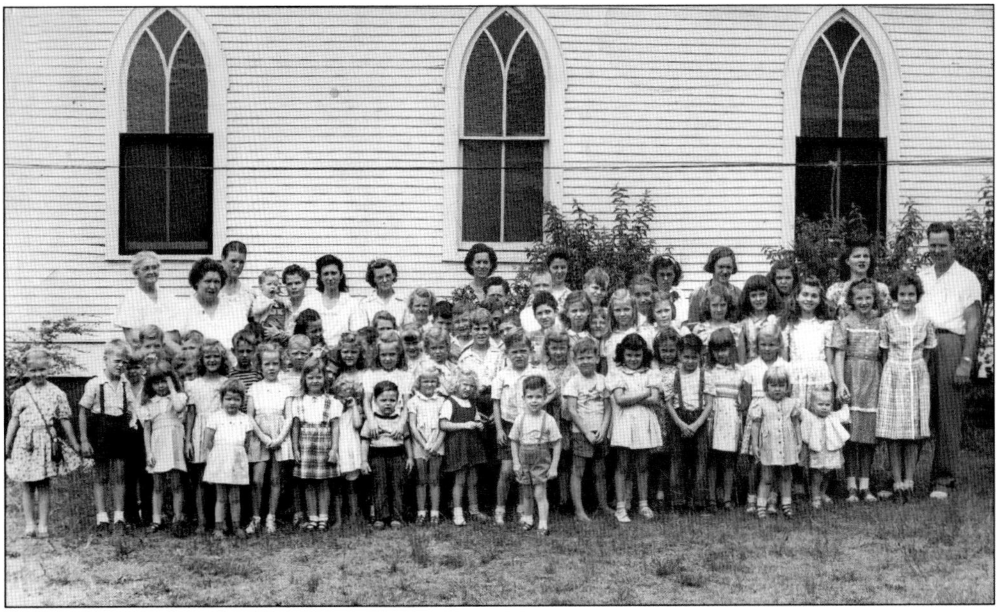

Members of the Ellendale Methodist Church pose outside the sanctuary in 1940. The church was established in 1908, and the congregation met in the old community school before building the sanctuary seen here in 1920. The current sanctuary was completed in 1967 just behind the location of the original sanctuary.

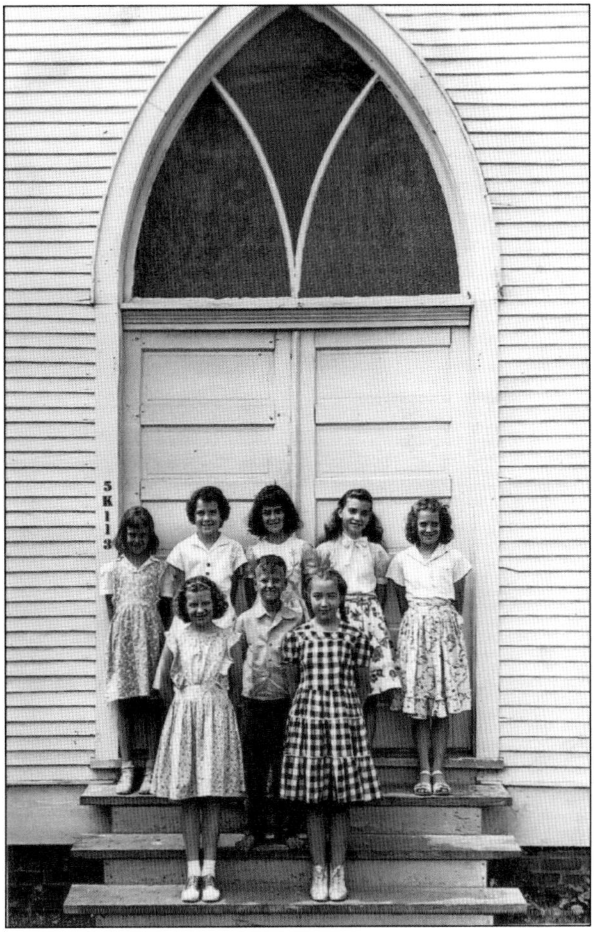

Churchgoers pose in front of the doors of the Ellendale Methodist Church. The church started out as a circuit church ministered by J. M. Hamlin. The first full-time pastor was Clark Bell, who served from 1938 to 1942. In 1954, the parsonage next to the church was completed, followed by the fellowship hall in 1963.

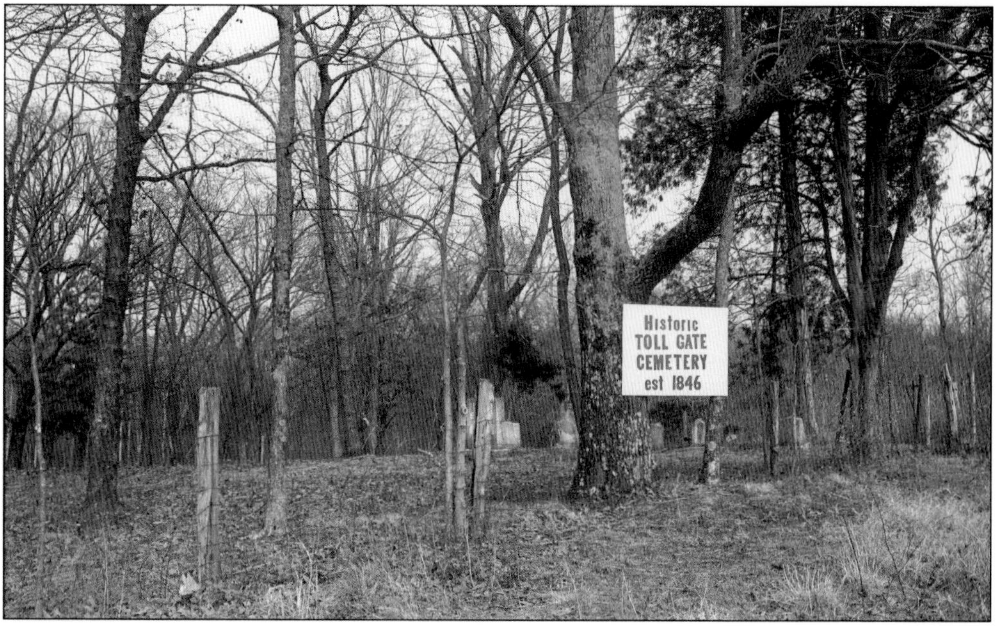

The Tollgate Cemetery was established in 1846 just east of Germantown Road on Stage Road. The tollgate for the Memphis-to-Somerville plank road was directly in front of the cemetery and operated in the 1850s, collecting tolls for use of the road.

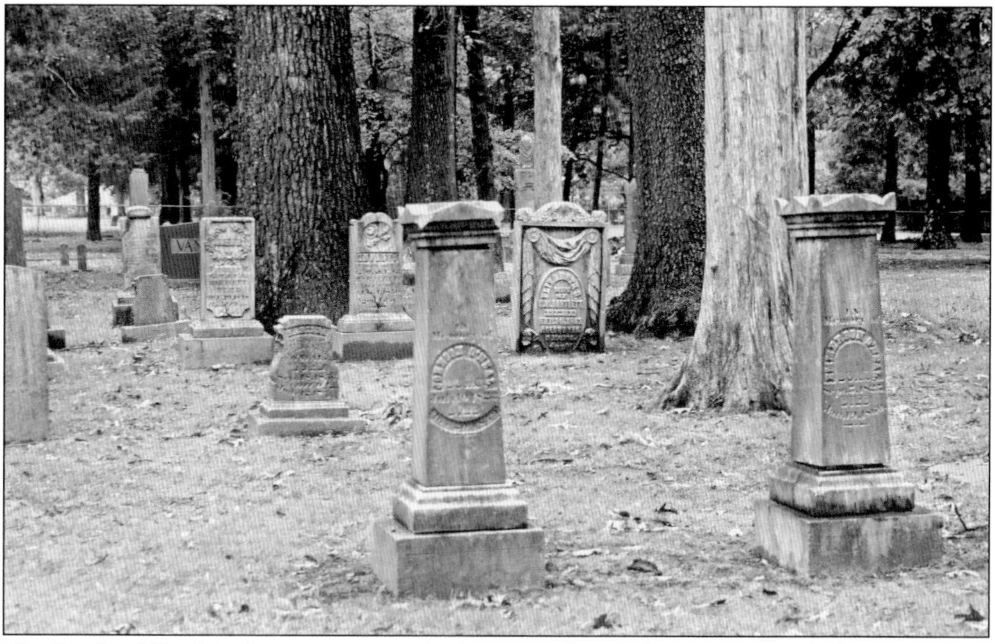

The Bartlett-Ellendale Cemetery, originally known as Pisgah Cemetery, was the location of the Warren Chapel, built in 1836. The cemetery bears the names of many of the earliest citizens of the city, including Blackwell, Bartlett, Warren, Locke, and Bond.

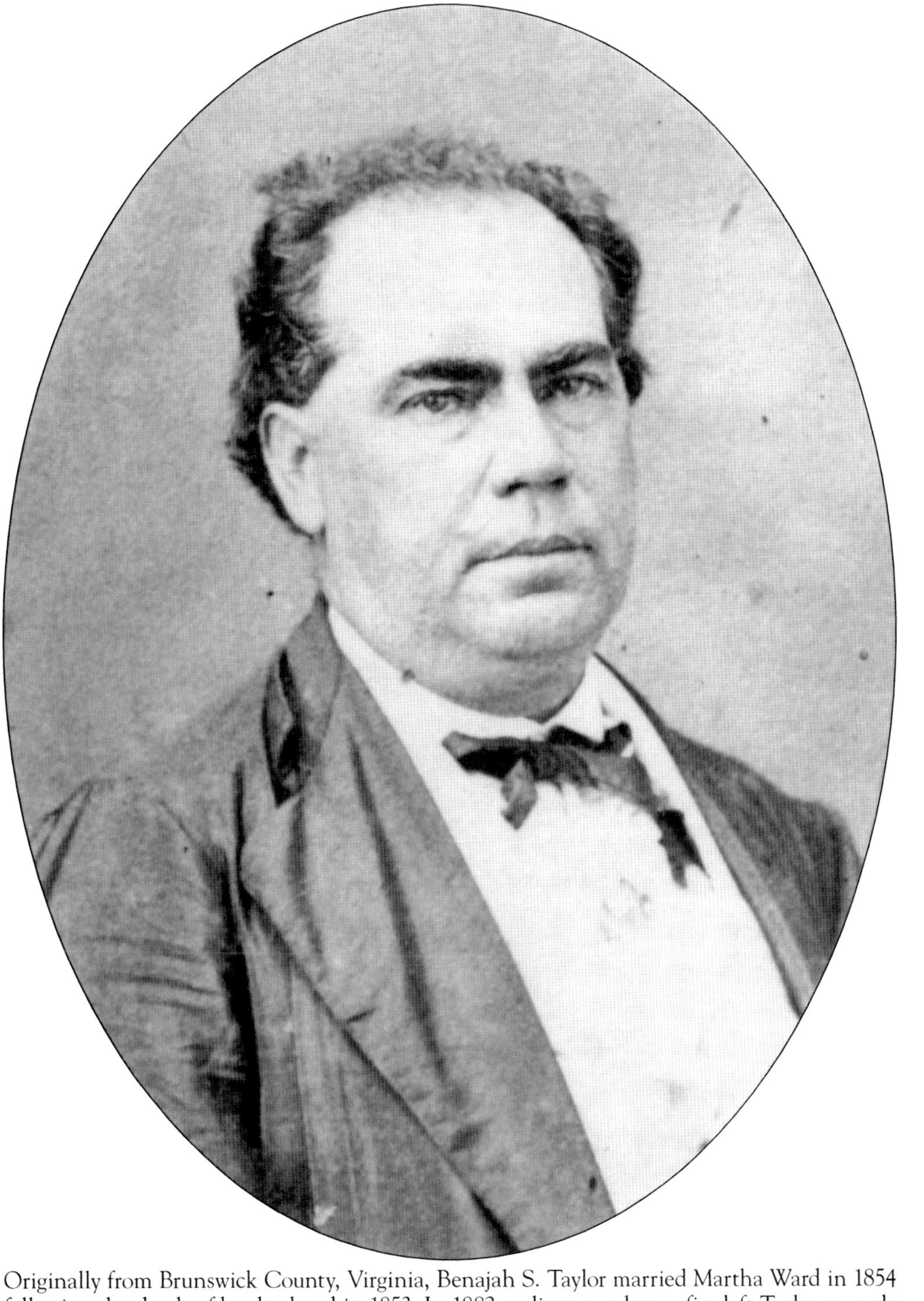

Originally from Brunswick County, Virginia, Benajah S. Taylor married Martha Ward in 1854 following the death of her husband in 1853. In 1882, a disastrous house fire left Taylor severely ill, and he passed away the next year. In the 1860s, he donated land on the south side of Stage Road to be used as an African American cemetery, which was known as Major Taylor Cemetery. Today the cemetery, located off Mercury Street, is long overgrown and abandoned.

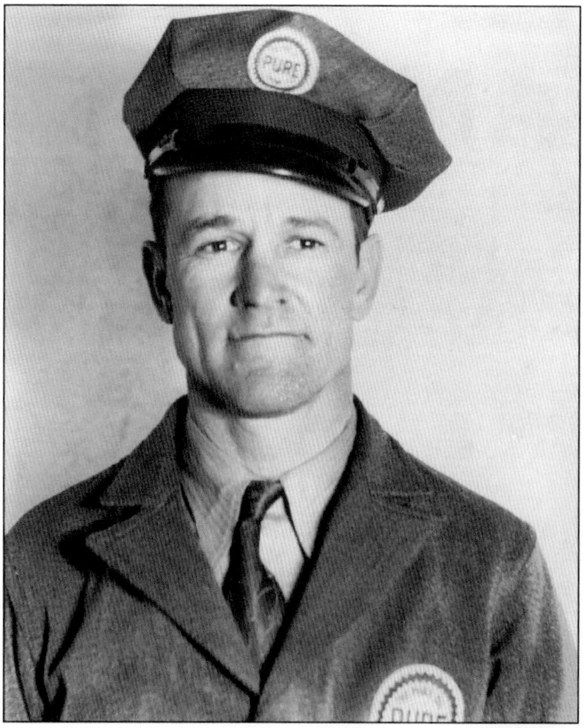

Thomas Evans Warr, shown at left in the 1950s, served many years as a Bartlett alderman, as a magistrate, and on the Shelby County Quarterly Court. The Warr Machinery Company was located at Bartlett and Stage Roads.

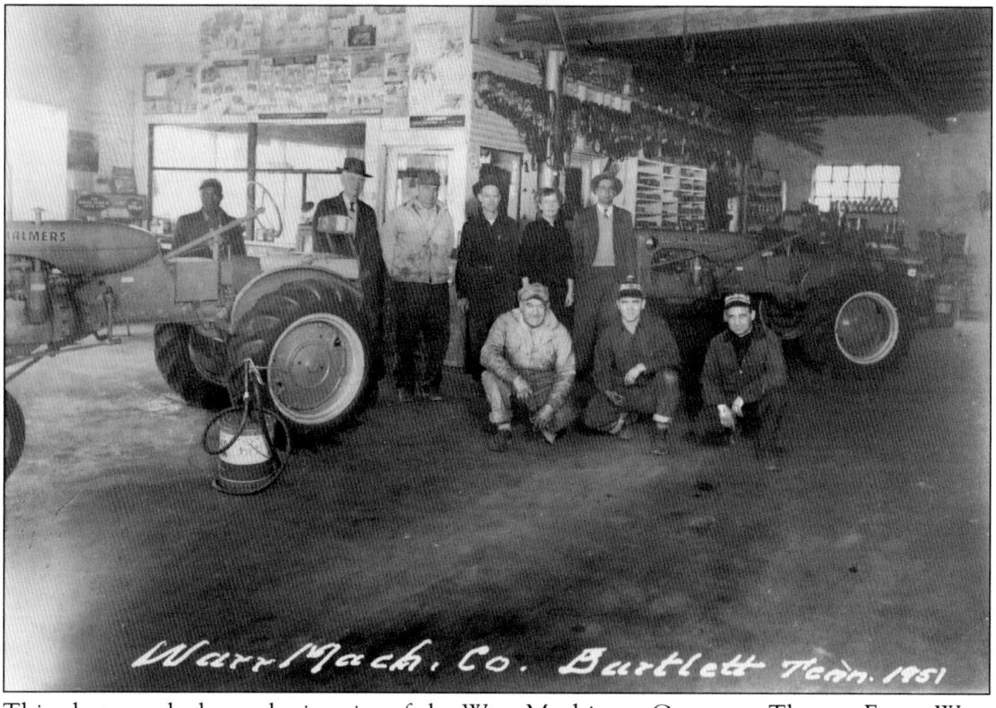

This photograph shows the interior of the Warr Machinery Company. Thomas Evans Warr remembered that Edward "Boss" Crump visited Bartlett in the 1930s and 1940s. Crump was the Memphis mayor in the early 1900s and was influential in Shelby County politics for many years.

Five

Schools

In Bartlett, as in many small towns, the high school played a very important part in the community. Many parents who never attended school themselves could, for the first time, send their children to school. In 1858, Prof. John Rousseau and his wife, Anna, moved to Bartlett, then known as Union Depot, and set up the first organized school in the town. Located on Stage Road near Alfaree Street, the boarding school operated until 1871, when the land and home were sold. Another of the first schools in Bartlett was taught by Rev. John Shelton from 1860 until just after the Civil War. The school was located on Sycamore View Road, then known as Brownsville Road. In 1885, the Bartlett Training Institute was opened with John and George Neuhardt as instructors. The school was held in the Bartlett Courthouse, which was vacant due to the district courts moving out of Bartlett in 1885.

In 1908, additional money was granted to Bartlett for the purchase of a horse-drawn wagonette to transport the students. The same year, Dr. Nicholas Blackwell, who had donated the land for the original courthouse, deeded the property and courthouse to the school. In 1917, his daughter, Willie Bugg Blackwell Miller, donated additional land west of the courthouse for the construction of a new building to be named Nicholas Blackwell High School. The new school had 100 students and seven teachers. Dora Gholson had served as principal of the Bartlett Courthouse School and remained in this position at the new school until 1922, when John H. George took over. In 1905, the Shelby County Industrial and Training School was built at the corner of Memphis-Arlington and Alturia Roads. The county-sponsored home was built to house boys who had no supportive family. They spent half their day in school and half working the agricultural fields surrounding the school. One of the superintendents was Thomas P. Westendorf, who before coming to Bartlett wrote and published many songs, including "I'll Take You Home Again, Kathleen," which was later covered by Elvis Presley. Ellendale School operated from the late 1800s until 1918 for children in the Ellendale area. In 1918, a new school was built on Third Street, and it operated until 1976. This building is today the Singleton Community Center. With Bartlett's rapid growth in the 1980s, many new schools have been built, including Oak Elementary, Appling Middle School, and Kate Bond Elementary. St. Ann School was established in 1960 and was the first Catholic School in the Bartlett area.

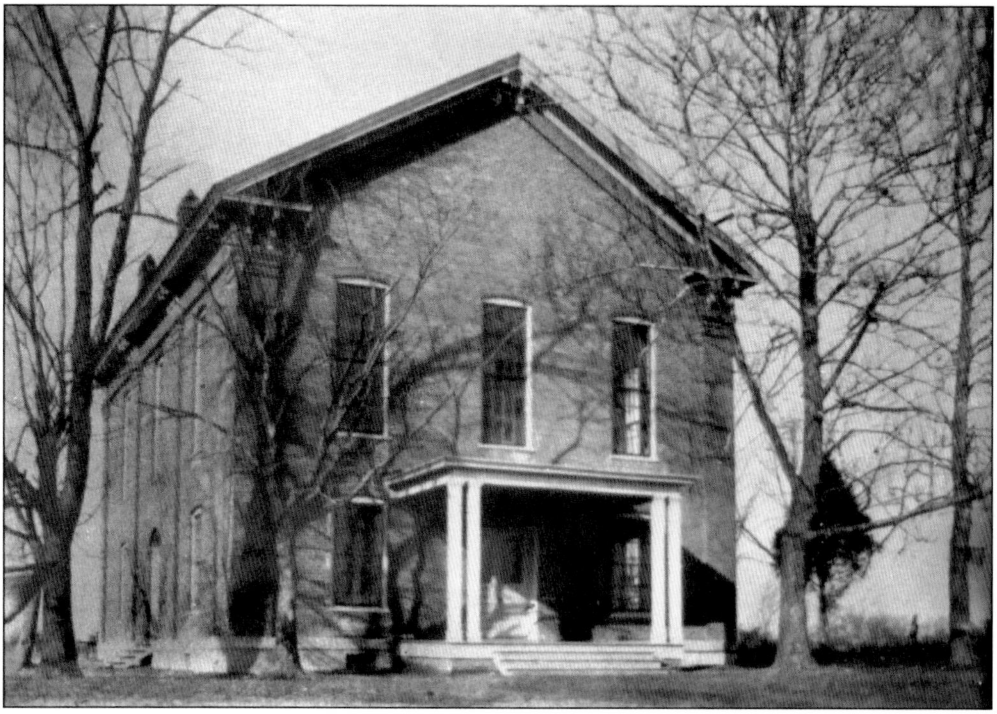

As Shelby County grew after the Civil War, citizens found the need for a circuit courthouse that was more centrally located. Bartlett was chosen, as it was near the center of the county. In 1870, James Oglesby built the Bartlett Courthouse, which cost $12,449. The courthouse operated from 1870 until 1885, when the courts were moved back to Memphis. After the courts left, the property was used as a school until 1917.

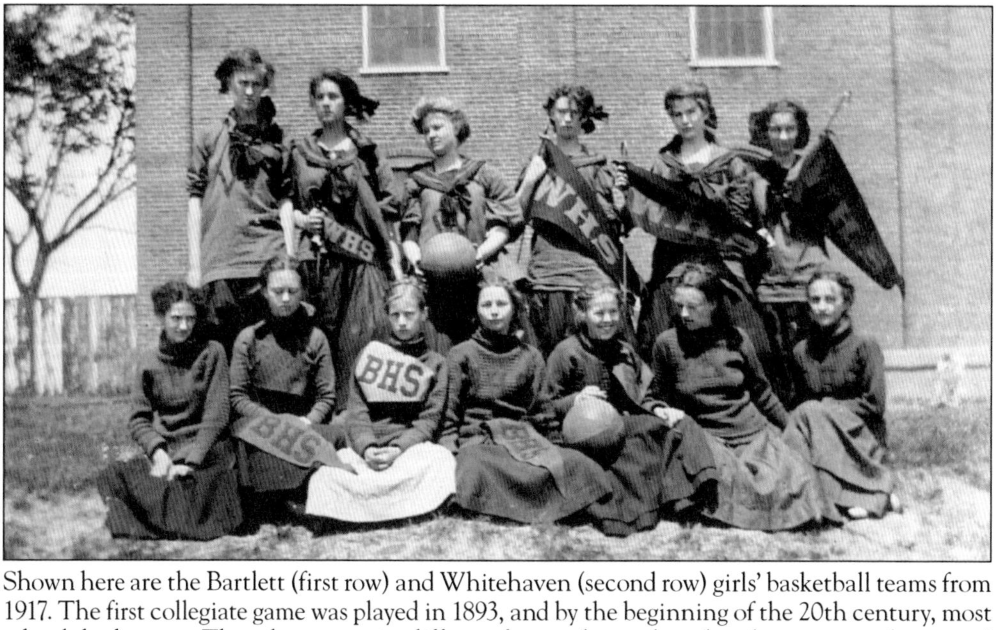

Shown here are the Bartlett (first row) and Whitehaven (second row) girls' basketball teams from 1917. The first collegiate game was played in 1893, and by the beginning of the 20th century, most schools had a team. The rules were quite different from today, with each girl staying in a designated area and only being allowed to dribble three times before having to pass to another player.

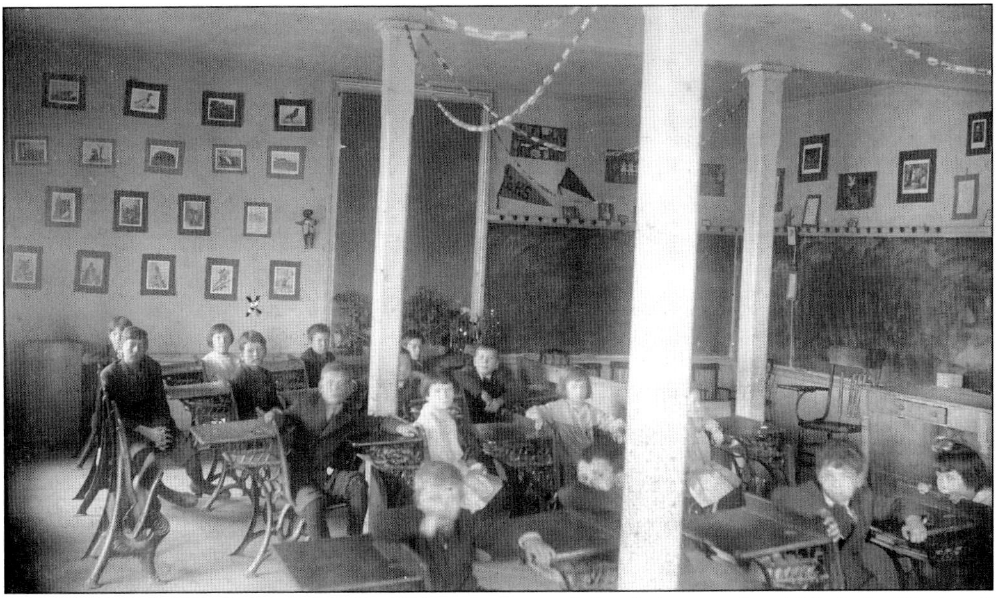

This was the last class to attend to Bartlett Courthouse School. A new school, Nicholas Blackwell High School, was built next door and opened in 1917. The student second from the left on the next-to-last row is W. J. Freeman, who was a town alderman for 35 years. The Freeman family arrived in Bartlett in 1853.

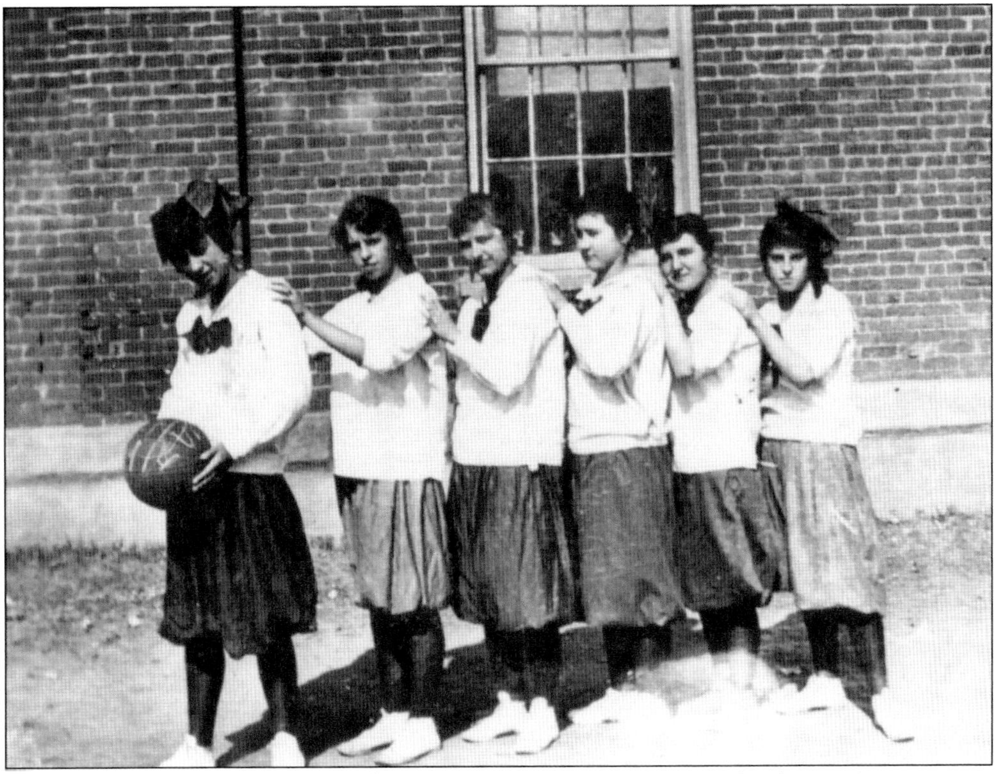

The girls' basketball team poses in front of the Bartlett Courthouse School in 1917.

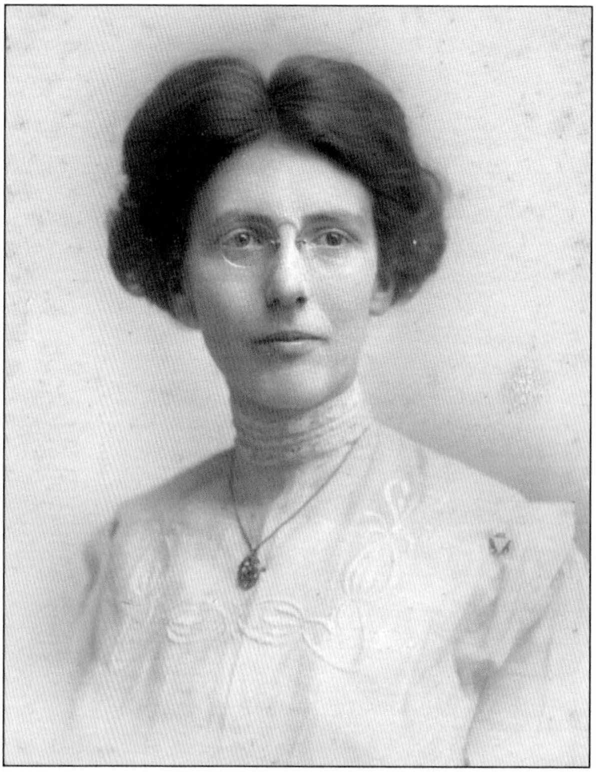

Dora Gholson was the principal for the Bartlett Courthouse School and the first principal for the 1917 Nicholas Blackwell High School.

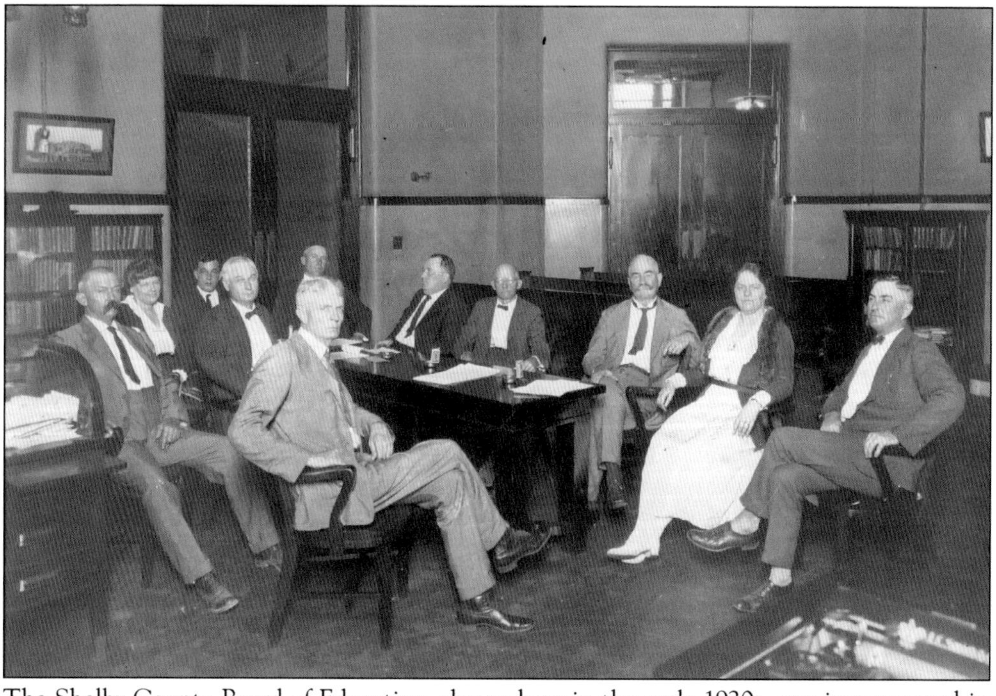

The Shelby County Board of Education, shown here in the early 1920s, was instrumental in creating a higher level of education in Shelby County. Many of the county's high schools were built between 1915 and 1925, including Millington, Collierville, Bartlett, and Whitehaven.

Members of the Nicholas Blackwell High School boys' basketball team in 1923 included Walter Elmore, Robert Bledsoe, Sam Blackwell, Edward Barton, and Wade Baxter.

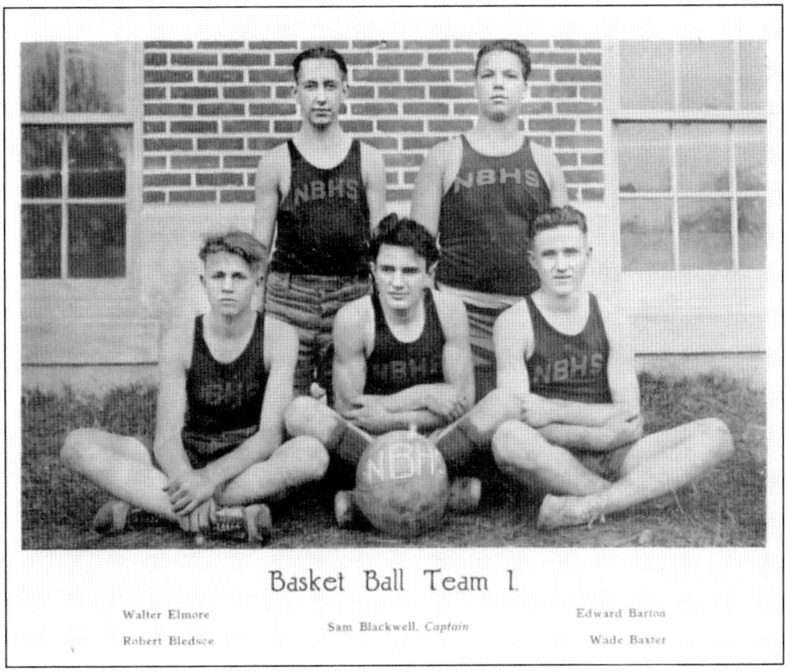

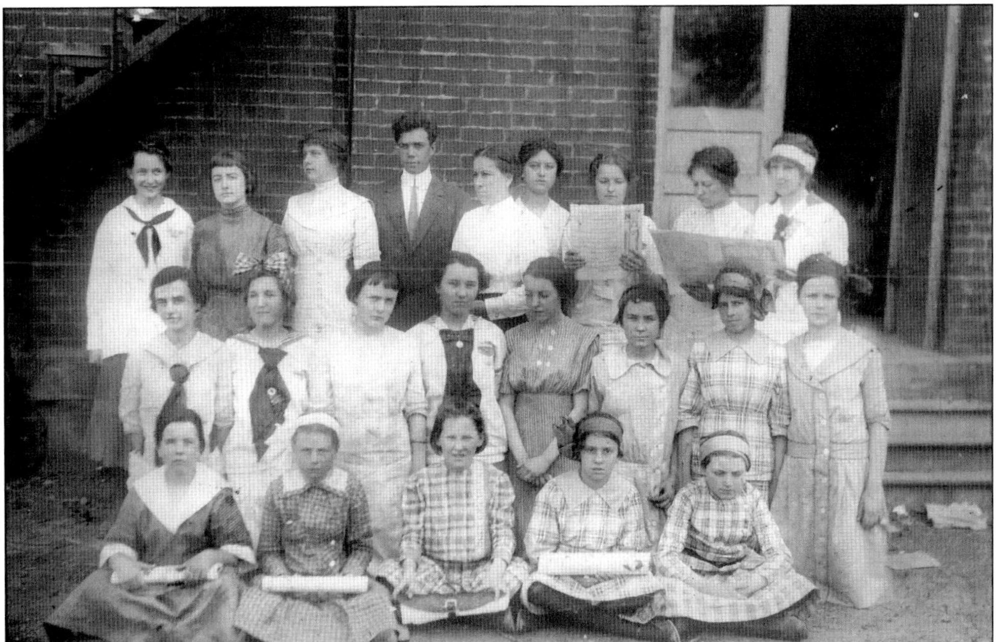

An early class photograph from the Bartlett Courthouse School is shown here, taken around 1912. Begun in 1885 with the move of the circuit courts to Memphis, the school operated until 1917, when Nicholas Blackwell High School was built.

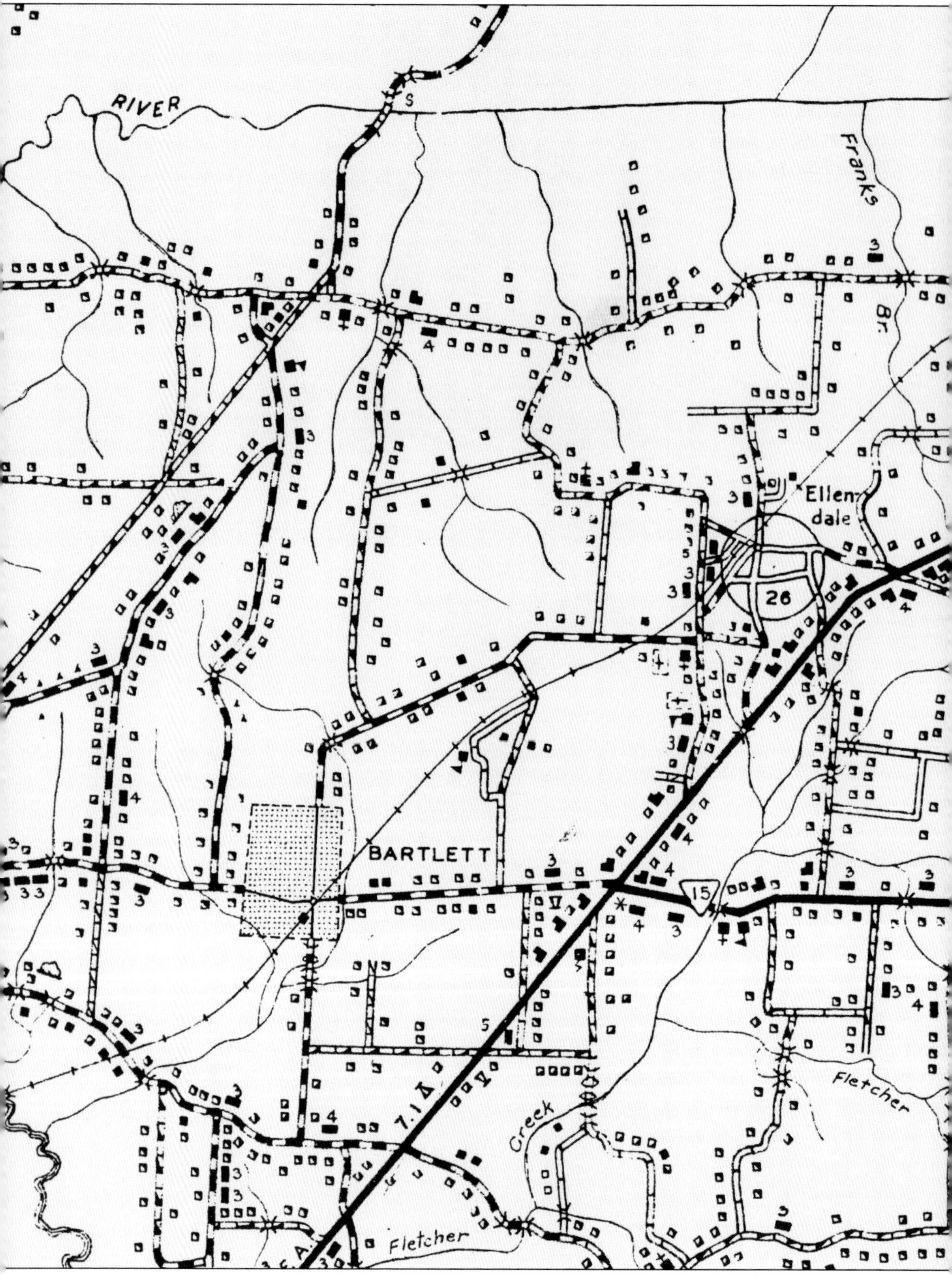
RIVER
Franks
Br.
Ellen-
dale
26
BARTLETT
15
Creek
Fletcher
Fletcher

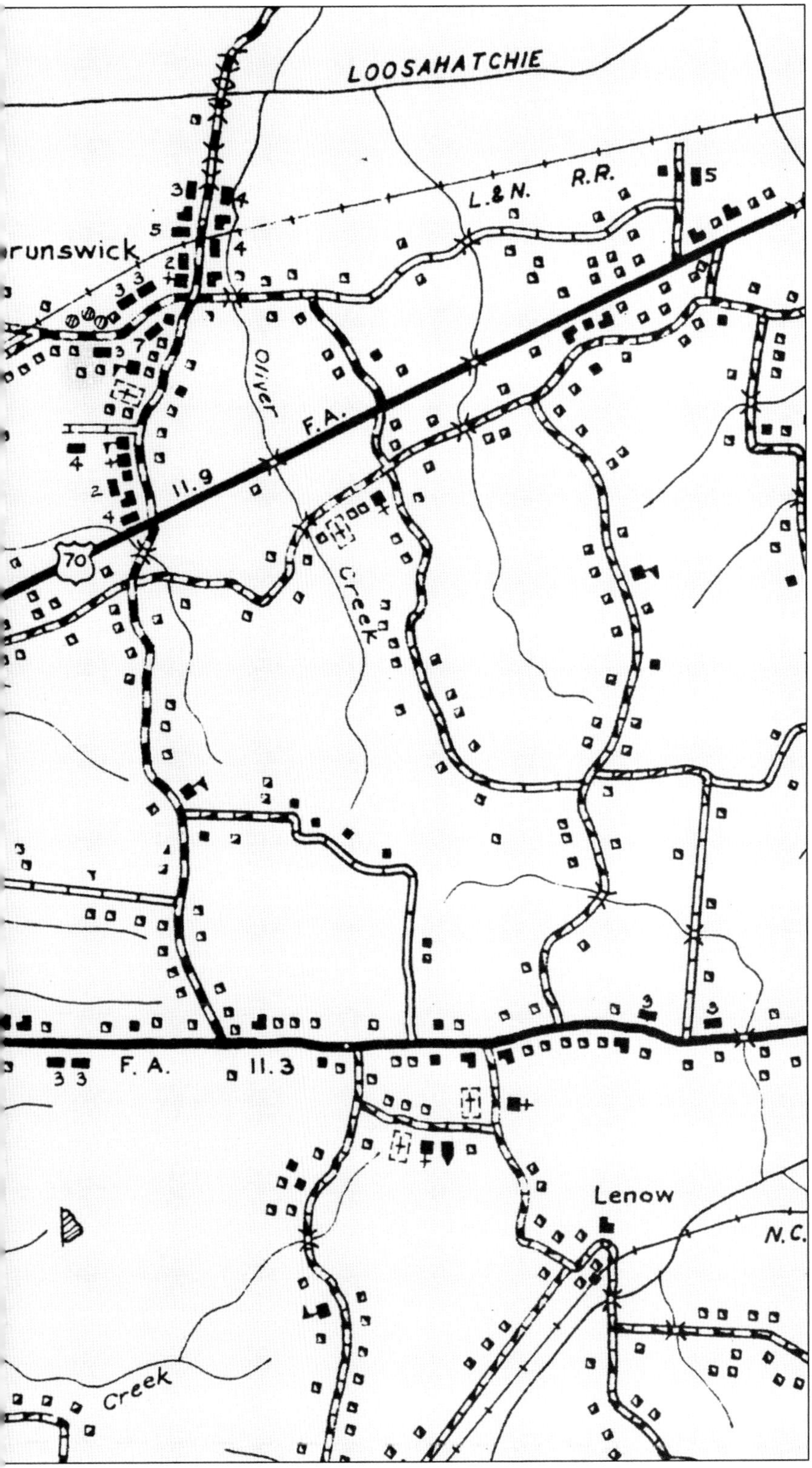

This 1950s map of Bartlett shows house locations. The town of Bartlett was rather small until the 1970s, when the area saw a tremendous rise in home building.

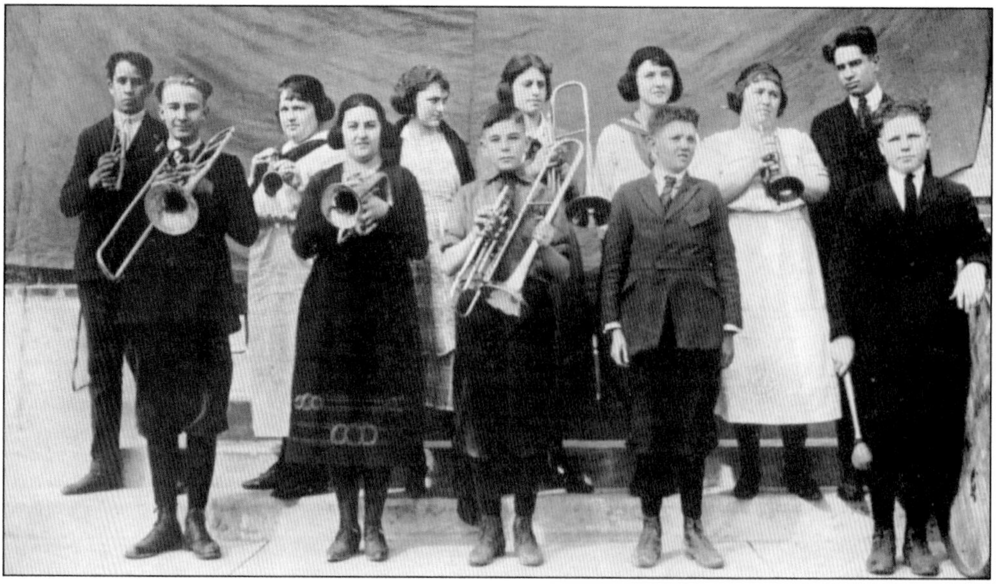

Members of the Bartlett music class pose for the 1921 annual. Music was provided in Bartlett schools as far back as 1880, when a music recital was performed for the community. Members included Francis Gotten and her brother Dave, A. G. Warner, and Albert Hays.

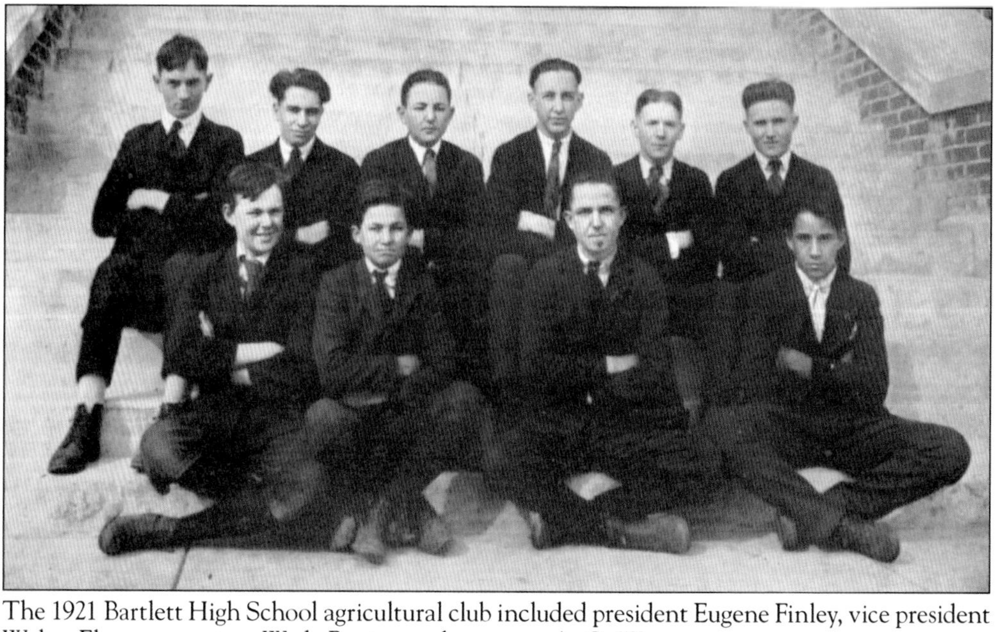

The 1921 Bartlett High School agricultural club included president Eugene Finley, vice president Walter Elmore, secretary Wade Baxter, and treasurer A. G. Warner.

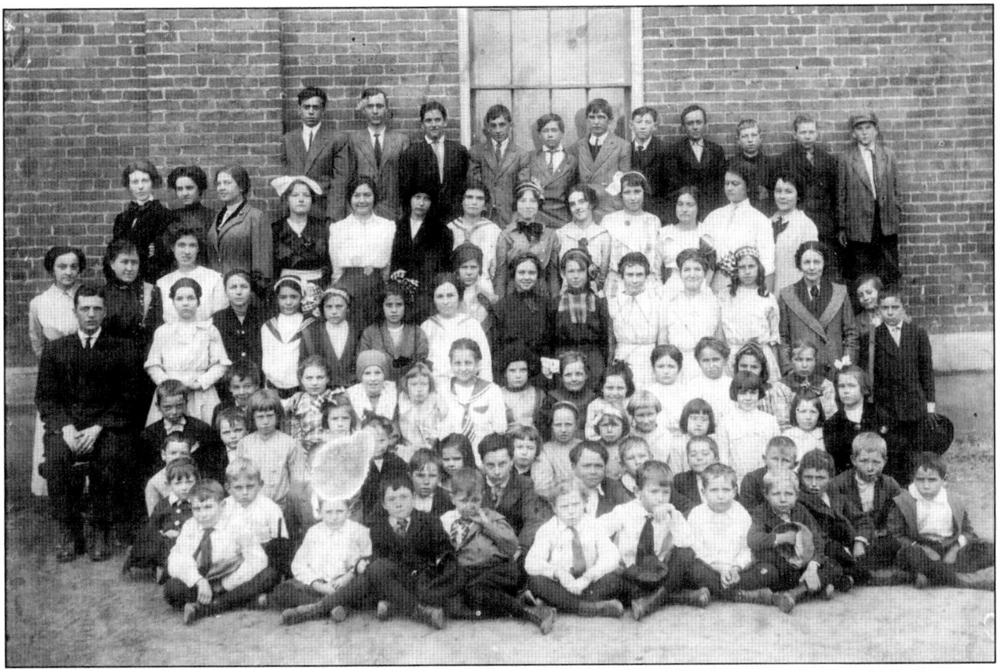

The 1912 class of the Bartlett Courthouse School poses for the yearly photograph. In 1907, the state legislature reorganized the county school system, replacing district commissioners with a county-wide school board. This helped to equalize school funding and lengthened the academic year.

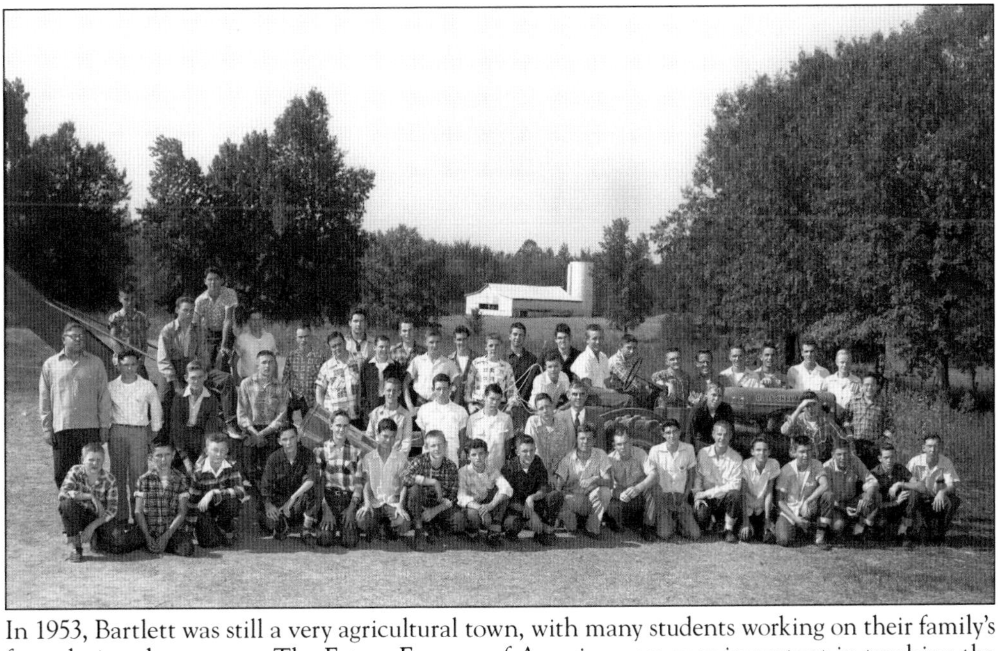

In 1953, Bartlett was still a very agricultural town, with many students working on their family's farm during the summer. The Future Farmers of America were very important in teaching the fundamentals of farming to high school students.

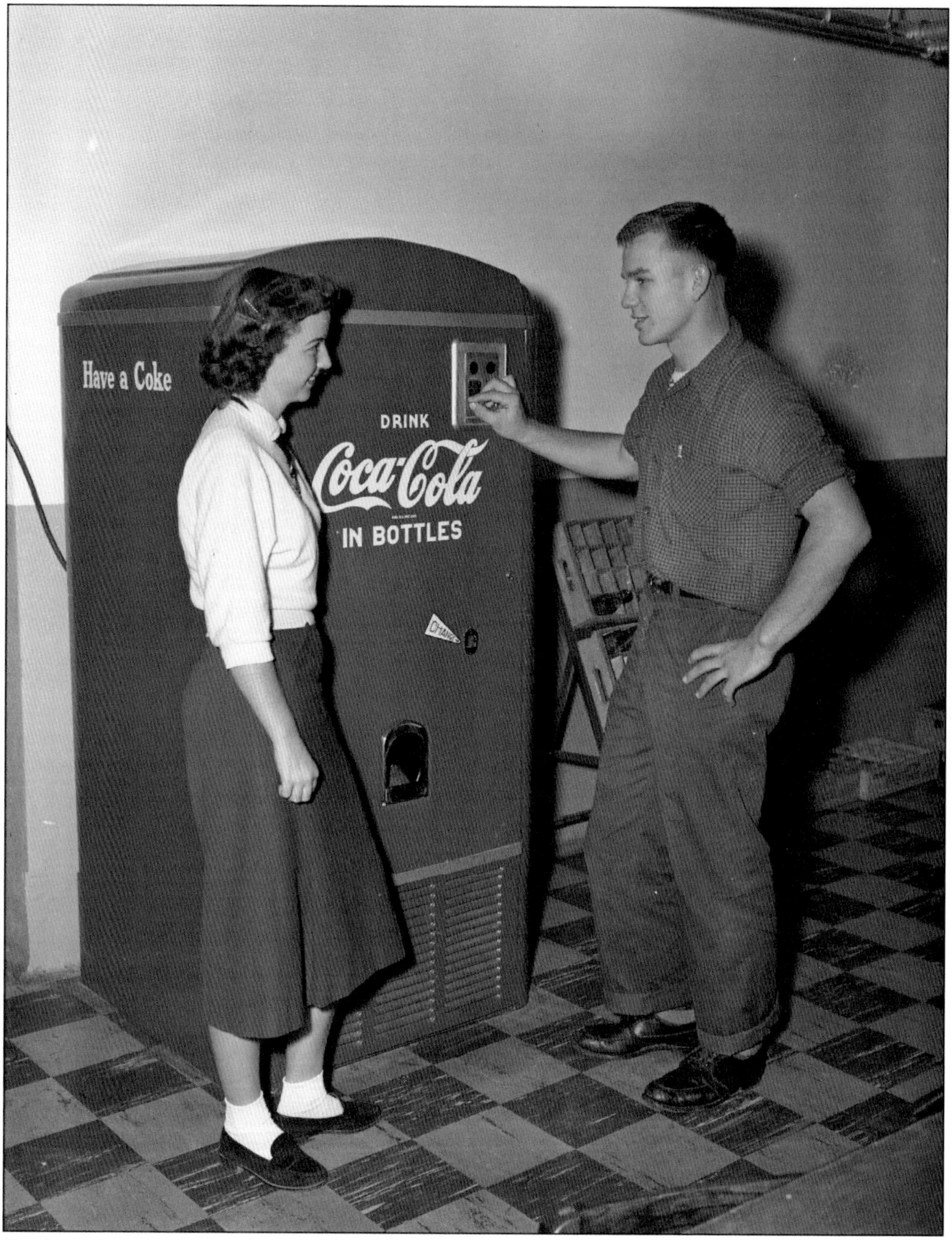

Students pose in front of a nickel Coke machine at Bartlett High School in 1953. Coca-Cola sponsored many events at Bartlett, from the yearly annual, known as the *Panther Parade*, to sock hops and football games. When Coke was originally sold in 1886, it was only sold from soda fountains. It was not until 1894 that one could get a Coke in a bottle.

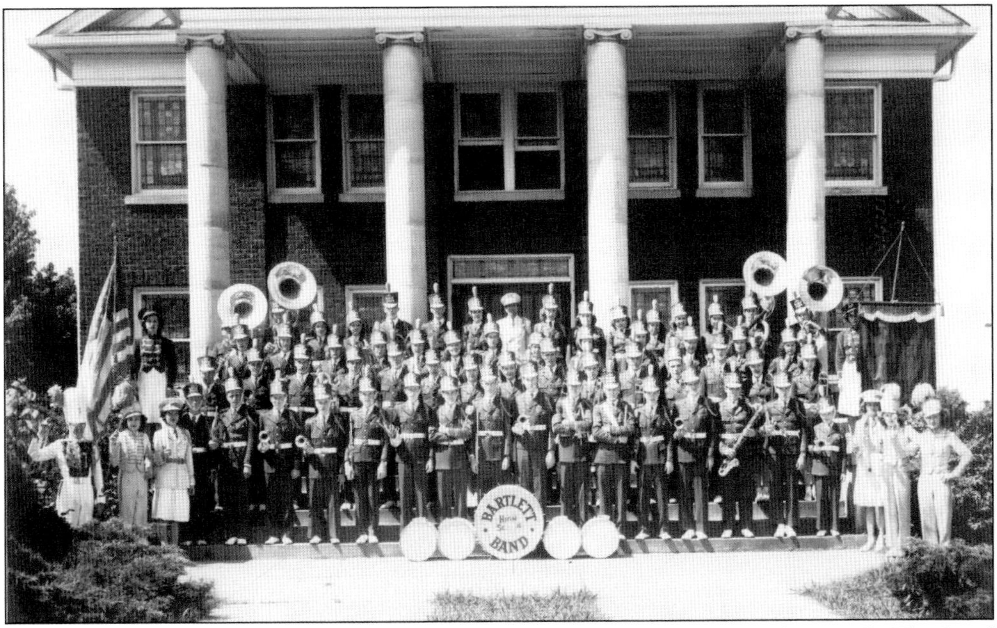

The Bartlett High School band is shown in front of the Methodist church in 1953. The band would often perform for the Memphis Cotton Carnival, held each May.

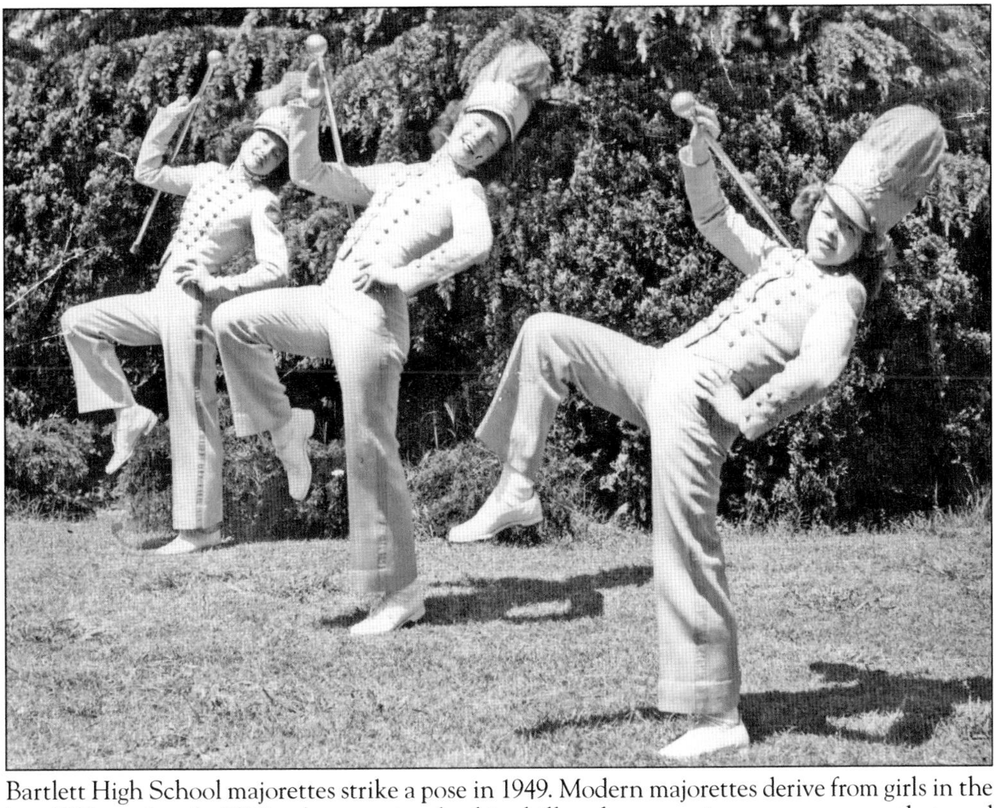

Bartlett High School majorettes strike a pose in 1949. Modern majorettes derive from girls in the late 1800s and early 1900s who were involved in drill and gymnastic teams or groups that used apparatuses similar to those found in rhythmic gymnastics, such as batons.

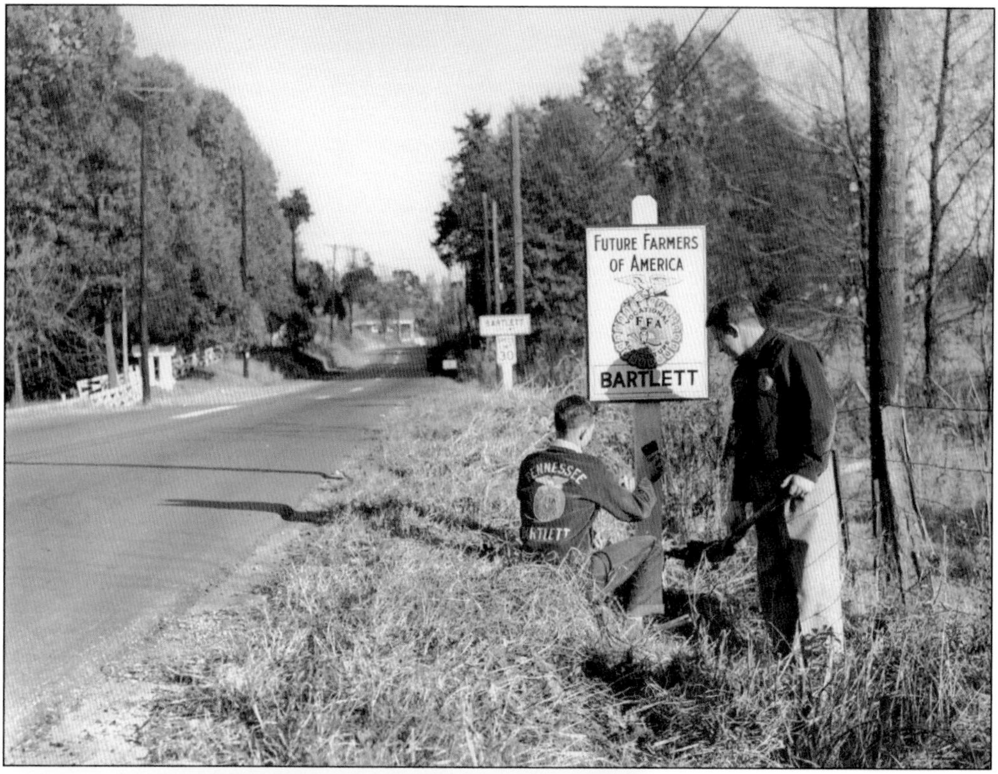

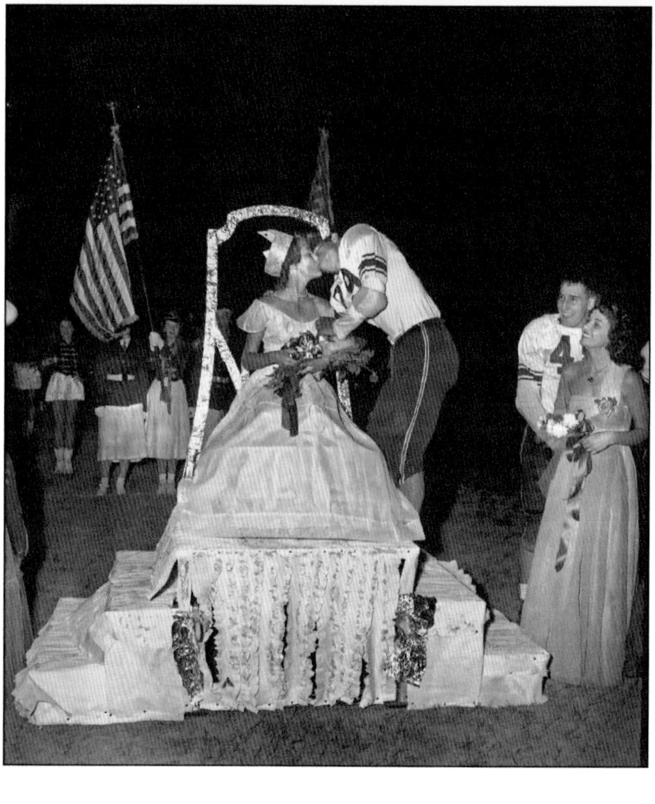

Under the guidance of their teacher and mentor David McPherson, the Bartlett High School Future Farmers of America was one of the leading chapters in Shelby County. Shown above in 1951 installing a welcome sign on Stage Road just west of Bartlett are, from left to right, Billy Klemm and Otto Rahm.

Homecoming, shown at left in 1953, was held during football season and culminated with the crowning of the homecoming queen.

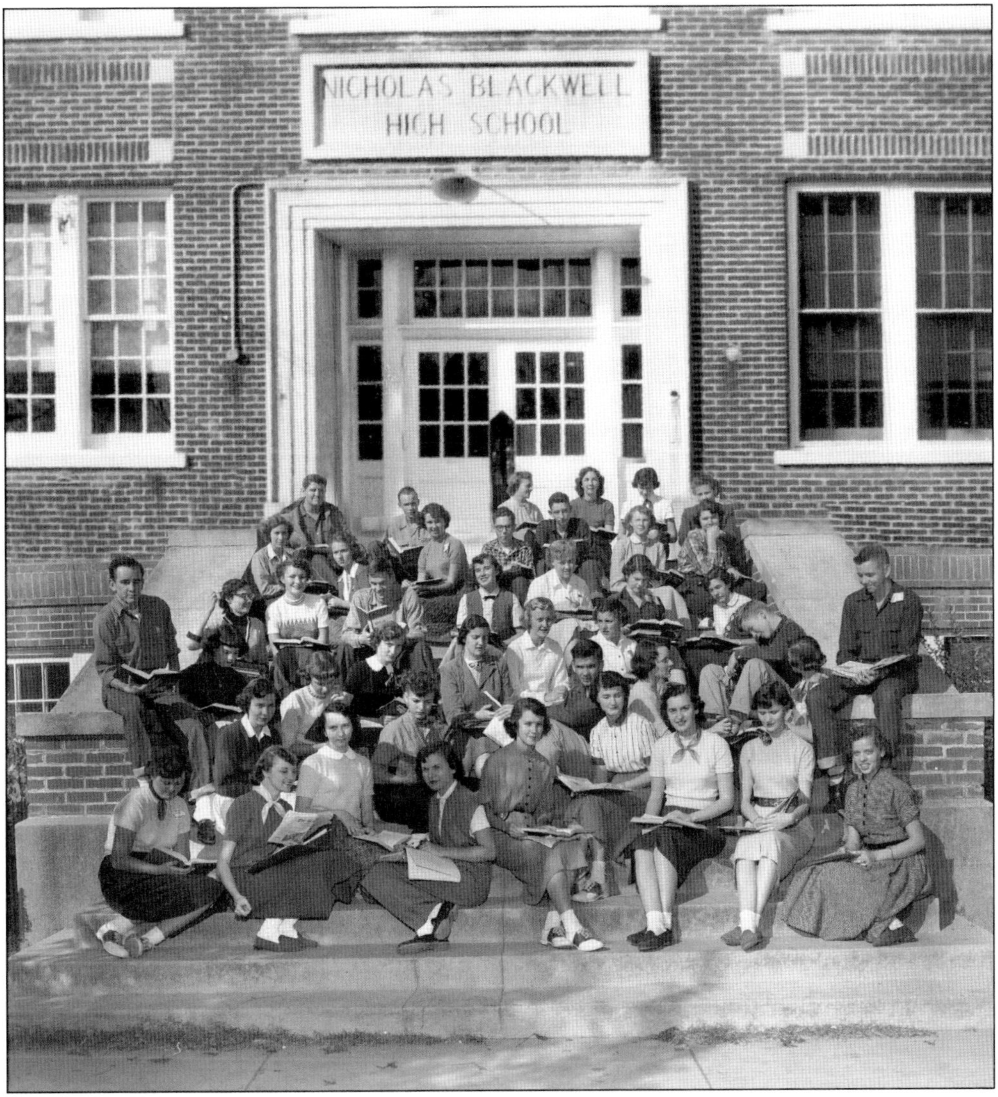

Students sit on the front steps of Nicholas Blackwell High School in 1953. The steps were known at the "Senior Steps," and underclassmen had to use the side entrances. The original 1917 building was demolished in 1977, making way for a modern building housing offices and classrooms. The first *Panther Pride* yearbook was published in 1949.

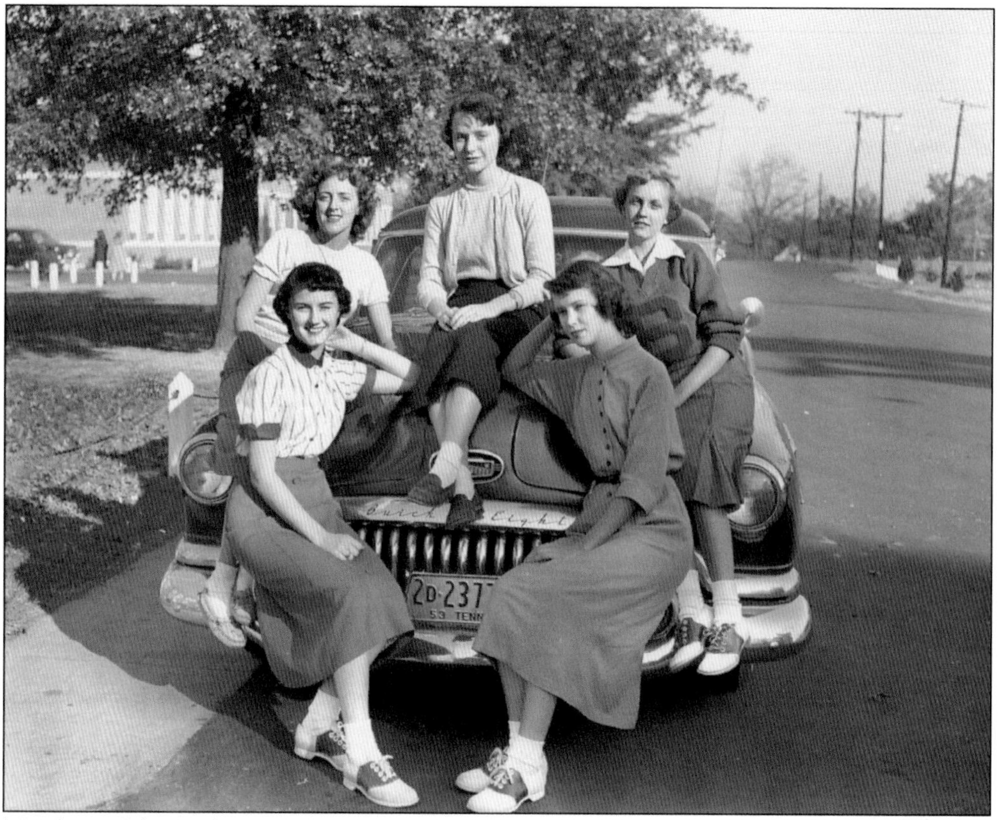

Members of the student government pose on the hood of a car for the yearbook photographer in 1953. In 1931, the English department decided the school needed a newspaper, and a contest was held for a name. The winning name was the *Gleaner*, meaning the students would glean the best and most interesting stories about the school.

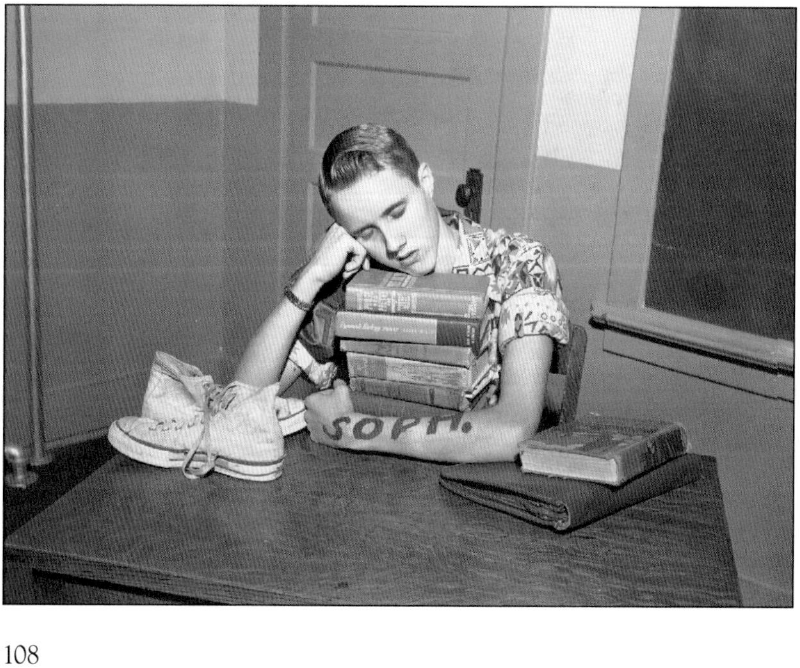

A sophomore's life could be tiresome, having to carry the seniors' books or use only certain doors to enter the school. The front steps were strictly for the seniors.

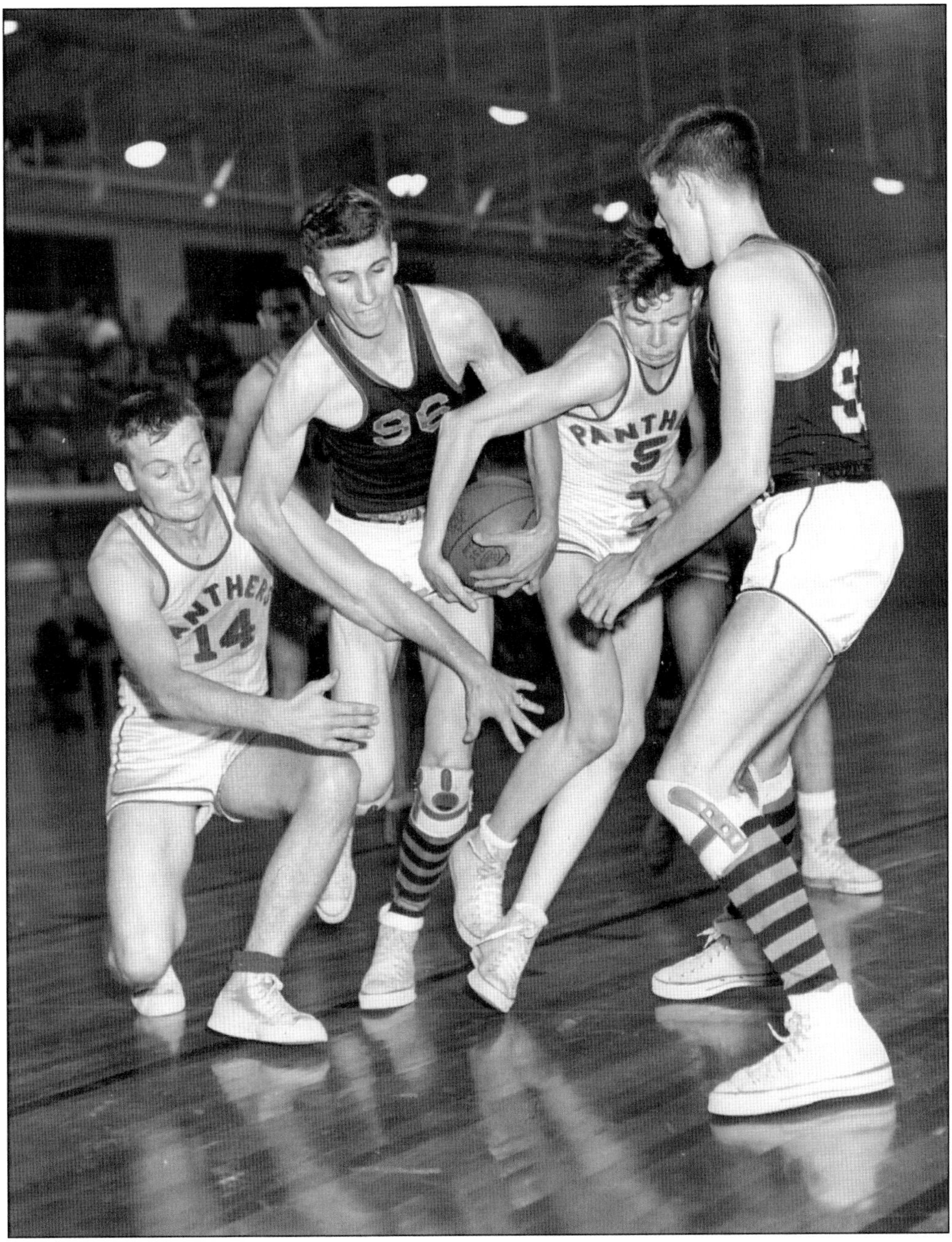

One of the biggest basketball rivalries among the Shelby County high schools was between Bartlett and Whitehaven. In this national award–winning photograph from 1951, the players fight over a loose ball. The players are, from left to right, Tom Brown, Billy Joe Jones, Eugene Sanders, and John McGee.

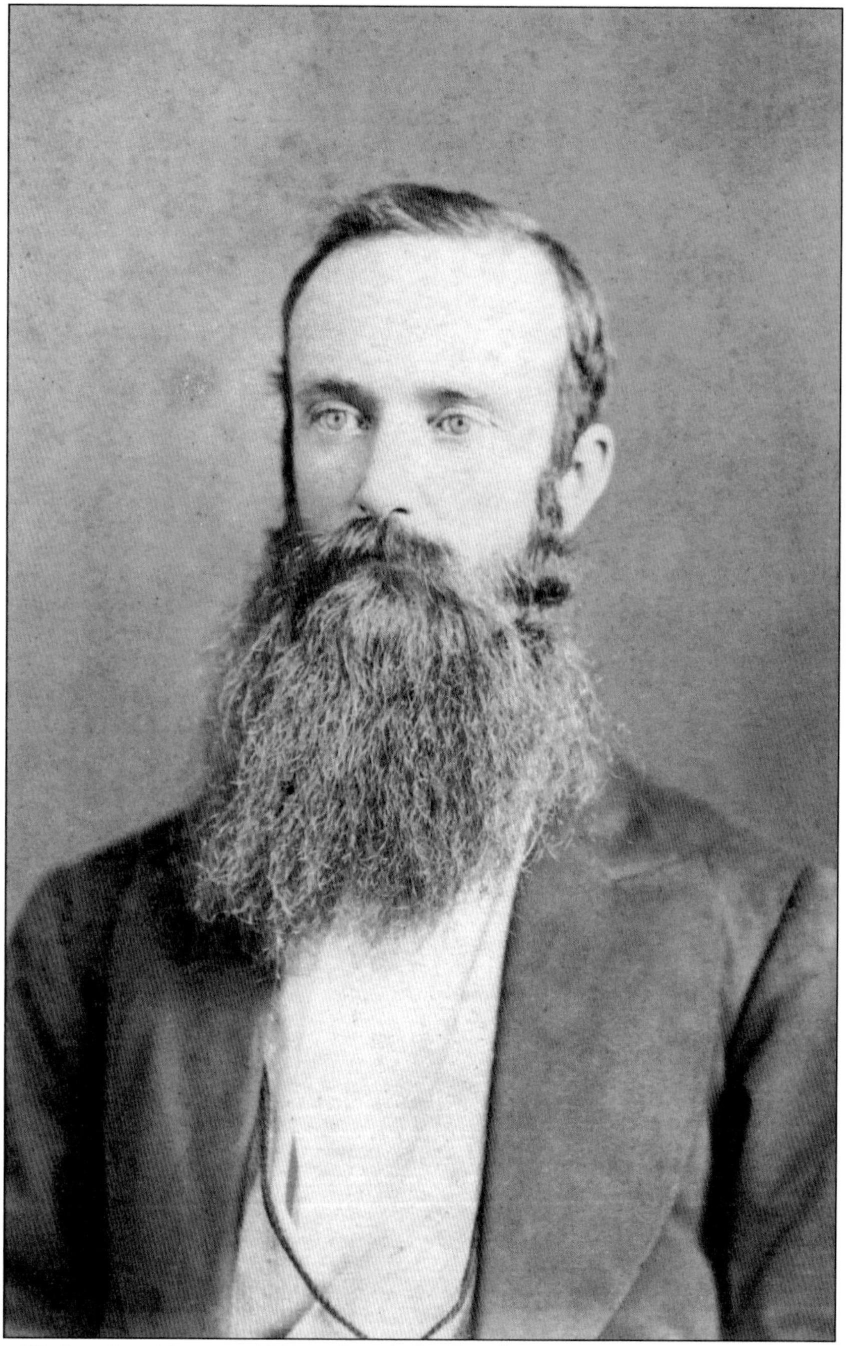

Nicholas Blackwell was born in 1838 and settled in Bartlett in 1865 after fighting in many of the major battles of the Civil War. He was elected Bartlett's first alderman and second mayor and was praised in the Memphis newspapers for his selfless work during the yellow fever epidemic of 1878. He donated land in the Bartlett Historic District for churches, schools, and meetinghouses. He was a devoted father to his only child, Willie Bugg, and cared for the orphan children of his brother George, who had died in 1862. It was fitting that in 1917 the new high school was named Nicholas Blackwell High School in his honor.

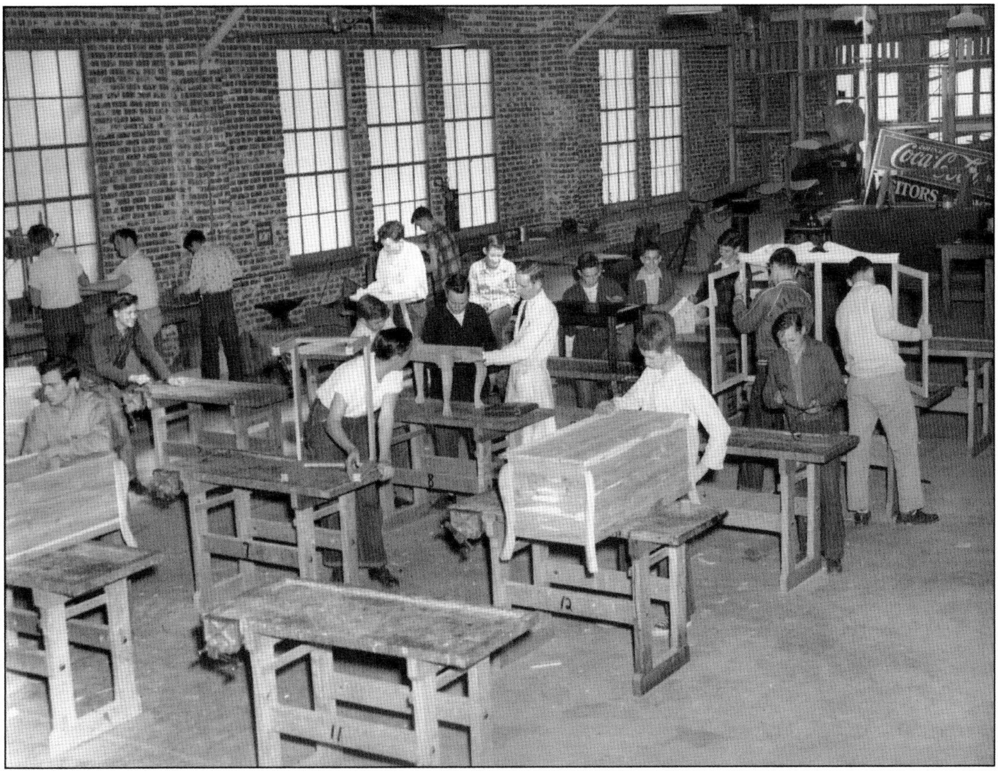

While most girls took home economics in the 1950s, boys had a year of shop class. Many a mother had a cedar chest or coat rack to show for her son's labor.

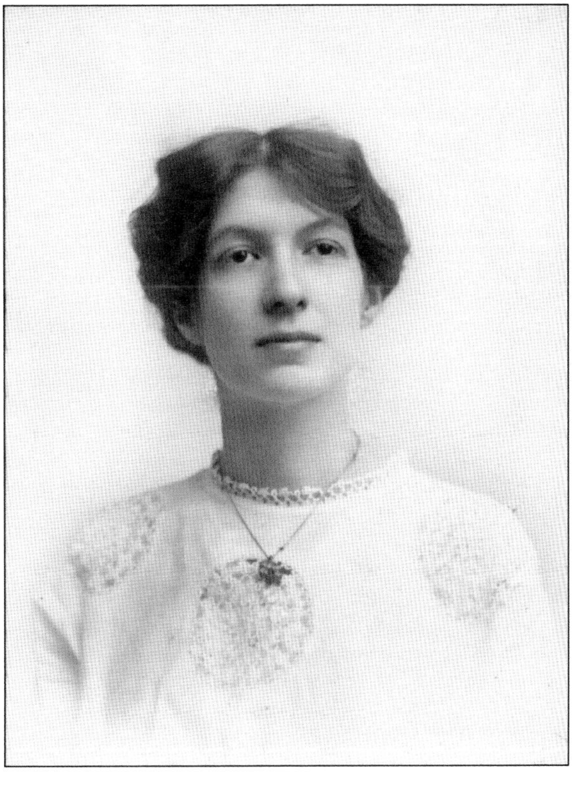

Mabel Richmond was a schoolteacher at Bartlett High School for many years. After she was unable to teach, she was the operator for the Bartlett volunteer fire department.

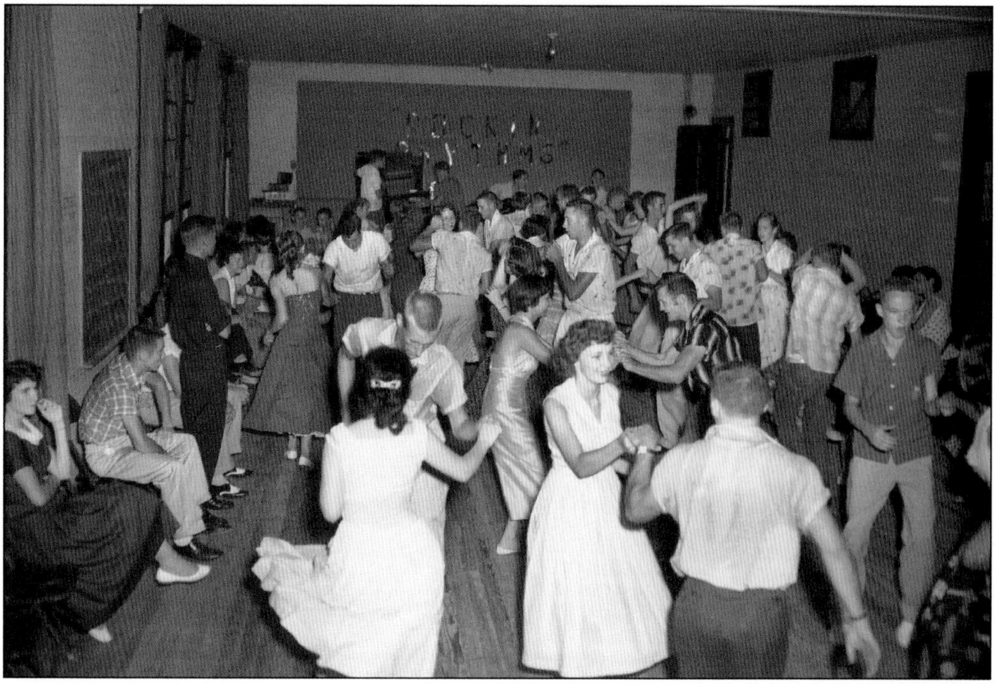

Riding the first wave of Memphis rock and roll, Bartlett students dance the night away to the sounds of the Rockin' Rhythms, a local Bartlett band consisting of Gene Acre, Jimmy Dye, and Pat Miller.

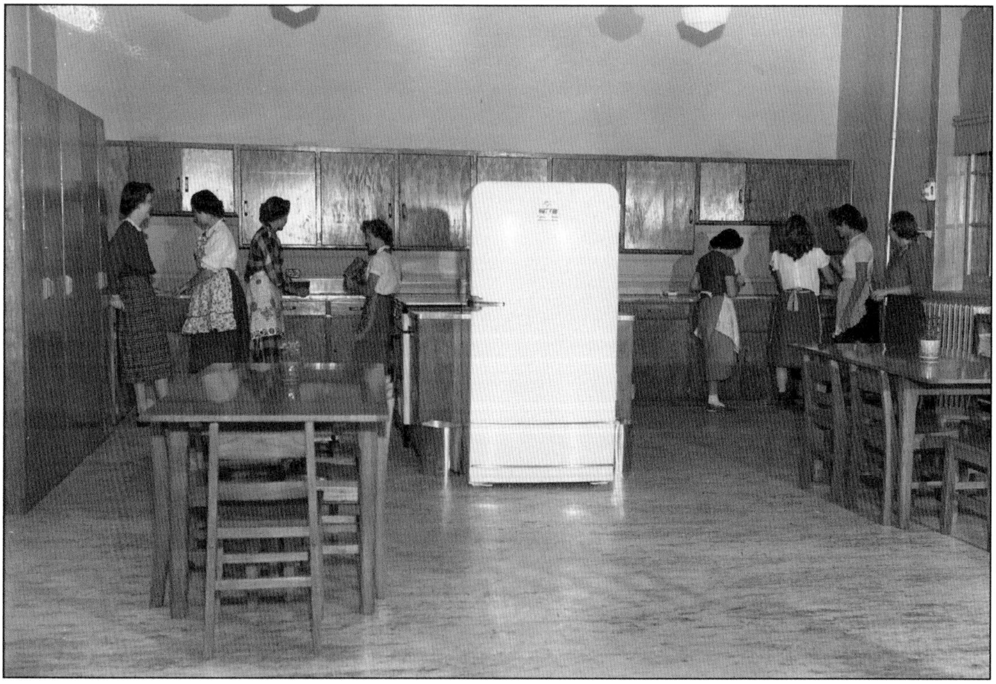

Most young ladies took home economics in the 1940s and 1950s. Taught for many years by Betty Whitworth and Hal Douglas, the classes offered cooking, sewing, and homemaking as general themes.

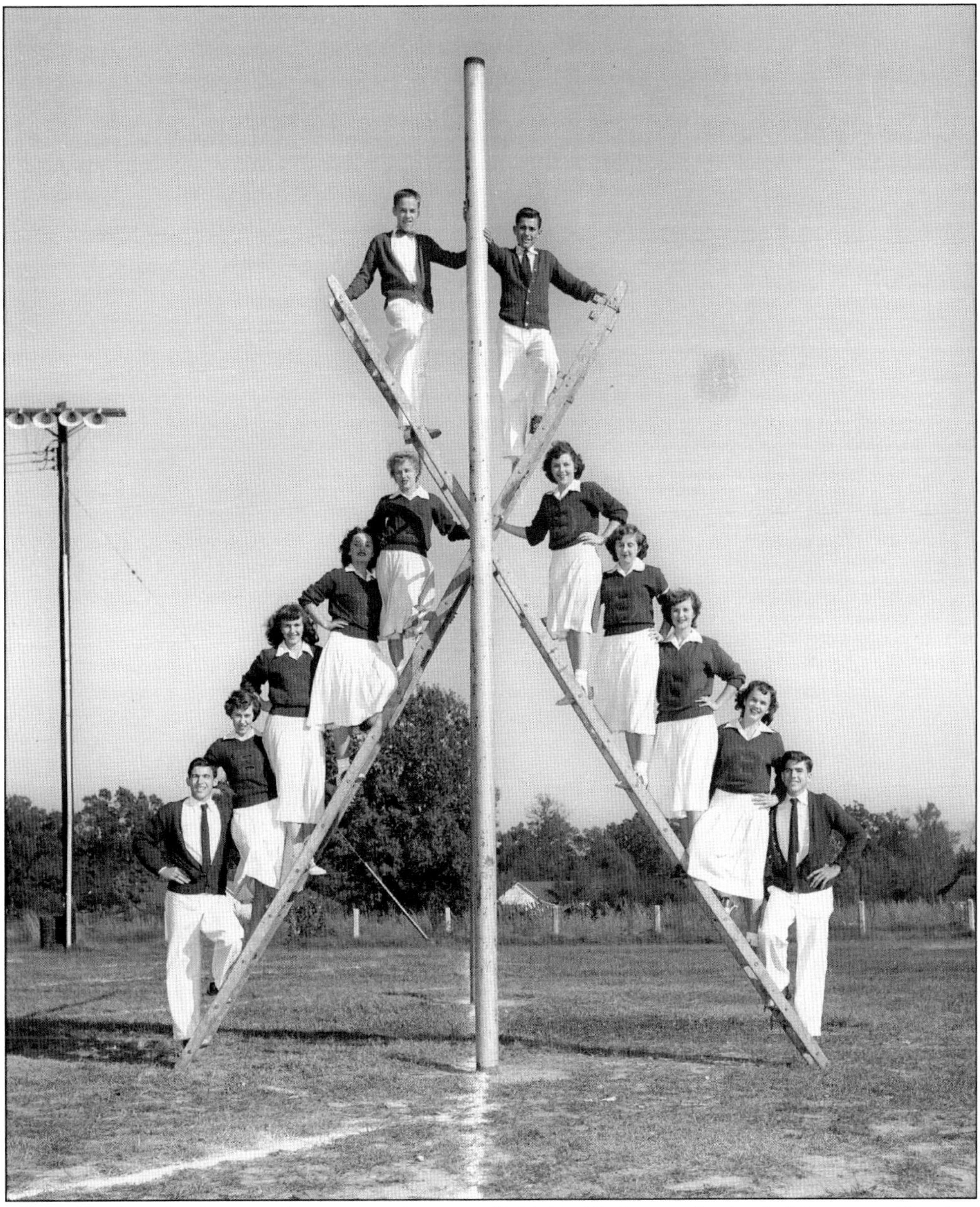

The 1951 cheerleaders are, from top to bottom, (left) Buddy Bancroft, Avola Simmons, Carolyn Porter, Jean Jeffries, Sara Howell, and John Carnes; (right) Tommy Howell, Edna Pike, Bobby Craig, Francis Marshall, Sue Bancroft, and Charles Carnes.

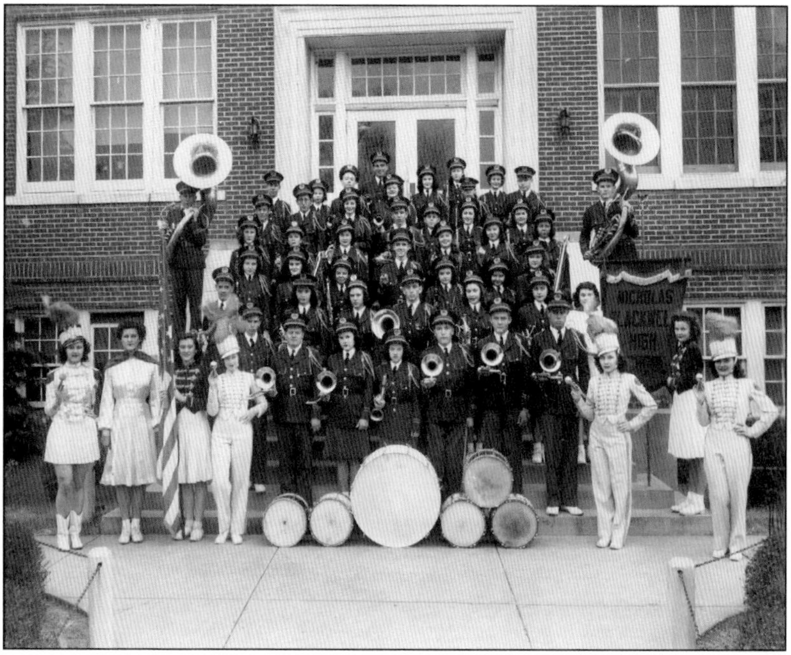

The Bartlett High School band poses on the Senior Steps in 1946. Beginning in 1934, the band performed an annual concert under the direction of A. E. McClain, who once told the parents, "The kids are yours, but the satisfaction of teaching them is mine."

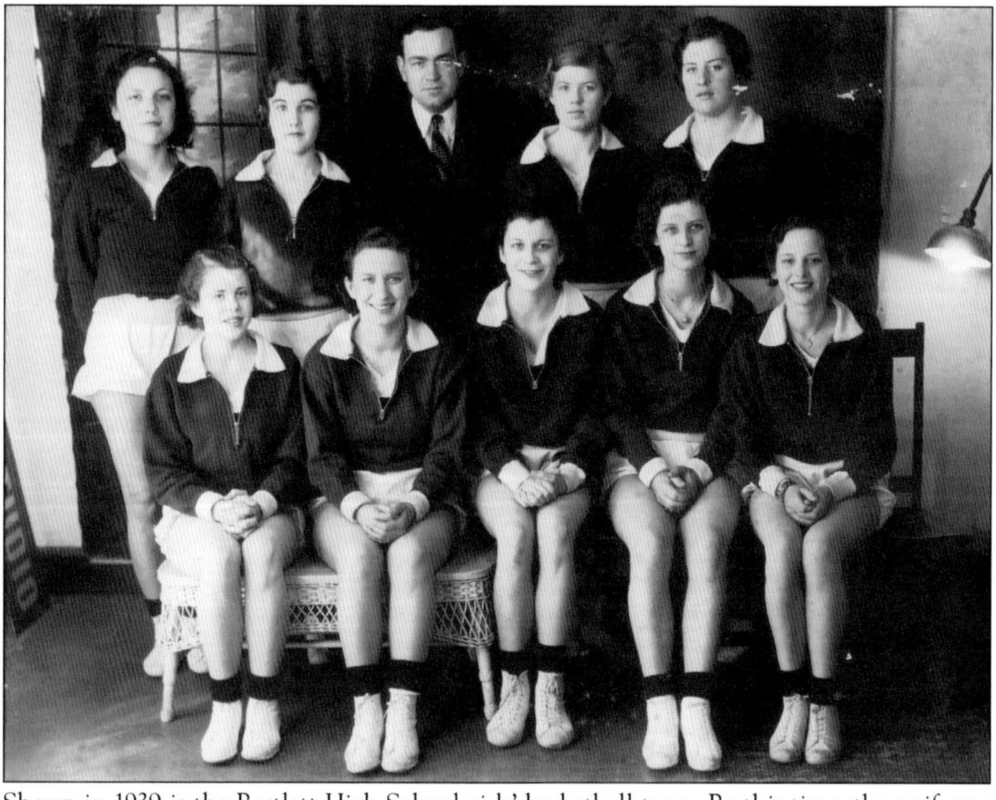

Shown in 1939 is the Bartlett High School girls' basketball team. By this time, the uniforms had become more similar to today's. In the past, the uniforms came just above the ankle.

The Bartlett High School football team gets some pointers from the coach in 1953.

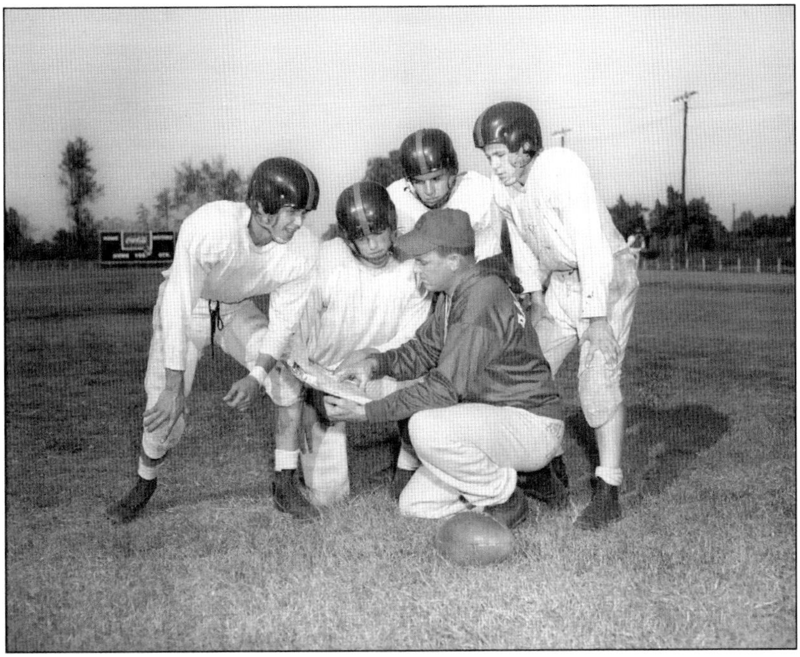

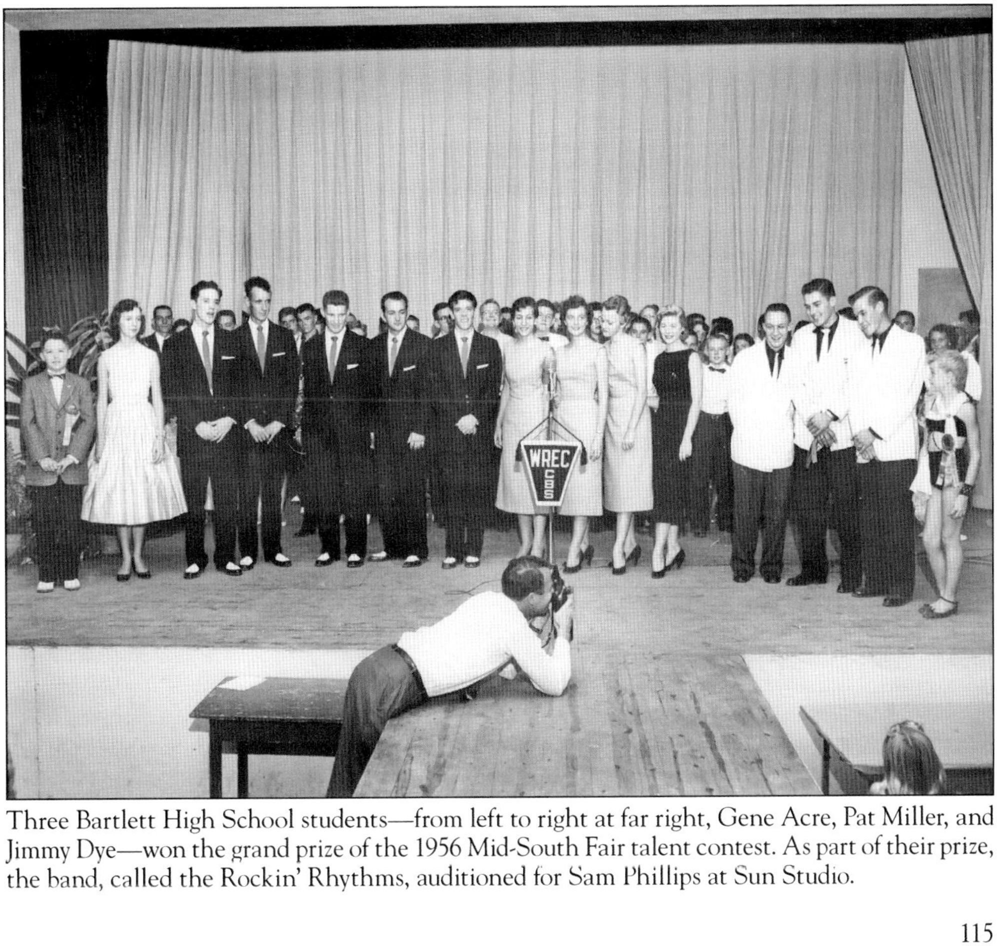

Three Bartlett High School students—from left to right at far right, Gene Acre, Pat Miller, and Jimmy Dye—won the grand prize of the 1956 Mid-South Fair talent contest. As part of their prize, the band, called the Rockin' Rhythms, auditioned for Sam Phillips at Sun Studio.

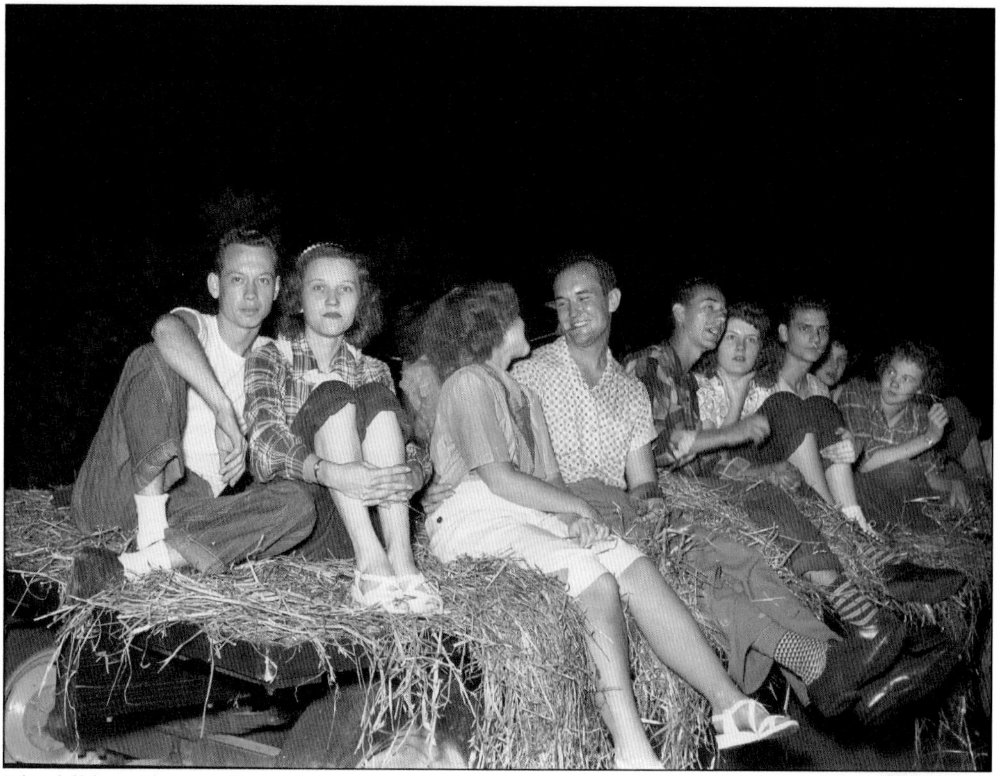

The fall hayride, seen here in 1949, was a tradition each year. The driver would carry the young couples around the neighborhood and usually end up at a bonfire.

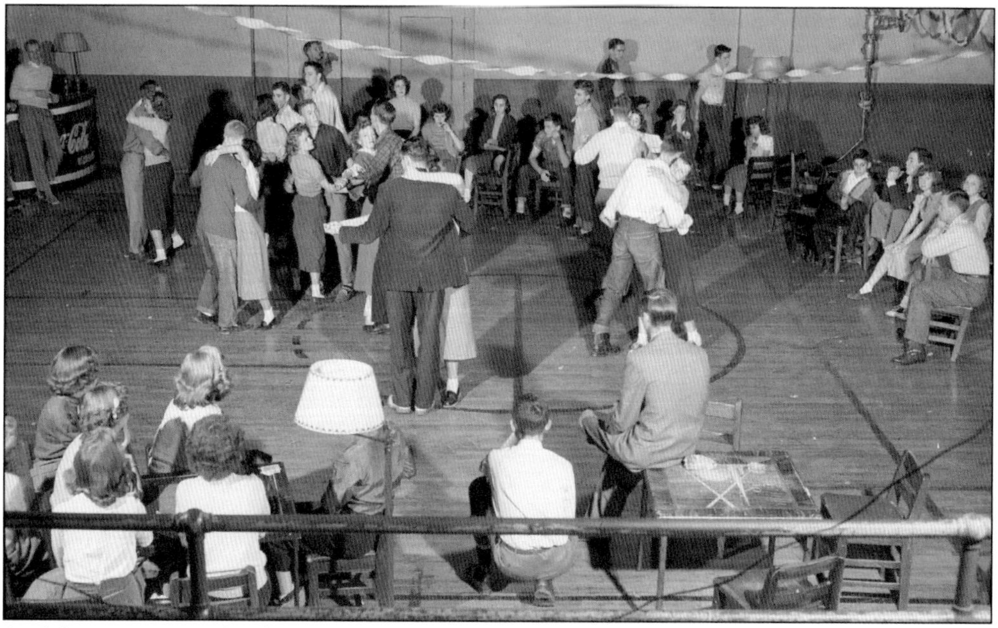

Sock hops were popular during the early 1950s, with the dances being held in the gymnasium.

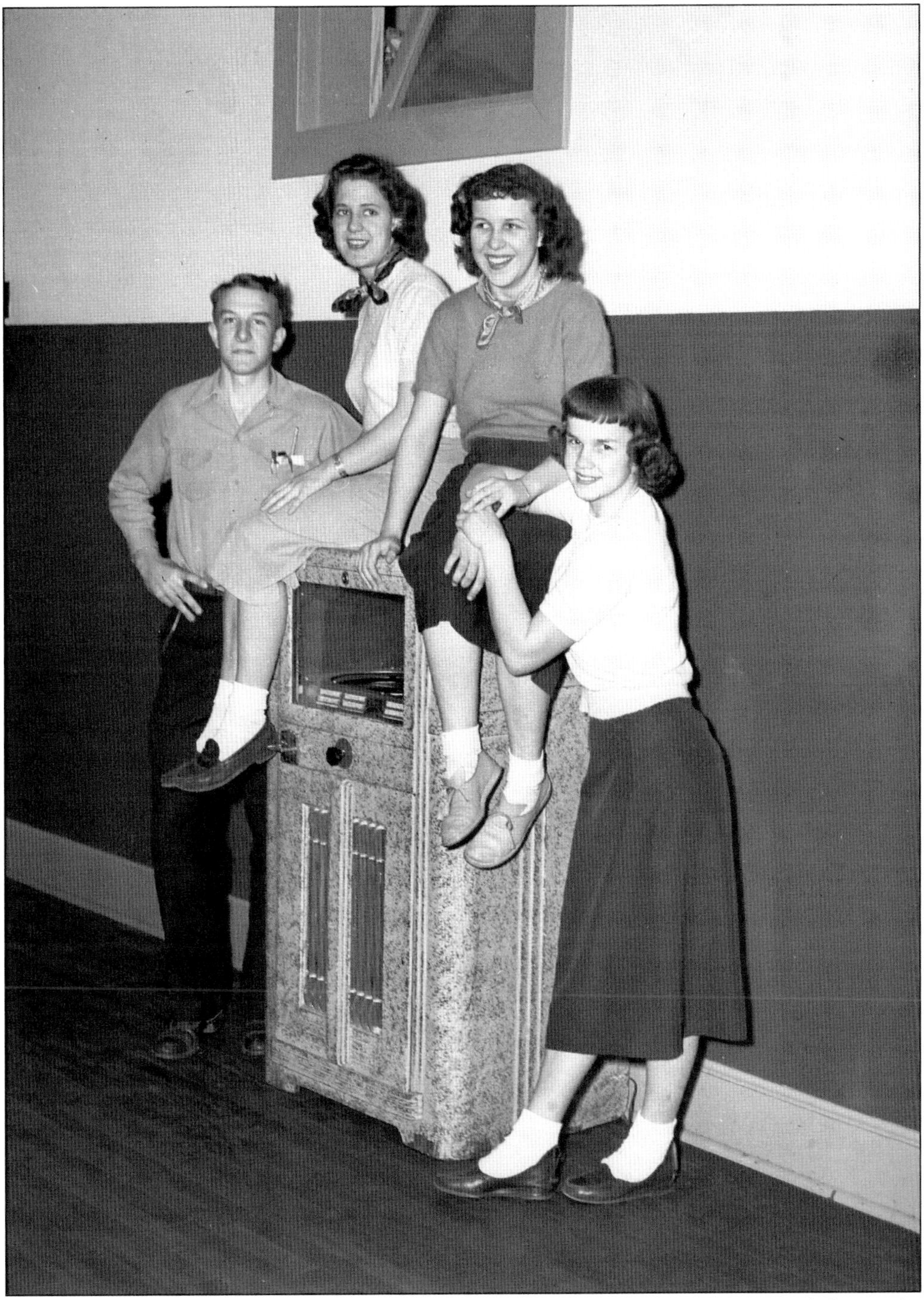

Bartlett High School junior class officers pose in front of a jukebox in 1950. From left to right are David Kime, Lucille Jamison, Lila Nell Sheffield, and Sue Bancroft.

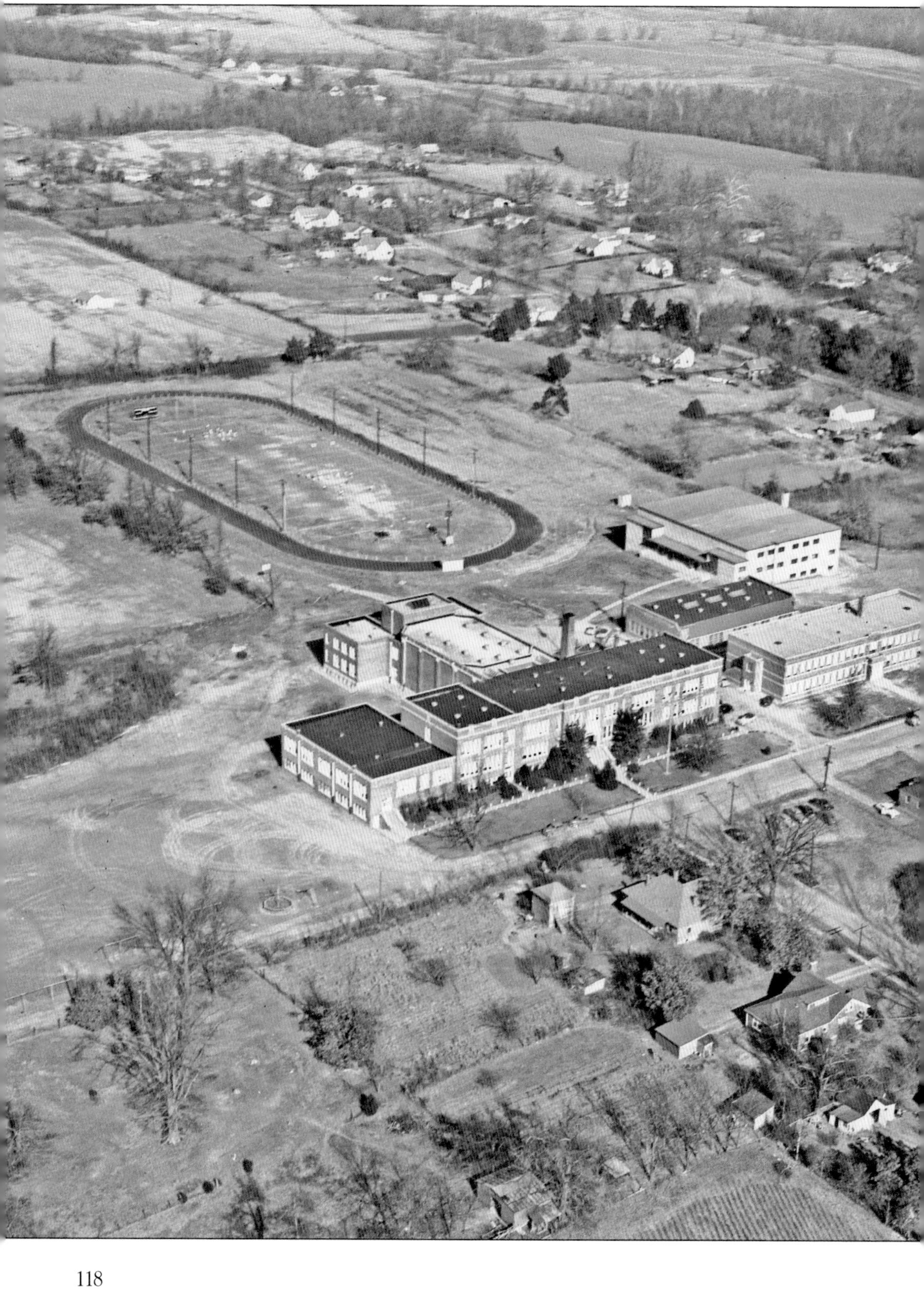

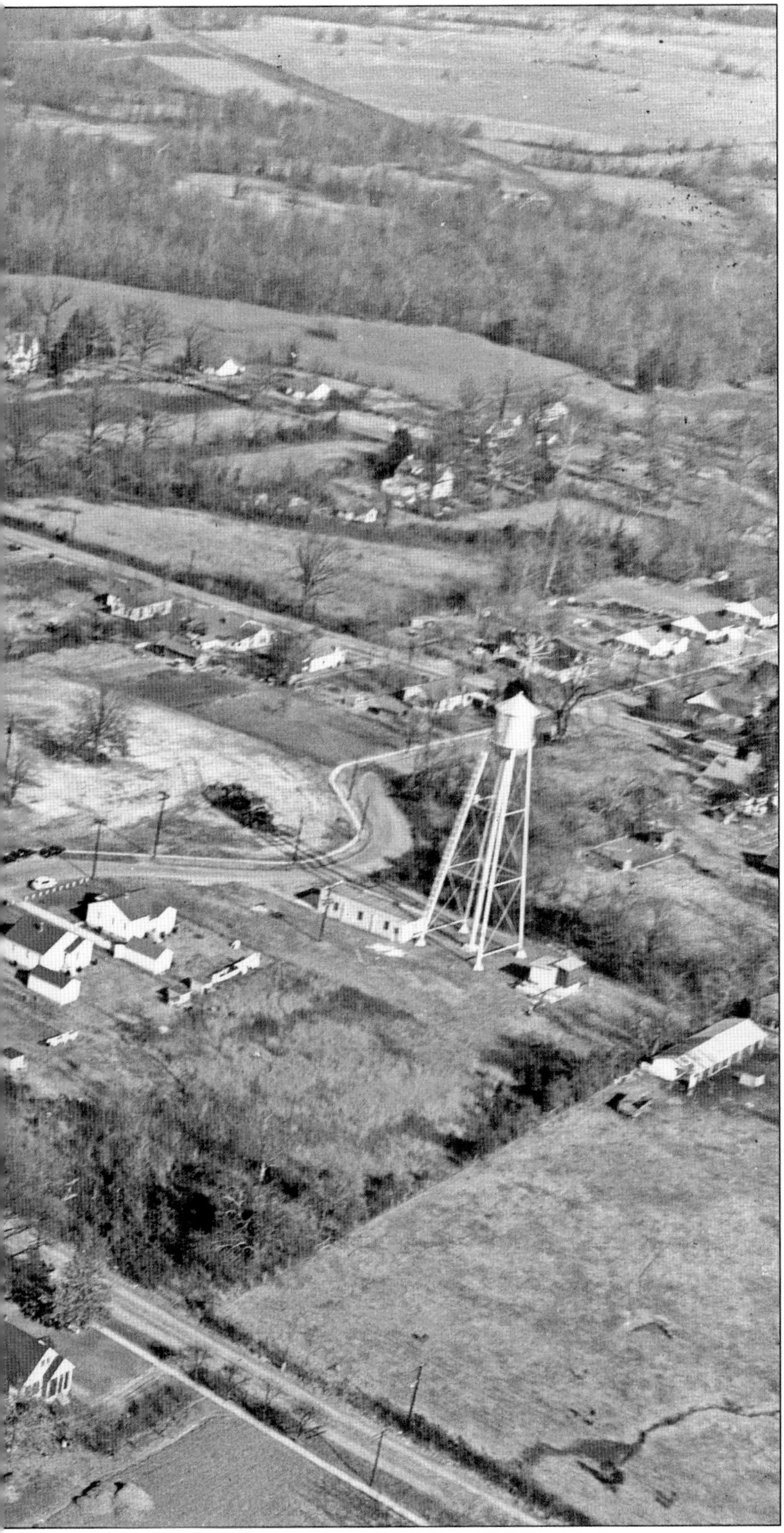

Bartlett High School in 1951 was still surrounded by farmland. In the upper right is the Bartlett Historic District, showing Court Street and Sycamore View Road. The curve in Woodlawn Street is where the Bartlett Courthouse once stood.

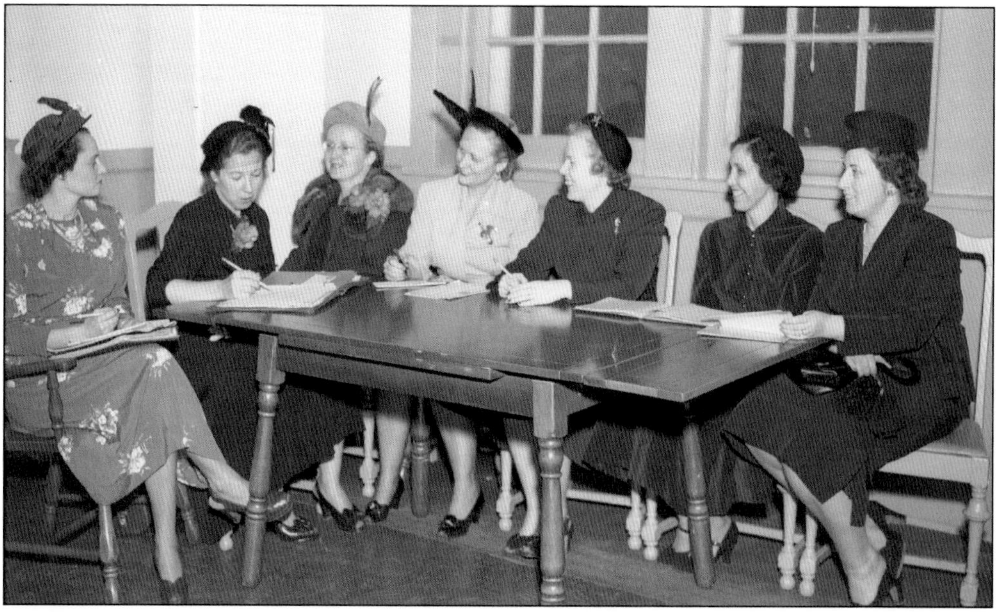

Members of the Bartlett PTA in 1950 were, from left to right, Mrs. Clyde Croft, Mrs. H. W. Slavick, Mrs. Clyed Harris, Mrs. Ralph Hunt, Mrs. Joseph Freeman, Mrs. Hugh Huffman, and Mrs. H. L. Perry.

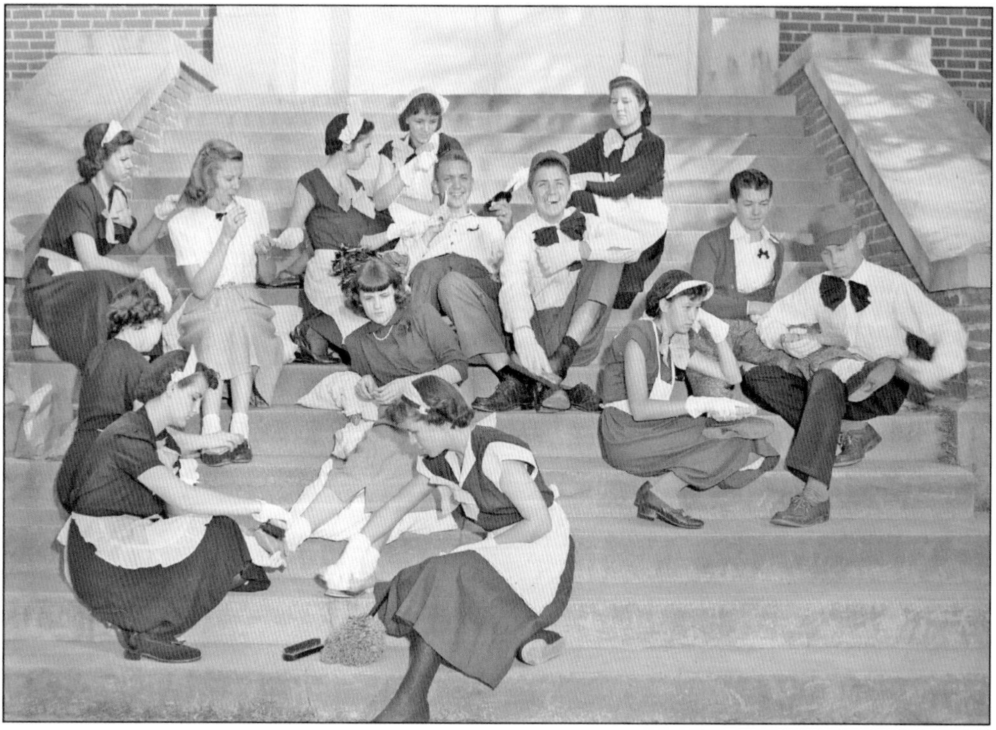

Senior Beta Club members get the full attention of underclassmen wanting to join the organization. Begun in 1934 in South Carolina, the National Beta Club is committed to recognizing and promoting high academic achievement, encouraging service to others, and developing character and leadership skills.

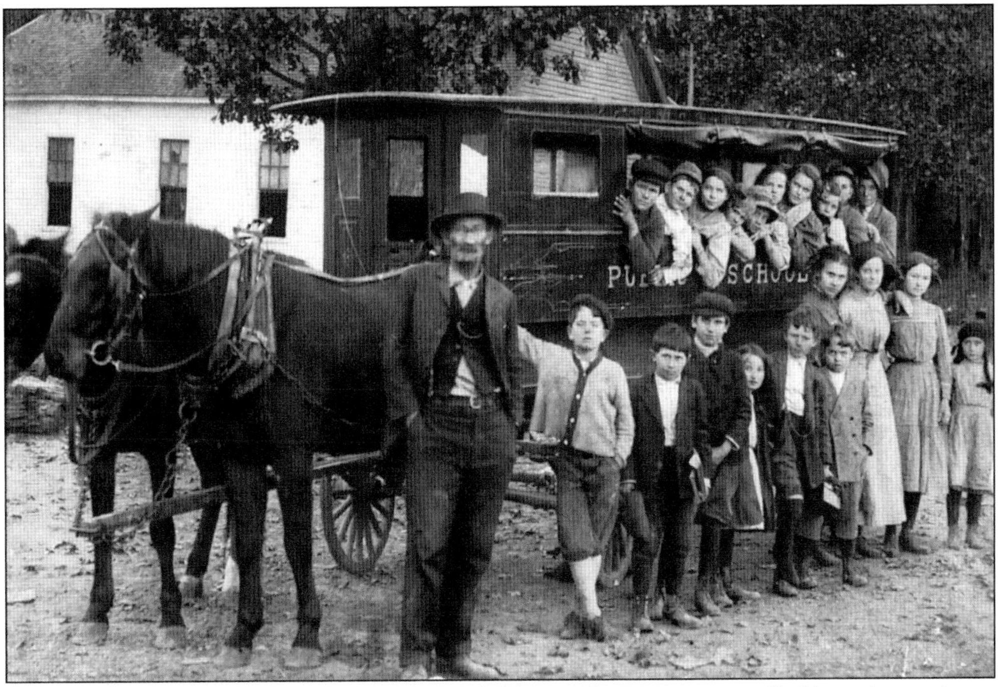

Before the advent of the modern school bus, children rode a wagonette pulled by either mules or horses. During the cold winter months, the wagons were enclosed, and heated bricks were kept on the floor. The first wagonettes were introduced in 1908, and they were eventually replaced by motorized buses in the 1920s.

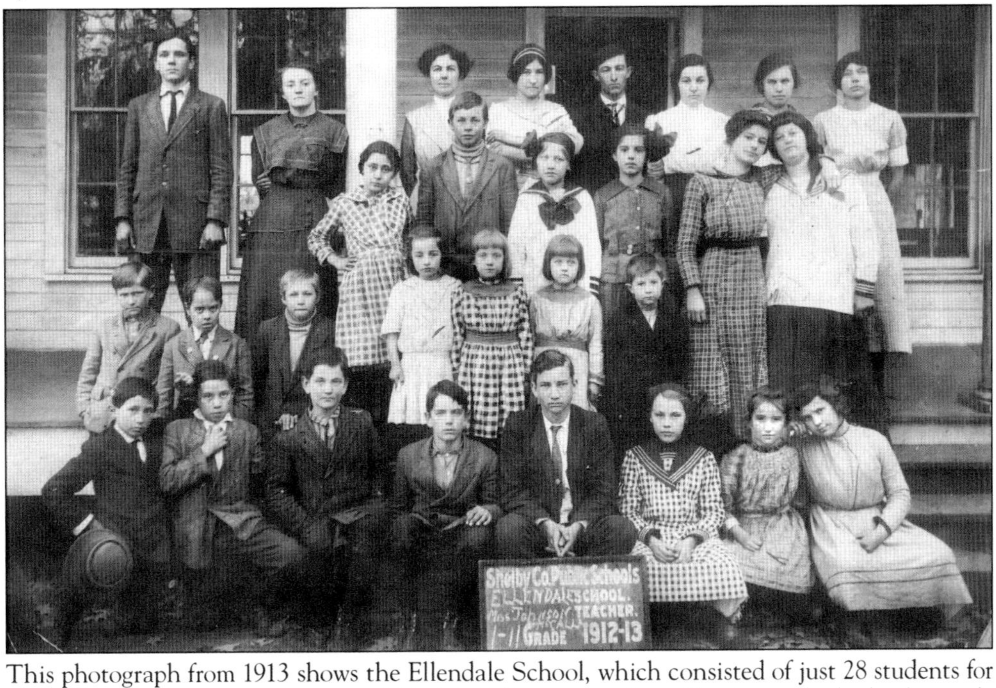

This photograph from 1913 shows the Ellendale School, which consisted of just 28 students for grades 1 through 11. Ms. Johnson and Ms. McCalla were teachers. Teachers, who had to be single and of good standing, typically earned $30 to $50 per month during the early 1900s.

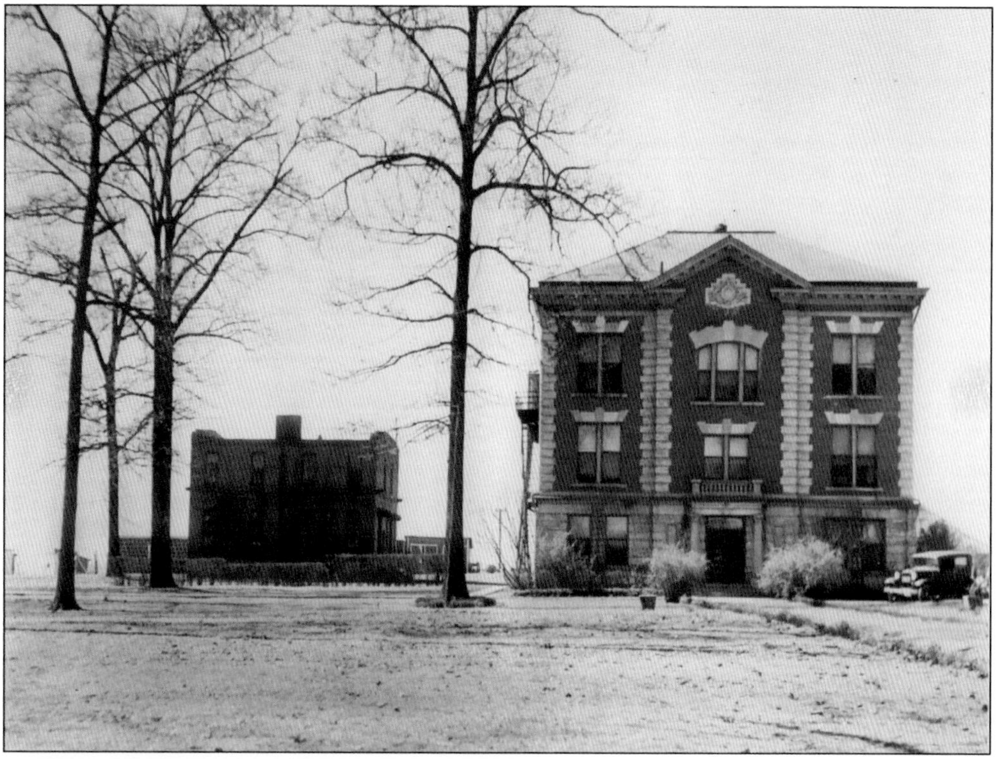

The Shelby County Industrial and Training School was constructed in 1905 on Memphis-Arlington Road as a county-sponsored home for boys with no supportive families or who were destitute. They spent half the day working on the farm and half in school. The school shut down in 1935, and the buildings were demolished soon after.

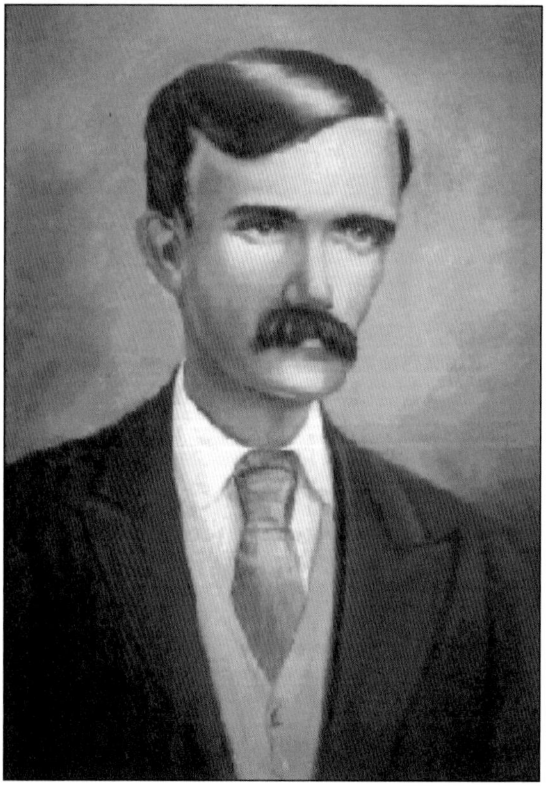

Thomas P. Westendorf, originally a schoolteacher in Plainfield, Indiana, was in charge of the Shelby County Industrial and Training School from 1905 until 1916. Born in 1848, he composed hundreds of songs throughout the late 1800s.

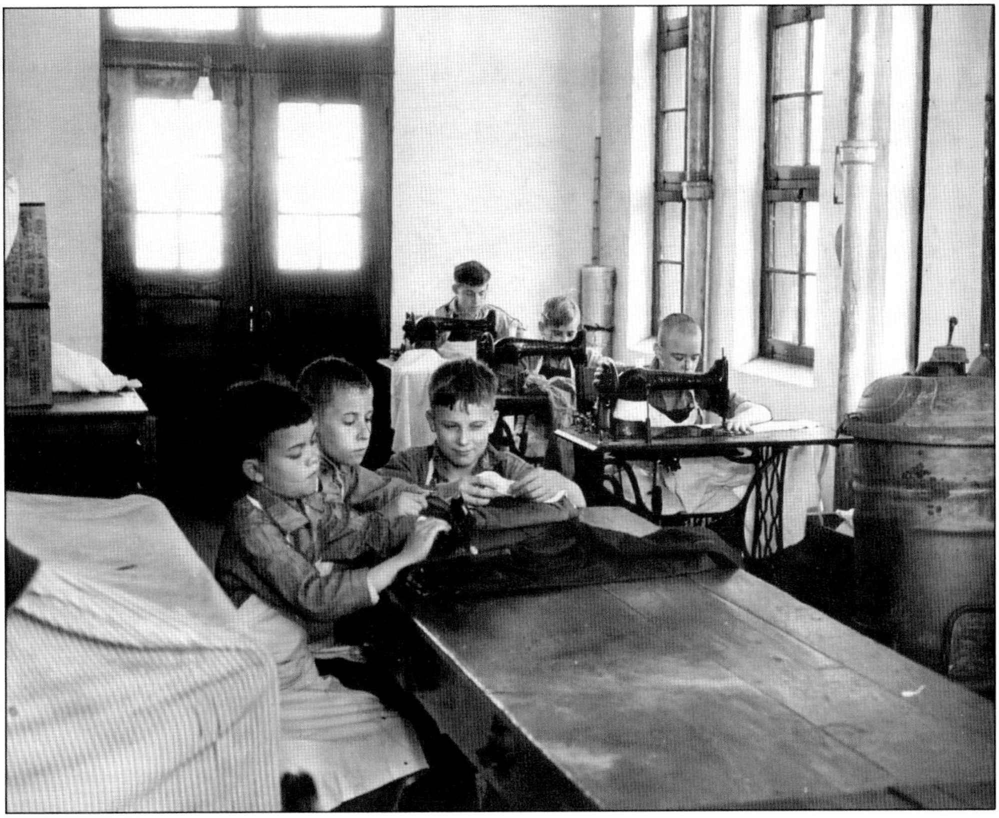

This photograph from 1933 shows the interior of the Shelby County Industrial and Training School. Here the students are learning to sew.

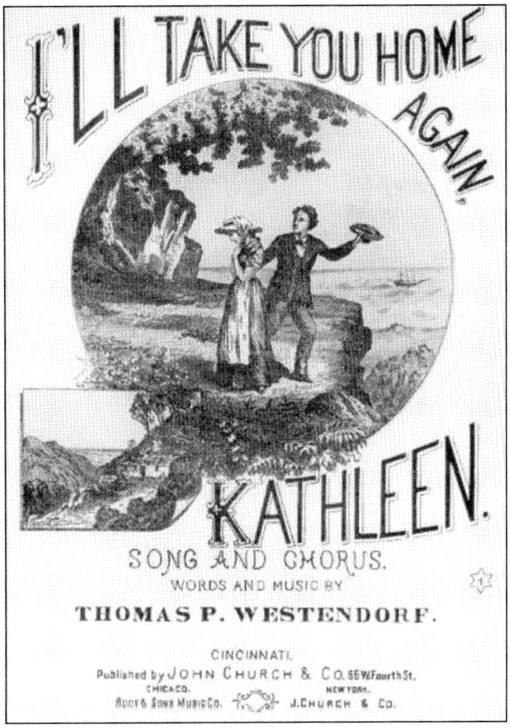

Thomas P. Westendorf's most popular song, "I'll Take You Home Again, Kathleen," was written in 1875 for his wife (who was, however, named Jennie). It is in the form of an answer to a popular Irish ballad of the time, "Barney, Take Me Home Again." The song was covered by Bing Crosby, Merv Griffin, Michael Crawford, and in 1971, Elvis Presley.

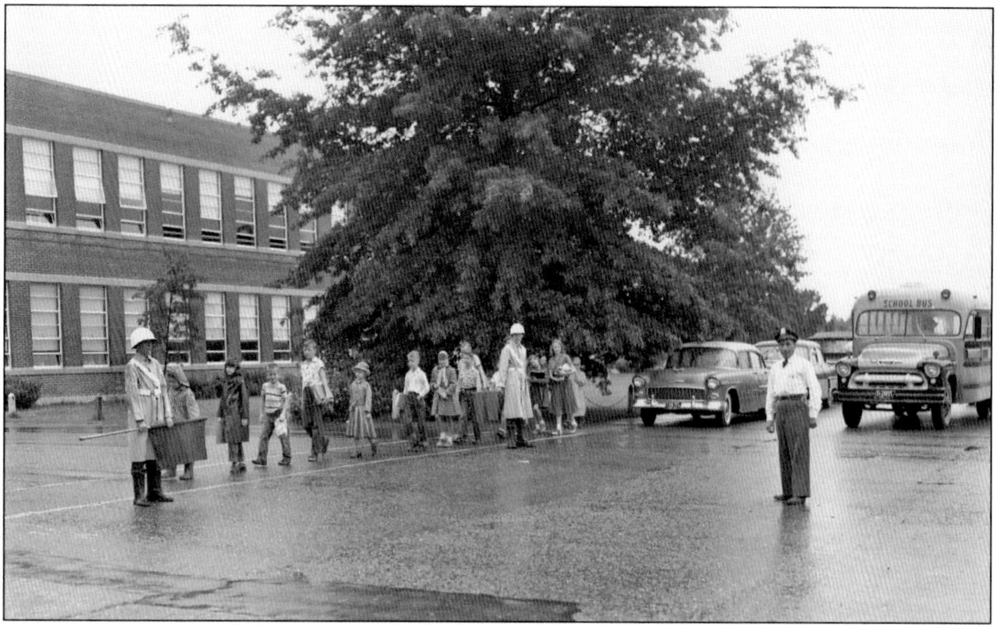

When the original Bartlett High School was built in 1917, all grades were taught in the same building. In the early 1960s, Bartlett Elementary was built just west of the high school. In 1991, a new elementary school was built on Billy Maher Road; today it serves 850 students. There are now six elementary schools, three middle schools, and three high schools serving the Bartlett area.

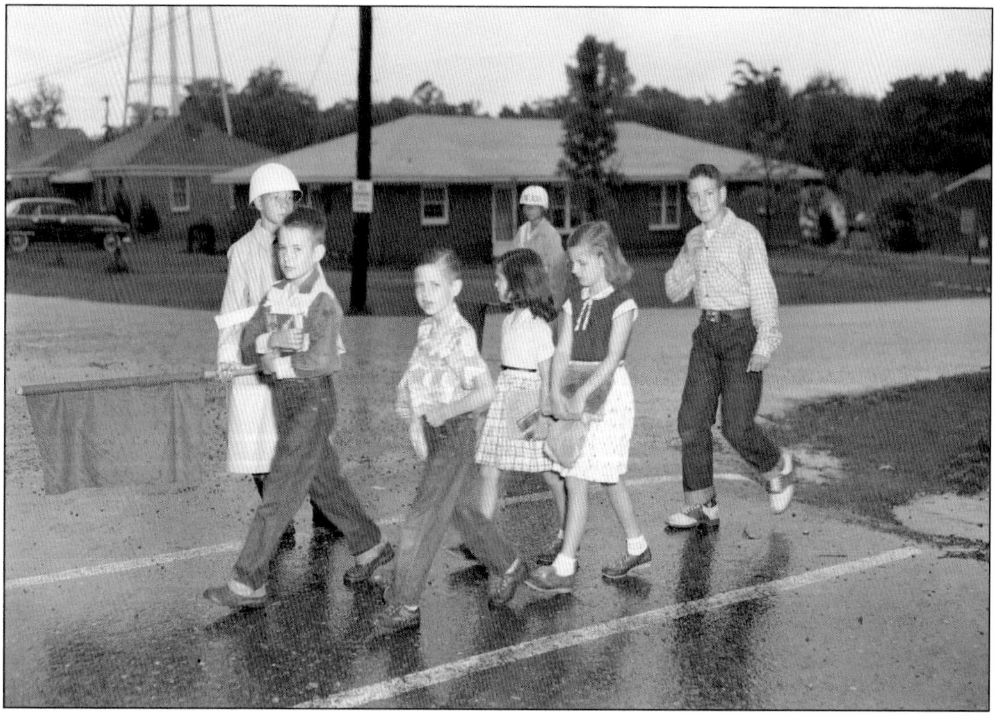

Students cross Woodlawn Street in the late 1950s on their way to Bartlett School. Oswald H. Thomas, whose family settled in Bartlett in the 1870s, was one of Bartlett's first bus drivers beginning in the 1930s.

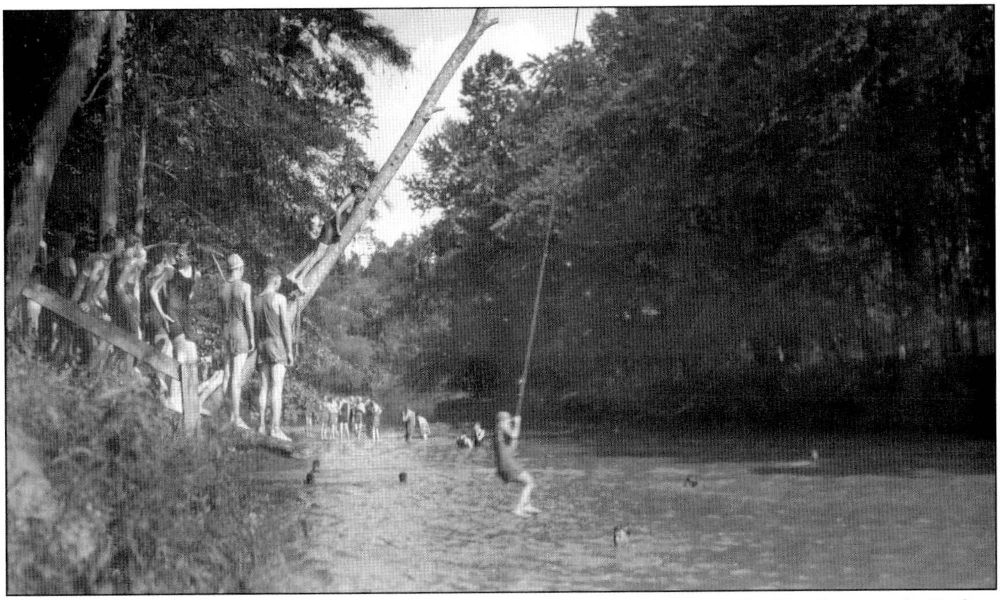

The Wolf River, shown here in the 1920s, was a popular swimming spot for Bartlett youth. Before the days of commercial development, which dumped chemicals and topsoil into the river, the waterway was clean and safe for swimming.

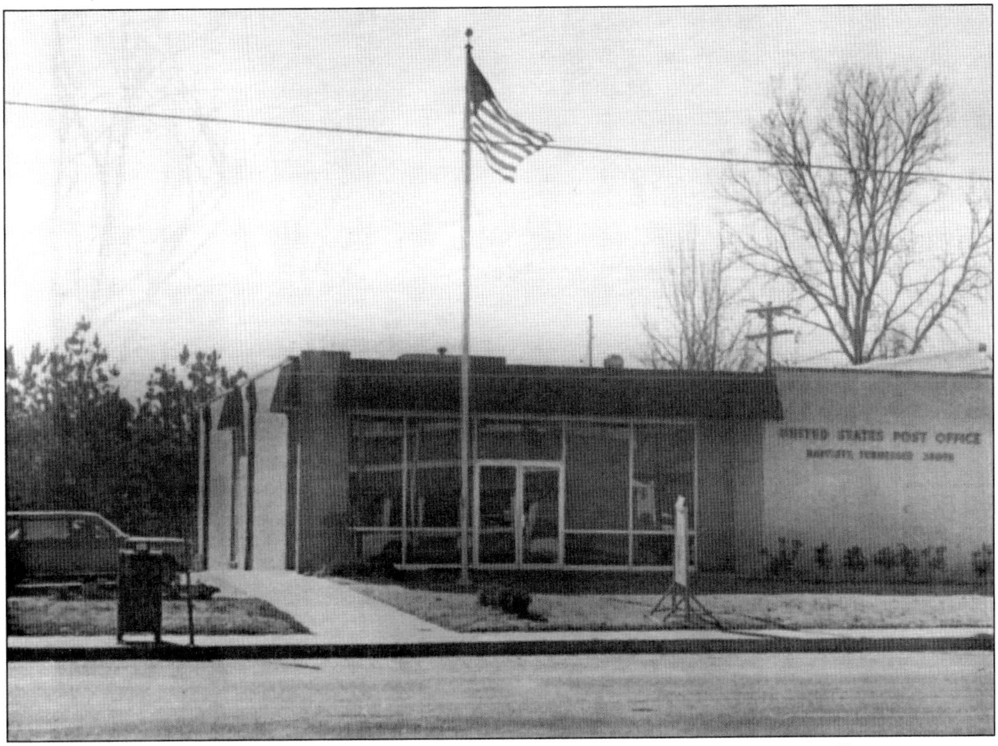

Bartlett's first post office was established in 1857 with John C. Gay as postmaster. For many years, the post office was kept in various stores on Stage Road. In 1968, a new permanent post office, shown above, was built on the south side of Stage Road next door to the library. In 1976, a larger, more modern post office was built on Elmore Road.

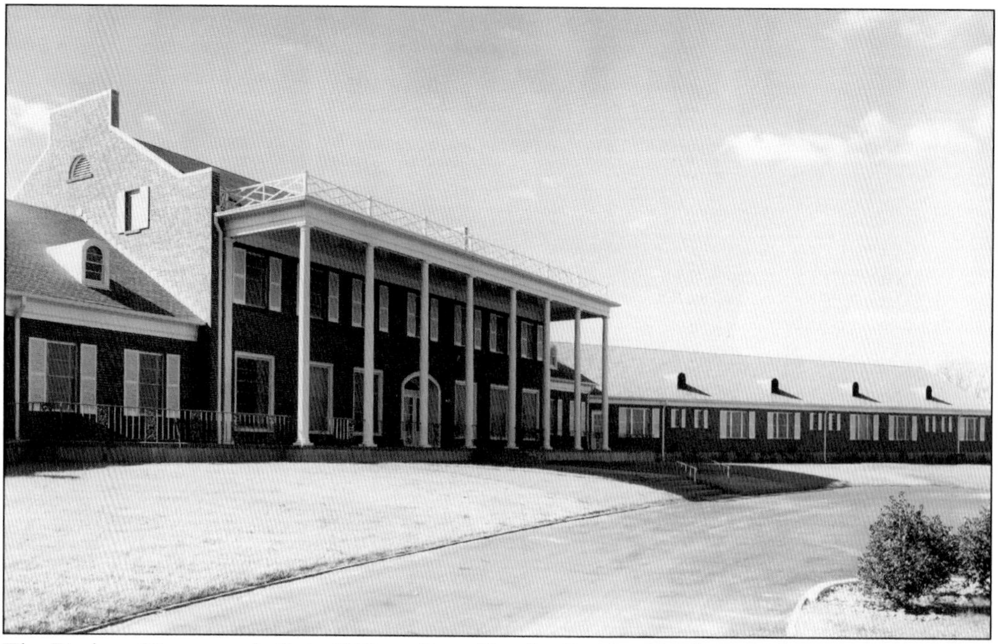

The Durham Home was built in 1957 on Stage Road at Bartlett Boulevard. The retirement home, built by H. W. Durham, was in operation for 30 years before being demolished to make way for the Bartlett Towne Center. The money from the sale of the Durham Home helped to create the H. W. Durham Foundation, which provides grants to assist senior citizens. Many of the antique furnishings from the Durham Home are now on display in the front parlor of the Bartlett Museum.

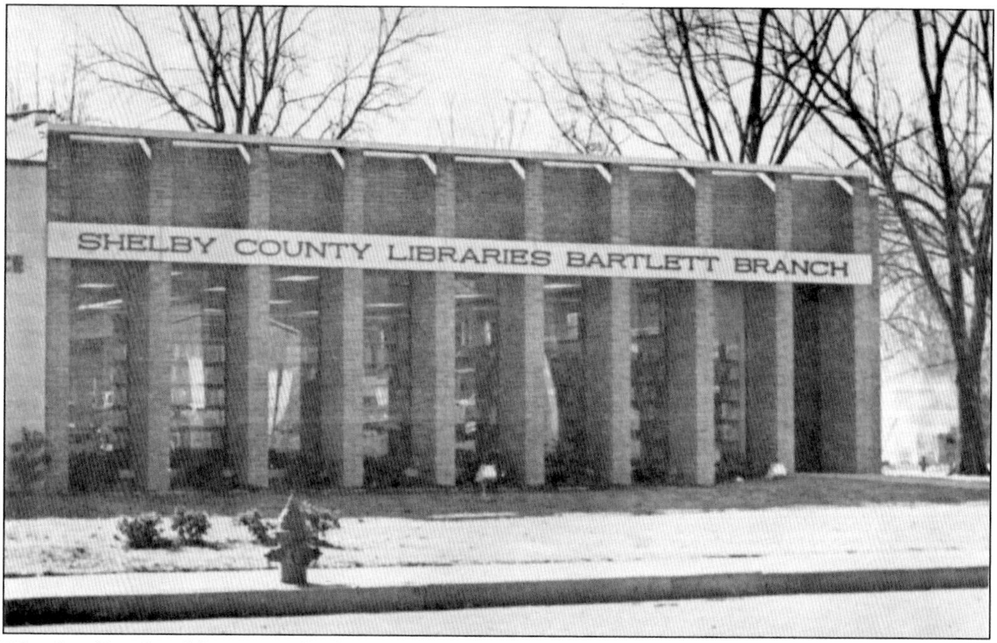

The first Bartlett library was built in 1967 and was located at 5803 Stage Road. The library cost $78,000 to build and was replaced in 1980 with a new $500,000 library next door to city hall. In 2007, Bartlett dedicated a new library in the Bartlett Station Municipal Center, formerly Bartlett Baptist Church.

TIMELINE

1793 Tennessee is adopted as a state.
1818 Andrew Jackson and Isaac Shelby, as agents for the state of Tennessee, purchase West Tennessee from the Chickasaw Indians for $300,000.
1823 William Polk purchases 5,000 acres north of Stage Road.
1823 Richard Smith purchases 2,560 acres in what would become Ellendale.
1824 George Doherty purchases 3,000 acres south of Stage Road to Germantown Road.
1836 Warren Chapel is built in Ellendale, the present-day site of Bartlett-Ellendale Cemetery.
1838 Goodwood plantation is established on Stage Road near Kirby-Whitten Road.
1839 John Shelby, nephew of Isaac Shelby, moves to Bartlett area.
1845 Cedar Hall built for Samuel Bond.
1847 Gabriel Maston Bartlett moves to Green Bottom on Memphis to Somerville Road.
1853 The Memphis and Ohio Railroad is built through present-day Bartlett, and Union Depot is established.
1853 Memphis to Somerville Road become a toll road. Wood planks are laid on the roadbed.
1864 Union general Lew Wallace sets up headquarters in Gabriel Bartlett's home.
1866 The town of Bartlett is incorporated. Gabriel Bartlett is elected the first mayor.
1869 The Nicholas Blackwell house is built.
1870 Shelby County establishes a circuit court in Bartlett.
1871 The Nicholas Gotten house is built.
1871 Bartlett's first newspaper, the *Bartlett Enterprise*, is established.
1878 Yellow fever hits Bartlett.
1885 The courts leave Bartlett for Memphis. The courthouse becomes a school.
1885 Bartlett loses its charter.
1905 Bartlett regains is charter.
1917 Bartlett High School is built.
1919 The Bartlett Courthouse is torn down.
1927 Highway 70 is cut through the Bartlett area, connecting Memphis to Nashville.
1934 Roy Dixon is elected mayor.
1940 Bartlett's depot is torn down.
1946 Cecil Barnett is elected mayor.
1964 Oscar Yates is elected the town's first full-time mayor.
1988 Bobby Flaherty is elected mayor.
1998 Ken Fulmar is elected mayor.
2002 Keith McDonald is elected mayor.
2010 Bartlett's population is 49,500.